Indispensable Outcasts

The Working Class in American History

A list of books in the series appears at the end of this book.

Indispensable Outcasts

HOBO WORKERS AND COMMUNITY IN THE AMERICAN MIDWEST, 1880–1930

Frank Tobias Higbie

UNIVERSITY OF ILLINOIS PRESS

URBANA AND CHICAGO

This book is printed on acid-free paper.

Library of Congress Cataloging-in-Publication Data
Higbie, Frank Tobias.
Indispensable outcasts : hobo workers and community
in the American Midwest, 1880–1930 / Frank Tobias Higbie.
p. cm. — (The working class in American history)
Includes bibliographical references and index.
ISBN 0-252-02794-9 (cloth : alk. paper)
ISBN 0-252-07098-4 (paper : alk. paper)
1. Seasonal labor—Middle West.
2. Migrant labor—Middle West.
3. Migrant agricultural laborers—Middle West.
4. Progressivism (United States politics)—History.
5. Middle West—History.
6. Labor—United States—History.
7. Working class—United States—History.
I. Title: Hobo workers and community in the
American Midwest, 1880–1930.
II. Title.
III. Series.
HD5856.M65H54 2003
331.5'44'097709041—dc21 2002009172

For Loretta

❖

CONTENTS

❖

ACKNOWLEDGMENTS

It is often said that scholarship is a lonely profession, but I have not found this to be true. In the course of writing this book I have benefited from the generosity of a great many scholars, librarians, archivists, friends, and public servants. Many of them offered suggestions that have guided my telling of the story of hobo labor, and knowing that they have an interest makes the story worth telling in first place.

As I began to wander around the Midwest looking for obscure sources, Arnold Alanen and Peter Rachleff gave me good advice, directing me to many excellent archives. Salvatore Salerno invited me to his home and generously opened his research files to me. Barry Singer of the Superior Public Library; Donna Fredrickson, Spink County Clerk of Courts; and Michele Franey, Finance Officer of the City of Mitchell helped me find local government records. In particular, Ms. Fredrickson took time out of her schedule to search the court house for old, dusty records, which we eventually found in an attic room. I would also like to thank Ruth Bauer Anderson at the Minnesota Historical Society, Joel Wurl at the Immigration History Research Center, Marilyn Finke at the Central Plains Region National Archives, Mike Smith at the Walter Reuther Library, and Deb Lyon at the Center for Western Studies at Augustana College.

Surviving graduate school—during which this project first took shape—would have been impossible without supportive family, friends, and colleagues. My parents, Peter and Frances Higbie, provided invaluable moral and financial support and tolerance for my errant political views. Many thanks also to Mike and Sharon Gaffney, who opened their home to me as a new family member during this time. A circle of friends and colleagues—Steve Vaughan; Lisa Gatzke and our godson, Jackson; Tom Jordan; Julia Walsh; Caroline Waldron; Robert Merithew; Steve Jahn; Mary Vavrus; Kathy Mapes; Randi Storch; Merrill Miller; Val Littlefield; Rick, Ana, and Richard Langlois; Jonathan Sterne; Carrie Rentschler; Dave Breeden; Nan Hyland; Nicole MacLaughlin; Dan Graff; Charles Allen; Dawn Coppin; Elizabeth Majerus; Pat Simpson; and many others—broke the isolation of graduate school and kept me sane. Most of them, and many others, were members of the Graduate Employees' Organization, IFT/AFT, AFL-CIO. With them I learned just how hard it is to organize a union, even among stable, well-fed people. Thanks especially to Karen MacKenzie, Tom Amato, and Terry Reed of the Illinois Federation of Teachers, each of whom helped me learn the art of organizing.

During my research, I became friends with Kristine Stilwell and have benefited immensely ever since. She directed me to many wonderful collections of primary source material, helping to make the final draft of this work much richer, especially the memoirs of Robert Saunders and Thomas Bogard, the Peter Tamony Papers, numerous newspaper articles on women hoboes, and other sources that she acquired during her own dissertation research. I have enjoyed our long discussions of the arcana of hobo studies and cannot thank her enough for her generosity and friendship.

I have also benefited from the generosity of a number of other colleagues and institutions. At the University of Illinois, fellow graduate students and professors read early drafts of my work, and I would like to thank Nils Jacobsen, Miller Karnes, Joseph Love, Frederic Jaher, Lynnea Magnusson, Craig Koslovsky, Joe Perry, and Ruth Fairbanks. Dorothee Schneider directed some of my early research and continued to give me excellent advice throughout the project. Some of my research time was supported by fellowships from the University of Illinois Graduate College and the University of Illinois Department of History.

My dissertation committee was a wonderfully entertaining and supportive group. Anthropologist William Kelleher pushed me to look beyond the explanations I was most comfortable with. Kathryn Oberdeck offered many excellent suggestions and shared insights from her own work that helped me understand my subject more clearly. Always ready with a smile and moral support, Vernon Burton also taught me the importance of region and community. James Barrett taught two of my first classes at the University of Illinois and has been a great mentor and friend ever since. His research, writing, teaching, and politics have proven to be excellent guides.

At the Newberry Library I have found many supportive colleagues and have especially benefited from conversations and friendships with James Grossman, Alfred Young, Elliott Gorn, Leon Fink, Carolyn Podruchny, Sara Austin, Mary Wyly, Mary Janzen, Carla Zecher, Jim Ackerman, Doug Knox, Rob Galler, Paul Gehl, Jennifer Koslow, Rebekah Holmes, and Michael Bellesiles. A reading of my work by the Newberry Fellows' Seminar provided intense and refreshing feedback at a time when I was stuck. I would also like to thank Newberry librarians Martha Briggs, Hjordis Halvorson, John Brady, John Powell, and Janis Dillard for their bibliographic assistance and Susan Fagan for her help with interlibrary loans. Emily Kelley of the Atlas of Historical County Boundaries Project created the maps of laborers' job histories.

I also must thank the two anonymous readers at *Social Science History* for their excellent comments, as well as the readers for the University of Illinois Press, Cindy Hahamovitch, David Montgomery, and one anonymous reader, each of whom offered encouragement and insightful criticism. Kevin Carollo and Matt Mitchell provided excellent editing of several chapters. My copy editor, Carol Anne Peschke, was helpful and patient. Dick Wentworth, my editor at the press, has guided the manuscript through the intricacies of publication and waited patiently while I took too long to make revisions. Thanks also to Theresa L. Sears, managing editor at the Press.

Lastly, and most of all, I want to thank Loretta Gaffney: friend, confidante, cheerleader, critical reader, copyeditor, and so much more. She took time away from her own research and writing to read every chapter of this book (usually more than once). She made many valuable suggestions and generally tolerated disruptions of home life and vacations. Her presence in my life has made everything so much more fun and worthwhile, and I'm looking forward to many more years together. In the immortal words of Joe Hill, "It's great to fight for freedom with a rebel girl."

Parts of chapter 1 appeared in "Indispensable Outcasts: Harvest Laborers in the Wheat Belt of the Middle West," *Labor History* 38:4 (Fall 1997): 393–412. An earlier version of chapter 2 appeared as "Crossing Class Boundaries: Tramp Ethnographers and Narratives of Class in Progressive Era America," *Social Science History* 21:4 (Winter 1997): 559–92.

❖

ABBREVIATIONS

ADN	*Aberdeen (South Dakota) Daily News*
AFL	American Federation of Labor
AWIU	Agricultural Workers Industrial Union
AWO	Agricultural Workers Organization
IBWA	International Brotherhood Welfare Association
IPUMS	Integrated Public Use Microdata Series
ISR	*International Socialist Review*
IW	*Industrial Worker*
IWW	Industrial Workers of the World
MCPS	Minnesota Commission of Public Safety
MDLI	Minnesota Department of Labor and Industry
MHS	Minnesota Historical Society
NDIRS	North Dakota Institute for Regional Studies
NDSP	North Dakota Socialist Party
NPL	Non-Partisan League
SCJ	*Sioux City (Iowa) Journal*
SHSW	State Historical Society of Wisconsin
UA	*Union Advocate*
USCIR	United States Commission on Industrial Relations
USDA	United States Department of Agriculture
USES	United States Employment Service
USIC	United States Industrial Commission
WHMC	Western Historical Manuscript Collection
WSHS	Washington State Historical Society

Indispensable Outcasts

INTRODUCTION

> There is here, beyond a doubt, a great laboring population experiencing a high suppression of normal instincts and traditions. There can be no greater perversion of a desirable existence than this insecure, undernourished, wandering life, with its sordid sex expression and reckless and rare pleasures.
>
> —Carleton H. Parker

> One of the things I went out west for was to earn more money to send home. You had to do that, that was one of the things we had to do, us kids did. We thought of ourselves as men after awhile, but the first thing was your mother there with the younger children.
>
> —Vincent Raymond Dunne

ON A WINTER DAY in the early twentieth century, the reformer Alice Solenberger met an unemployed laborer on a downtown Chicago street. Solenberger recognized the "Irishman" as one of the many men who had applied for work recently at the Chicago Bureau of Charities. As the director of the bureau's central district, she was familiar with Chicago's homeless men, and she considered the Irishman a typical seasonal laborer: Each year he worked steadily from the spring to the fall in the countryside earning enough to carry him through a winter of unemployment in the city. But this winter he had been "unusually extravagant" and was broke by December. He visited the Bureau of Charities daily for a week, seeking even the most menial positions, but none were open. He then disappeared for several weeks.

By the time of his return to Chicago and his chance meeting with Solenberger, it was the height of the ice harvesting season and there was plenty of work for those who needed the money badly enough. But the Irishman told Solenberger that he was no longer looking for work. The reformer assumed he had found a steady job and asked about it. "No, I mean I've *got money,*" the laborer replied, "I don't need to work any more." Solenberger asked whether some relative died and left him an inheritance. "Relative! No, I ain't that lucky. You don't understand. I mean that I've got money that I worked for. I got a job that last day I was at the charity office and I worked nearly two months. Just stopped it here last Saturday. It was good pay and I've got a-plenty of it now. That's why I ain't working on the ice. I don't need to."[1]

This was logic that Solenberger could not understand. She pressed the Irishman about saving for his old age, or for sickness. He offered several alternative explanations focusing on his youth, his lack of family commitments, the fact that summer work would open soon enough, and even his dislike of working on the ice. When none of these satisfied Solenberger, he offered apologetically, "I'm real sorry to disappoint you, Miss, since you seem so set on the idea of me working on the ice, but to tell the truth I really wouldn't think it was *right* to do it. I'd just be taking the work away from some poor fellow who needs it, and it wouldn't be right for a man to do that when he has plenty of money in his pocket."

Solenberger's exasperation at what she considered to be "the philosophy of a great many seasonal workers" suggests the deeply divergent outlooks on work and personal responsibility held by middle-class social investigators and their working-class subjects during the Progressive Era. The laborer saw no particular merit in work for work's sake. He placed his current unemployment in the context of a responsibility to other workers: Given a finite supply of work, anyone who worked more than necessary denied others the chance to earn a livelihood. Solenberger saw this as a mere rationalization, the result of years of irregular employment. "They really do not believe in [working continuously]," she wrote, "nor will many of them admit any necessity for saving more than enough to carry them from one season to the next." For Solenberger, like many other middle-class observers, seasonal work could only lead to degradation. But for the unnamed "Irishman," seasonal work was a fact of life, a way of getting by, not an end in itself.

This moment of cultural confusion speaks to a larger problem. Although most readers will understand why Solenberger complained about the laborer's excuses for not working, it is more difficult to imagine why the laborer felt he ought to quit a job simply because he had enough money to take him through the rest of the winter. Of course, we might agree with Solenberger that this was just an excuse for one man's laziness. But the Irishman was certainly not alone.

During the late nineteenth and early twentieth centuries, millions of people worked in highly seasonal occupations, piecing together a living by whatever means they could find. This book focuses on the large segment of the seasonal workforce to which Solenberger's Irishman belonged: the young, immigrant and American-born men—often called floaters or hoboes—who worked in logging, crop harvesting, construction, and other seasonal industries (see figure 1). In his widely read study of the Progressive Era, Robert Wiebe wrote of them, "Scorned, feared, yet desperately needed, migrant workers comprised the indispensable outcasts of rural America."[2] Whereas Wiebe dealt with seasonal laborers in a pithy turn of phrase, this study recasts Progressive Era history around the conflicts they symbolized and experiences they embodied.

Scattered across the American countryside in work camps and on farms, subject to exploitation at the hands of employers and employment agents, and disrupting quiet prairie towns with revolutionary direct action, seasonal laborers were the quintessential "social problem." Like our contemporary social problems, this one inspired radically different interpretations. Was the laboring life a "perversion of a desirable existence," as the economist Carleton Parker argued, or a rite of passage that turned boys into men and sustained the left-behind household, as Vincent Dunne remembered?[3] Was "the philosophy of a great many seasonal workers" simply a way to rationalize laziness, as Solenberger would have it? Or did it express an ethic of mutuality and working-class consciousness that Solenberger could not fathom?

Figure 1. Men outside a Bridge Square employment bureau in Minneapolis, 1908. Photo by Luxton's Library of Historic Photographs. From the collections of the Minnesota Historical Society (neg. 25589, HG4.2/rs).

These questions are complicated by Progressive Era Americans' use of the image of the hobo to various, contradictory ends. The social reformers who studied labor market structures, interviewed laborers, and lived undercover as workers not only described living conditions but helped to define class division itself as they moved between middle-class and working-class worlds. Radical organizers built community among laborers, encouraging them to challenge their marginal position. For organizers the "hobo" could be both the ultimate symbol of capitalism's human toll and the militant vanguard of working-class liberation. Although working for a time as a migrant seasonal laborer was common for working-class and rural men, these men faced horrendous sanitary and work conditions. Wages were good, but the erratic supply of jobs kept laborers near the edge of survival, perpetually looking for more short-term jobs. In a sense, both Parker and Dunne were right about laboring work: It could be a "perversion" of normal life and a way to maintain that normal life. The paradox presented by seasonal laboring men was that they were at once strangers and familiars, homeless and linked to communities, marginalized socially and central to the extractive economy. Both their labor and degradation were pillars of American society.

The remainder of this introduction outlines the theoretical issues I see as central to deciphering the history of seasonal laborers' experiences. Chapter 1 examines the network of extractive agriculture and industry that linked the upper midwestern city and countryside. It also traces the conflicted role of seasonal wage labor for the region's agricultural economy and farm households. Chapter 2 turns to the politics of social investigation, analyzing the ways investigators gave meaning to class distinctions by telling the story of their own experiences as undercover workers and by repackaging the life stories of the workers they studied. Chapter 3 reassesses the geography of work and community among the floating laborers. In addition to examining census and other data to estimate the racial and ethnic characteristics of this difficult-to-define group of workers, this chapter explores the place of floaters in radical and labor movement discussions about society and considers the lives of female hoboes and the gay subculture among men on the road. Chapter 4 turns to the politics of community in the Great Plains wheat belt, specifically the organizing efforts of the Industrial Workers of the World (IWW) from 1908 to 1924. Here we see localized struggles to control seasonal labor, "battles," as the local press called them, which provide a window onto the clash between notions of community, manliness, and class in small-town America. The final chapter returns to the question of "the philosophy of a great many seasonal workers," to use Alice Solenberger's phrase. How did laborers frame their own life experiences to contemporaries and in retrospect? Using published and unpublished memoirs, oral histories, song, and folklore, this chapter maps the complexity of "manliness." On this uneven terrain of memory, protest, and celebration, working-class experience emerges as positive expressions of solidarity, unhealed wounds, and half-hidden social practices. As individuals and as members of social movements laboring men were active in shaping the meaning of their experiences. The lessons they drew often were quite different from those drawn by outside observers.

The lack of a single term to describe those who worked in seasonal industries suggests the difficulty of relating their history. Examining late-nineteenth- and early-twentieth-century commentaries and investigations, and later historical and sociological interpretations, one finds a vast array of names for these people. In addition to the myriad occupation-specific titles such as *harvest hand, gandy dancer* (railroad worker), and *lumberjack,* there are the general terms: *hoboes, tramps, bums, homeless men, vagrants, transients,* or *mendicants; migratory, floating, casual, unskilled,* and *seasonal workers or laborers; rounders, go-abouts, down-and-outers, the underclass, the working poor, the unemployed,* and, of course, *the working class.*

The term *hobo* suggests further complications. Its origin is obscure. Some suggest that it derives from *hoe boy,* or agricultural laborer, others that it is a shortening of *homeward bounders,* referring to Civil War veterans, many of whom became seasonal workers in the West. One itinerant worker claimed the term originated from the French *haute beau,* or "high beauty," and another from the Latin phrase *homo bonus,* or "good person." Still others believed it was simply a clipped version of the railway workers' greeting "Hello Boy."[4] Even when people agreed that a hobo was a transient worker, they disagreed on the significance of his transience and the strength of his commitment to work. To make distinctions between transients, observers developed a familiar typology based on terms used by transients themselves. Generally, these followed the idea that *hoboes* wandered to find work, *tramps* worked only to facilitate wandering, and *bums* neither wandered nor worked. The reader will find that I often echo Progressive Era language, especially when it is relevant to the conflicting interpretations of laboring men's experiences. However, I also use *seasonal laborers* and *laboring men* because the term *laborer* was a common generic term in both rural and urban settings.[5]

Just as the world of laboring men threw common categories into disarray, a study that combines rural and urban realities confronts the traditional division between rural history and labor history. Despite the varied origins of harvest hands—some rural, some urban, some workers, and some farmers—nearly all of them moved seasonally between the city and the countryside. Moreover, labor historians' focus on workers in key industrial sectors overlooks a large number of rural people who also worked for wages. As late as 1920, 5 percent of all gainfully employed Americans were farm laborers "working out" for wages on nonfamily farms. In comparison, transportation industries and mining of all kinds accounted for 7 percent and 2.5 percent of all gainfully employed workers, respectively.[6]

The invisibility of midwestern rural workers in American history is tied equally to the biases of historians and the special place of the midwestern countryside in our national identity. For instance, southern historians routinely address rural labor relations because slavery was a predominantly rural labor system, and large-scale plantation agriculture was common in the region. Similarly, western agriculture developed early as a capital-intensive rural industry employing large numbers of migrant laborers. In other words, it is easier to see class in the southern and western countryside because it has a familiar profile: an enslaved, oppressed, or proletarianized working mass dominated by property owners. In contrast, the midwestern countryside was the heartland of the family farm, a region of independent producers where, at least theoretically, any man who wanted to work hard could become his own boss. It is an enduring vision of the good life for men and their families, all the more powerful for its intensely masculine appeal.

Faced with an apparent contrast between a countryside dotted by independent producers and cities dominated by the expanding power of industrial employers, labor and rural historians have tended to mind their own backyards. The traditional concerns of labor history—unionization, working-class politics, and the development of class-based identity—have been almost entirely urban-focused. Similarly, in staking out their own historiographic turf, some rural historians argue that rural experience cannot be subsumed into the urban-biased grand narrative of American history. For instance, one of the best general books on wheat harvesting portrays the harvest labor system as a perfect symbiosis between workers and farmer-employers that was disrupted by outsiders who did not understand the nature of farm work.[7] My study is guided by a more critical historiography of labor relations in the rural North, along with recent studies that have moved across the rural-urban divide by focusing on work relations within the farm household, the connection between rural and urban work in transforming regional economies, and the migration patterns and work experiences of immigrant and African American workers.[8]

Rural and labor history also must be linked because the era of mass immigration and industrialization transformed the countryside as surely as it did cities. The seasonal laborers of the upper Midwest lived in a world of expanding capitalist production that needed both their labor and the raw materials they dug from the earth or harvested. Demand for labor and commodities set the context for all migrations, whether they were transoceanic or just across state lines. Yet even as the urban-based economy penetrated and transformed remote rural areas, it did not completely overwhelm rural patterns. In places such as the upper Midwest, the so-called modern world still relied on the nonmodern cycles of agriculture and seasonal change. As a result, seasonal work was a way of life; very few people held year-round employment. In this context, rural and urban America fed each other's need for workers: A change of season often meant a change of job and a move between the countryside and the city.[9]

These connections existed in politics as well as social life. Historians usually think of the developing labor and farmer movements as wholly separate, and in fact direct ties often were tenuous. As Leon Fink argues in his study of the Knights of Labor, a potential alliance between Kansas Knights and Populists was unsuccessful because immigrant working men and U.S.-born farmers had conflicting opinions on machine politics, women's rights, and prohibition.[10] Despite the divisions between trade unionists and Populists in Kansas City and elsewhere, citizens of the rural West used railroad workers' and miners' organizations to build a variety of popular movements opposing corporate power in their communities. Many of the leaders of these local movements became activists in the People's party.[11] By the early twentieth century, farmer, tenant, and worker protests in Kansas, Oklahoma, Arkansas, and Louisiana became less differentiated as the Socialist party, the IWW, and other unions organized the region. In the upper Midwest farmers and workers found common ground in the Socialist and Nonpartisan movements. As Fink notes, working-class and farmer political movements fed off each other's energy to such an extent that they were both "part of a larger, evolving political storm."[12]

The crises of urban and rural life continued to occupy public attention throughout the early twentieth century despite the eclipse of the Populist and industrial union movements in the 1890s. In the industrial sector, workers and employers waged a running battle over pay, job security, and union recognition. The frequency of strikes rose to historic peaks from 1900 to 1920, while membership in trade unions grew nearly tenfold.[13] It was in this context of labor unrest that the IWW, or Wobblies, led several strikes of textile workers, lumberjacks, miners, and wheat harvesters, bringing attention to unskilled and immigrant workers. Founded as an avowedly revolutionary union movement in Chicago in 1905, the IWW slowly developed from a propaganda organization into a functioning union federation. Initially, the Socialist party supported the IWW, and its left wing remained an enthusiastic backer of the union. But moderate Socialists, especially elected officials, like mainstream trade unionists, preferred to keep their distance from the upstart movement.[14]

Labor historians generally agree that the IWW was a minority movement that never seriously challenged the American Federation of Labor (AFL).[15] However, it is crucial to note that for many years the IWW was the only union attempting to represent laborers in timber, railroad construction, and agricultural work, especially west of Chicago. Even where mainline unions eventually did try to organize laborers, the IWW had been there first and left a lasting impression on many workers. For a time, the IWW and its farm labor union, known as the Agricultural Workers Organization (AWO), Local 400, neared social acceptability, holding conventions in wheat belt towns and drawing praise from liberal political leaders and trade unionists who recognized the burning need for any kind of organization among common laborers. The political leanings of a sizable minority of farmers, ranging from Populist to Socialist, ensured a level of tolerance not usually ascribed to rural employers. When the union reached its peak, membership included farm-born and city-born laborers in nearly equal numbers, according to an outside observer.[16]

Although strikes grabbed the headlines, personnel managers, social scientists, and government officials began to worry about a quieter phenomenon: the pervasive tendency of laborers and semiskilled workers to quit their jobs at the slightest instigation. Heavily mechanized manufacturers often had to hire many times the total number of jobs available over the course of a year simply to keep their factories fully staffed. Whereas employers in meatpacking altered their labor force daily and even hourly in response to availability of raw materials, the new assembly line manufacturers found that high labor turnover cost them in terms of training and inefficiency. As one personnel executive noted vividly in 1916, "Just as quicksand cannot be kneaded in the hands into a solid lump, so also will it be found difficult to take hold of an ever-changing mass of employees and transform it into a homogeneous, intelligent, contented body."[17] The significance of the crisis of turnover was grasped by the labor economist John R. Commons, among others. Although scientific managers had rationalized industry by changing the movements of individual workers and the production process as a whole, Commons noted, they failed to see "that one of the greatest costs of labor is not the inefficiency of the individual but the lack of goodwill of labor as a whole."[18] Commons and others called for a shift in managerial thinking that would gain favor in the 1920s. The new thinking saw irregular employment, poverty, and class conflict as a drag on efficiency. The proponents of so-called welfare capitalism argued that a community of interest between industrialist and worker was not simply more humane but also more efficient. American democracy, community, and capitalism could be strengthened by enlightened management practices and an expanded state role in stabilizing the economy.[19] Yet while rationalization of production brought larger worksites to factory production during the 1920s, it also decreased industry's need for extra workers to cushion the swings between slack and busy seasons. Thousands of workers lost the seasonal jobs they relied on to make a living. This change, along with the slow decline of the mining, logging, and railroad industries, foreshadowed widespread unemployment during the Great Depression of the 1930s.

The crisis of labor turnover also had a rural complement, which was itself part of a wider discourse of crisis in rural life. As Mary Neth argues in her study of the roots of agribusiness, prosperous farmers with links to financial and political power were keen to develop agriculture as a modern industry. Their outlook on farm production often conflicted with the interests of poorer farmers and rural laborers. At the turn of the twentieth century, testimony before the U.S. Industrial Commission emphasized that farm employers had difficulty finding what they considered good workers, largely because of low wages and unsteady employment. A South Dakota stock farmer noted, "Our average hired men are not quite what they used to be. . . . They are determined to work fewer hours, though they are paid better wages than we used to pay them, or that I used to get when a hired man myself." He suggested the reason was irregularity of farm employment. "They cannot rely upon employment the year round, and so those who like to have employment steadily go into other" lines of work. A representative of the National Farmers Alliance and Industrial Union noted that farm laborers in Minnesota preferred railroad work to farm work because the hours were shorter and the work steadier, despite slightly lower wages.[20]

Less than a decade later, the Country Life Commission worried that native-stock American men were no longer assured that hard work would lead to farm ownership—one of the fundamental elements of citizenship, in the opinion of the commission. Instead, poor rural living conditions and low farm profits combined with the lure of the cities to depopulate the countryside and undermine the agrarian bulwark of American democracy. Just as studies of urban labor problems mixed criticism of economic structures with condemnation of workers' laziness, the Country Life report noted, "So long as the United States continues to be a true democracy it will have a serious labor problem." Competent labor always moved up the agricultural ladder. Others with energy and ambition were lured to the cities by higher wages, shorter hours, and greater "opportunities for social diversion and often of dissipation." Meanwhile, incompetent farm owners lost their farms and became tenants who "farm for a living rather than as a business, and . . . laborers become watchers of the sun rather than efficient workers." The commission reported that immigrants often were better workers than their U.S.-born neighbors because the "American is less pressed by dire necessity to labor and save."[21] The problem of rural labor, then, was very much linked to questions of laborers' work ethic. Without some mental or material compulsion, these observers argued, workers would not work. Many farmers and their business allies in small rural towns defined this relative shortage of laborers willing to work for "going wages" as an absolute shortage of farm workers. In response they issued urgent calls in the newspapers of large cities for additional harvest labor, often with the result of flooding the labor market and reducing workers' ability to hold out for higher wages.[22]

Rural workers' unwillingness to work for going wages and the high turnover rate among urban workers were two sides of the same coin. As agriculture and industry rationalized production, wage earners felt increasingly constrained and resisted whenever and however they could. Usually, this meant quitting and moving from countryside to city in search of better work. As William Cronon argues in his study of Chicago and the West, "The journey that carried so many travelers into the city also carried them out again, and in that exchange of things urban for things rural lies a deeper truth about the country and the city. The two can exist only in each other's presence. Their isolation is an illusion." Cronon's powerful work clearly describes the links between rural commodities and their urban markets (focusing especially on the role of merchants and middle-class consumers in these links), but he touches little on the lives of ordinary men and women.[23] If we view the region not from the floor of the Chicago Board of Trade but from the eyes of a young laborer working in seasonal industries and agriculture, we get a different picture of the links between rural and urban life.

❖ ❖ ❖

As we follow workers crossing between rural and urban sectors, we also must refine our approach to community and work. Labor and social historians have drawn on workers' autobiographies and oral histories, the manuscript censuses, government reports, and other sources to reconstruct the social structures and daily life of shoe, textile, meatpacking, and steel workers, to name but a few. However, nearly all these studies are confined either geographically to one city or occupationally to one industry. It is possible to conduct a study of lumberjacks or harvest hands in one county. But because these workers moved regularly, a study of those who stayed in one place would ignore those who moved on. Unfortunately, it is difficult to follow these mobile workers in any systematic way. Outside of a handful of published and unpublished memoirs, we have only fragments of whole lives often translated by agents of the state, philanthropists, and oral historians. Seasonal laborers were among the "non-persisters" who disappeared from the databases of social mobility historians.[24] Yet as labor economist William Leiserson argued in 1916, the "army of migratory and casual laborers" included "practically every wage earner" at one time or another.[25] If the geographic metaphor for community is the neighborhood, seasonal laboring men as a group were at once part of tens of thousands of neighborhoods and outcasts from all communities. They came from somewhere, but they resided nowhere. Indeed, seasonal laboring men helped make stable communities possible by arriving at times of peak labor demand and then moving on at season's end.

Similarly, this study contrasts with the work by historians who view transient workers through the lens of homelessness and the tramp subculture. Although we share an interest in describing transient workers' experiences and middle-class reform efforts around the tramp issue, *Indispensable Outcasts* places greater emphasis on personal and ideological connections among settled and transient communities in the cities and the countryside.[26] Laboring men worked in out-of-the-way places, they were marginalized by their poverty and extreme mobility, and yet they were very much like other working-class and rural men. To the extent that they inhabited or created a culture different from the wider culture, it was not so much a result of their isolation from society as a result of a tension between their marginality and their similarity to the rest of society. To trace this tension we have to examine both the ideological and experiential aspects of *community* and the *labor market*. Variously, these terms may represent physical spaces, social relationships, or ideological constructions that order social relations. However, the concept of community is remarkable for its versatility and lack of definite meaning. As Raymond Williams notes, "unlike all other terms of social organization (state, nation, society, etc.) [community] seems never to be used unfavorably, and never to be given any positive opposing or distinguishing term."[27]

Conflicts over who was included in and excluded from community often translated into conflicts over work and the labor market, and vice versa. Historians and economists have studied labor markets largely in terms of the division between skilled and unskilled workers, the exclusion of women and African Americans from certain trades, and more generally in terms of the creation of institutionalized divisions within the working class.[28] Indeed, divisions of ethnicity and race were key to where, when, and how often seasonal laborers found work and what kind of work they performed. As Cindy Hahamovitch and Gunther Peck have shown, immigrant *padrones,* or labor agents, helped direct members of their own ethnic groups to particular employers and industries.[29] Similarly, railroad, logging, mining, and farm employers had notions of which ethnic groups performed best at different types of work, although these notions had less impact during a labor shortage.

Like community, we can see the labor market as a place, as social relationships, or as an ideological formation. For instance, nearly every city in the upper Midwest had a space that acted as the labor market during peak seasonal demand. In some towns this was the rail depot; in others it was the town square, the courthouse steps, or a bank office. The labor market also signifies relationships between buyers and sellers of labor. These relationships nearly always were unequal; however, sellers did have some advantages at times of great demand. For instance, grain farmers could not long stave off harvest hands' wage demands when their crops stood ripening in the field. In extreme cases, the "army of the unemployed" became the cavalry riding to the rescue.

It was the ideology of the labor market, however, that interacted most significantly with community. Just as full citizenship was contingent on such factors as sex, race, and length of residence, the laboring man without property could hardly refuse work without also marking himself as outside of the community; a good citizen was one who would work, start a family, and stay put. Middle- and upper-class observers believed that vagrants were a threat to the community because they undermined workers' commitment to wage labor and along with it "normal sex," that is, monogamous heterosexuality. As the freelance social investigator Josiah Flynt noted, "The menace of the tramp class to the country seems to me to consist mainly in the example they set to the casual working man—the man who is looking around for an excuse to quit work—and in the fact that they frequently recruit their ranks with young boys."[30] In this view, the health of the community required workers to have jobs and men to have families.

No doubt men and women who worked for wages had a different perspective on the issue. They certainly understood the need to earn wages to ensure the health of their families and communities. But their experiences with seasonal and irregular work demonstrated that unemployment was an inevitable part of life, and many harbored dreams of escaping the labor market altogether in small business, homesteading, and farming. In the upper Midwest, where work was highly seasonal and opportunities for homesteading and farming existed well into the second decade of the twentieth century, laborers might conceive of themselves as only temporarily subject to the labor market. Because of these opportunities, workers' class consciousness often was built around a desire to escape the labor market, a desire not to be a worker. Criticism of wage labor as "wage slavery"—by no means limited to radicals—was both an echo of agrarian republicanism and a sign of dissatisfaction with modern labor relations.[31]

At the same time, communities could provide laborers with an important margin of freedom from the labor market. Family groups, friends, and subsistence activities such as gardening, hunting, and fishing allowed men and women to remove themselves from the labor market temporarily. As Sarah Deutsch's study of Hispanic migrants in the southwestern United States argues, members of rural communities strategically engaged in seasonal wage labor in coal mines and on railroads with the goal of supporting traditional village life.[32] Similarly, Earl Lewis's study of migrants to Norfolk, Virginia, shows that they maintained ties to family and friends in the countryside, drawing on financial and moral support to survive the transition to urban life, and returning to their rural homes in hard economic times.[33] The boundaries of racial and ethnic communities, then, cut the labor market in two directions. On one side, group identity helped structure the experience of work. Employers and labor contractors used race and nationality to direct particular workers to particular types of jobs, and workers themselves used ties of kinship and community to find work and sustain themselves. On the other side, laborers' ability to resist exploitive labor market conditions increased in the early twentieth century as urban immigrant communities solidified. Communities could be shelters from work as well as conduits to it.[34]

At the heart of communities and families are cultural understandings of what men and women should do with their lives. Labor historians increasingly have recognized that the ways workers think of themselves as men and women decisively shape class identity. For many, gender is no longer an adjunct to class analysis but central to it. For instance, Alice Kessler-Harris argues that household gender arrangements have defined when and where people become wage laborers and therefore structure the workplace struggles usually identified as the locus of class. As Joy Parr writes in her study of workers in two Canadian industrial towns, "gender is an ever present connection in both economic and social existence." The sexual division of labor structured not only relations within working-class families but also those between male and female workers, employers, and the state.[35]

Following these insights, I place gender at the center of my analysis of the hobo workforce. Part of the conventional wisdom among labor historians is that nineteenth-century craftsmen adhered to a mutualistic "ethical code [that] demanded a 'manly' bearing toward the boss" and fellow craftsmen alike. According to David Montgomery, a craftsman worthy of his co-workers' respect "refused to cower before the foreman's glares—in fact, often would not work at all when a boss was watching." Skilled workers' technical knowledge afforded them this possibility because they could not be easily replaced, and despite the adverse effects of mechanization, autonomy and skill remained important attributes of what was considered manly work in the twentieth century.[36]

How men at the bottom of the skill ladder claimed or mobilized manhood is a more complicated matter. To be sure, laborers had their notions of manly behavior, but their position in the job hierarchy seldom allowed them to confront employers' power openly. In his study of early-nineteenth-century canal laborers, Peter Way identifies a destructive masculine "rough culture" of drinking, gambling, and fighting as central to laborers' culture. "By working hard and laughing in the face of danger, canallers were actually engaged in self-exploitation," Way argues. Irish laborers' vaunted ability to consume large quantities of alcohol, he suggests, should be seen as employer-inspired drug addiction.[37]

In contrast to Way's fascinating but overly negative reconstruction of working-class life, David T. Courtwright advances a more extreme argument in his synthetic study of the masculine origins of American violence. Thanks to natural selection, he writes, "Young men are prone to violence and disorder." Because the United States had a surplus of young males, "America had a built-in tendency toward violence and disorder."[38] Seasonal work on the all-male industrial frontier, he argues, was "genetically and personally suicidal" because early death without children awaited anyone who remained a laborer very long. He concludes that the "shrewder and better educated saw the futility of the floating army and got out quickly," while others either "burned out, landed in jail, or ended beneath the dissecting knife on the coroner's slab."[39]

Courtwright's social Darwinism reminds us that nineteenth-century notions about the innate inferiority of the working classes are still with us today. Nevertheless, the rough, destructive elements of laborers' culture were real enough. It is all too easy to romanticize hobo workers as freewheeling "knights of the road." Seasonal laborers' working conditions usually were unpleasant, unhealthy, and dangerous. Their food, always monotonous, was at times even poisonous. They faced robbery and extortion at every turn, legally from employment agents and illegally from hold-up men and train crews. When they quit their jobs and went into town for a "rest," they often spent their money on prostitutes, gambling, and excessive drinking. Moreover, while laborers enjoyed the social advantages of being men (e.g., geographic mobility), male power did not always benefit them. They were both perpetrators and victims of the physical violence that was an element of male social power generally.[40]

Nevertheless, I find a more complex relationship between rough culture and the young men working as seasonal laborers. Although they often were hard-pressed by poverty and although some engaged in violent crimes and self-destructive behavior, they were not pawns of economic and genetic forces. Among the most common explanations of laboring men's rough behavior is the fact that they lived in a bachelor subculture nearly devoid of the supposed tempering influence of women. In the words of the economist Carleton Parker, "the labor class lost the conventional relationship to women and child life, lost its voting franchise, lost its habit of common comfort or dignity, and gradually became consciously a social class with fewer legal or social rights than is conventionally ascribed to Americans."[41] But was this rough, womanless condition permanent or just a stage in young men's lives? What counted as manly behavior varied according to a man's age, his position within the household, and the conditions under which he labored. As Joy Parr argues, manliness is not "unitary or fixed but cross-cut into contending and complementary possibilities by class and age, fashion and belief, and the changing priorities of production and reproduction. . . . The entitlements of the single fellow and the family man emerge as distinctively as those of man and woman."[42] In addition, the laborer's world was far from womanless. Wives, lovers, sisters, and mothers maintained households to which men returned during the off season. Women fed strangers who came to their back doors looking for a handout. And, as Joanne Meyerowitz and Kathy Peiss have shown, in the urban dance halls young working women met up with young men ready to spend their hard-earned money for a night on the town and often established what used to be called "transient free unions."[43]

We can also see laborers' so-called womanless condition in light of their youth and the predominance of males in the population of the rural Midwest as a whole. In rural Minnesota there were 116 men to every 100 women in 1910, and in North Dakota 123 men to every 100 women. In addition, a greater proportion of rural women than men were married.[44] Given these statistics, bachelor men could hardly be thought of as automatically outcast from rural communities. Rather, as Cecilia Danysk argues in her study of hired hands in the Canadian prairies, bachelorhood was a legitimate masculine role as long as it was temporary, lasting until a young man earned enough money to marry and buy land. In the meantime, the community viewed single men "with tolerance, concern, and benevolence, and often with a certain bemused affection."[45] Like Way's rough canal laborers, bachelor homesteaders and hired hands valued physical strength and an individualism attenuated by the need for collective work. But because women also demonstrated physical strength in farm work, rural bachelors did not define themselves against weak women. According to Danysk, they defined their bachelorhood by their own lack of domestic skills, their inability "to take care of themselves, to cook, to sew, to keep clean, to converse politely, and to demonstrate other features of gentle civilization."[46] Despite their supposed lack of domestic skills, bachelor farmers, like men living together in track gangs, logging camps, and "bachelor shacks," had to cook and clean for themselves. Although traditional notions of what constituted men's and women's work remained, men working in all-male settings could hardly draw such distinctions too starkly.

Whether they were bachelor farmers or laborers living with an all-male crew, most laborers considered themselves part of a community and a household. Many were also an important part of family economies. Younger members of farm families contributed their labor to the family when needed and left the farm to work for wages during agricultural slow seasons.[47] Meanwhile, the sons and daughters of working-class families helped their families survive through wage work, peddling, scavenging, and other nonwage activities.[48] As Eric Monkkonen notes, "the institution of tramping provided one means to cushion the shock of unemployment . . . [because families] could send adult males out on the road."[49] Like seasonal workers in other regions, young men from working-class and rural families in the Midwest sought seasonal work away from their homes and families but rarely forgot what they had left behind. For those who lost touch with family, the absent household—and the nagging memory of their own failure to establish a family—often played the same role, structuring both the male and worker dimensions of their identity. Others created nontraditional families, either by "baching" with other single men or by living with male and female lovers. Laboring men's sense of their own place within broader social relations therefore was based in part on real, remembered, and constructed family relations and in part on the cultural understandings of what it took to be a man at different stages of life.

The middle-class investigators who studied laboring men accented different elements of manly behavior. Although middle-class propriety eschewed the rough culture of working-class men, it was hard for middle-class men not to see working men as somehow more virile and direct in their masculinity. By the late nineteenth century, as Gail Bederman argues, "middle class power and authority were being challenged in a variety of ways which middle class men interpreted—plausibly—as a challenge to their manhood."[50] The middle- and upper-class social investigators who took on working-class identities (the focus of chapter 2) were in a sense expressing uneasiness about their own and working men's manliness. By becoming a working man the investigator could have the best of both class worlds, experiencing the virility of working men and adding to his own knowledge and intellectual mastery of the social world.

❖ ❖ ❖

Although gender, race, and age structured the experience of laboring men, we cannot dismiss class as a defining element of their lives. Some kind of class analysis is essential for three important reasons. First, laboring men—whether farmer's sons or urban workers—shared the experience of working for wages in a seasonal labor market. Second, laborers, their families, employers, and reformers described laborers' experiences in terms of class. And third, the organized politics of migrant laborers and resident workers invoked class interest as a motivating element. The significance of these class positions, discourses, and politics is by no means self-evident. Just as historians now treat race and gender as categories that have changed over time, we must see the meaning of class as contingent on specific historical developments.[51] This is not to argue that class relations are somehow unreal; rather, it is to take greater account of the role of culture and politics in defining class positions, experiences, and consciousness.

These very concepts, experience and consciousness, which have been so fundamental to the new labor history, have been attacked as vague and misused. From Gareth Stedman Jones's argument that the political rhetoric of the Chartist movement made the English working class, rather than the other way around, to Joan Scott's claim that histories of experience obscure the more significant operations of discourse, the so-called linguistic turn in social history has forced a reassessment of historical practice. According to these scholars, social historians have mistakenly read statistics and narrative sources as evidence of class consciousness, as direct evidence of lived experience. Turning that approach on its head, those who emphasize discourse show how historical sources are themselves the agents of social reality, mapping out social formations, defining insiders and outsiders, and marking the limits of appropriate social behavior. They challenge the simple correlation between experience and its representation in historical sources. What we read as lived experience, they argue, is instead the footprint of cultural and ideological formations that structure reality.

However, the discursive approach is only one of many challenges destabilizing the concepts of consciousness and experience. For instance, feminist historians have criticized men's labor history for uncritically representing the gender ideology of the past as experience itself and thereby neglecting the history of women workers.[52] Given the various critiques of social history, how might we describe common peoples' lives with adequate nuance and complexity? How can we write a history that gives credence both to the power of economic and cultural structures and to the possibilities for people to make change?

Among the recent scholars who offer useful approaches to class analysis, the sociologist John Hall argues for a conception of class that focuses on relationships to markets rather than productive relationships alone.[53] Hall draws three important conclusions from this perspective. First, he observes that a person may confront different markets at the same time and therefore "may face multiple, potentially reinforcing or incongruent class situations at different moments in his or her life." Second, he notes that when people share the same relationship to a given market, they will not necessary have common interests or engage in concerted action. And finally, Hall argues that "cultural conditions rather than objective circumstances alone affect whether individuals jointly perceive their situations as deriving from a common external cause."[54] By focusing on the relationships of cultural institutions such as families, unions, and communities to commodity, consumer, and labor markets, Hall creates a dynamic framework for analyzing the actions of workers who do not neatly fit traditional models of proletarianization and class formation. This approach is especially useful for analysis of seasonal laborers who shared the experience of wage labor but came to it from diverse backgrounds.

If Hall's approach helps us see class as common actions in relation to markets, other theoretical approaches help define the extramarket relations that bear on the relative power people bring to markets as well as the cultural definition of the marketplace itself. We have already seen the important role of gender ideology and family relations in orienting men toward seasonal work. Similarly, racial ideology and identity played a role as employers allocated work to different ethnic groups, and white men sought to define themselves against other participants in the labor market. What is more difficult to explain is how and why culture and experience developed into class consciousness and action.

In this regard, Raymond Williams's work on class and culture is useful. Williams suggests that the relationship between social structure and social life is analogous to that of the musical score and the musical performance. Although a musical score is fixed, interpretation and error ensure that no two performances of the same score are identical. Similarly, in her work on German women workers, Kathleen Canning argues that people's identities form at the intersection of discourses that define various social roles and the bodily "experiences of desire and deprivation" felt by individual workers. Although cultural expectations limit the available models for social action, these models are never perfectly reproduced in life as it is lived. The disconnect between bodies as defined by discourse and bodies defined by lived experiences, these scholars suggest, is the place to look for working-class agency.

The men who worked in the seasonal industries of the Midwest might embody different social positions at different times in their lives: the bachelor homesteader, the husband and father, or the freewheeling hobo. Reformers, employers, and other laborers read these identities from the clothing, speech, actions, and physical attributes people exhibited: calloused or soft hands, lumberjack's mackinaw coat or farmhand's overalls, arriving in town as a ticketed rail passenger or hopping off a boxcar. However, laborers sometimes confounded expectations. Investigators discovered self-taught intellectual hoboes, newspaper reporters revealed boy hoboes as transient women in disguise, tramps bought nice suits and "passed" into respectable society. It is this lack of certainty that both frustrates and enables our efforts to understand the meaning of seasonal work. Although we benefit from what social investigators revealed about laboring men's lives, we often learn more about the social organization of power when investigators express surprise and confusion over laborers' actions and beliefs.[55]

The dominant social discourse marked laborers as dirty, lazy, and degraded outsiders. Although they were often hungry, cold, and at times physically and mentally broken, there is much more to their story. Between 1880 and 1930, the social meaning of seasonal labor shifted in response to the changing regional economy, developing ideas in economics and social reform, and the actions of laborers themselves. More specifically, what it meant to be a harvest hand or hobo changed as IWW organizers nurtured their culture of defiance. Workers individually and collectively took actions that defied the expectation that they would arrive in rural areas in time to bring in the harvest and then quietly go away without claiming a permanent role in rural society. In other words, they challenged the rules of the labor market itself.

Therefore, we should ask not only how social discourse marked the bodies of seasonal laboring men but also how laborers dealt with their cultural and physical marginalization. If society characterized laborers in various positive and negative ways, how much freedom did they have to choose among these identities? How did they make sense of their hunger, their pain, and their memories? What actions did they take based on these embodied experiences? There can be no easy answers to these questions. Seasonal laborers' life experiences can be understood only by balancing their various identities, caricatures, and representations, whether they be "farmers' sons," "rebel workers," or "hoboes, tramps, and bums." From disparate sources we must sift through the evidence, weighing social investigators' descriptions against laborers' remembered motives and feelings. Along the way, I hope to convince the reader that laboring men were by no means marginal to early twentieth-century America. Their life experiences, the social danger they symbolized, and the conflicts that arose from their actions were central to American culture, economy, and politics.

NOTES

1. Here and below, Solenberger, *One Thousand Homeless Men,* 141–45. Throughout the book, I have quoted at length from the words of seasonal laborers. Whether these passages were written by laborers themselves or reported through a third party, they often contain grammatical and spelling errors that I usually have chosen not to clutter with editorial comments. In a few cases, I have inserted letters or words within brackets to make the meaning more apparent.
2. Wiebe, *The Search for Order,* 17.
3. Parker, *The Casual Laborer,* 86; interview with V. R. Dunne, 11, MHS.
4. *Oxford English Dictionary* (OED): hobo, orig. Western U.S. "An idle shiftless wandering workman, ranking scarcely above the tramp" (Funk). On "haute beaux" see McCook, *The Social Reform Papers of John J. McCook,* hereafter *McCook Papers;* Benson, *Hoboes of America,* 15. On "Hello Boy" see Peter Tamony Papers, WHMC.
5. On hoboes, tramps, bums, and other categories of transient laborers, see chapter 3 and Anderson, *The Hobo.* Census enumerators in rural areas often listed "farm laborers" simply as "laborers." On the cultural significance of names and categories

see Green, *Wobblies.* Other studies of hoboes and homeless men include DePastino, "From Hobohemia to Skid Row"; Adrian, "Organizing the Rootless"; Bruns, *Knights;* and Kusmer, *Down and Out, on the Road.*

6. U.S. Bureau of the Census, *Fourteenth Census of the U.S.*, vol. 4, 35. Farm laborers as a whole (working out and at home) were 16 percent of all workers in 1910 and 10 percent of workers in 1920.

7. Isern, *Bull Threshers and Bindlestiffs,* 172; Swierenga, "Agriculture and Rural Life," 93–94.

8. An excellent study of early nineteenth-century farm labor is Schob, *Hired Hands and Plowboys.* Less widely known studies of farm labor and wheat harvest labor specifically include Cox, "The American Agricultural Wage Earner," 95–114; Paul S. Taylor, "Origins of Migratory Labor," 6258–98; Jamieson, *Labor Unionism;* Applen, "Migratory Harvest Labor"; Richard Mahon, "Wage Labor and Seasonal Migration in the Wheat Economy of the Upper Mississippi Valley, 1850–1875," 9 December 1988, Chicago Area Labor History Group, The Newberry Library, Chicago; McWilliams, *Ill Fares the Land.* Among the excellent recent work on rural history, see especially Gjerde, *The Minds of the West;* Neth, *Preserving the Family Farm;* Jellison, *Entitled to Power;* Fink, *Agrarian Women;* Dublin, *Transforming Women's Work;* Hahamovitch, *The Fruits of Their Labor;* Valdés, *Al Norte;* Mapes, "Defining the Boundaries."

9. Hatton and Williamson, *The Age of Mass Migration;* Montgomery, *The Fall of the House of Labor,* 70–71; Borchert, *America's Northern Heartland,* 31–78.

10. Fink, *Workingmen's Democracy,* 112–48.

11. Deutsch, *No Separate Refuge,* 24–26; Jameson, *All That Glitters,* 163–75.

12. Fink, *Workingmen's Democracy,* 112; see also Green, *Grass-Roots Socialism;* Hall, *Labor Struggles;* Morlan, *Political Prairie Fire;* Martinson, "'Comes the Revolution,'" 41–109.

13. Edwards, *Strikes in the United States,* 14–15; Lauck and Sydenstricker, *Conditions of Labor,* 11–20; Montgomery, *Fall of the House of Labor,* 332; U.S. Bureau of the Census, *Special Reports,* lxxxviii, and *Fourteenth Census of the U.S., 1920, Vol. 4, Occupations,* 34.

14. Montgomery, *Workers' Control in America,* 91–112; Salvatore, *Eugene V. Debs,* 205–212.

15. The standard histories of the IWW are Foner, *History of the Labor Movement,* and Dubofsky, *We Shall Be All.* Two older works still prove useful: Brissenden, *The I.W.W.;* and Gambs, *The Decline of the I.W.W.* Regional histories of the IWW include Tyler, *Rebels of the Woods;* Sellars, *Oil, Wheat and Wobblies.* A more interpretive history that has influenced my approach to the IWW is Salerno, *Red November.* Kornbluh, *Rebel Voices,* provides an excellent collection of primary sources. The union's official history is told in Thompson and Murfin, *The I.W.W.*

16. Schrager, "'The Early Days,'" 191; Lescohier, "With the I.W.W.," 371–80. The IWW launched the AWO in 1915 and changed its name to the Agricultural Workers Industrial Union, Local 120, in 1917.

17. Alexander, "Hiring and Firing," 128–44. Slichter, *The Turnover of Factory Labor;* Graziosi, "Common Laborers," 512–44; Montgomery, *Workers' Control,* 34–37, 40–44, 116–22; Montgomery, *Fall of the House of Labor,* 238–39; U.S. Commissioner of Labor, *Eleventh Special Report.*

18. Commons, "Introduction," in Slichter, *The Turnover of Factory Labor,* xiv.

19. Fraser, "The 'Labor Question,'" 55–84; Brody, *Workers in Industrial America,* 48–81; Fink, *In Search of the Working Class,* 201–35; McCartin, *Labor's Great War,* 24–37.

20. Neth, *Preserving the Family Farm,* 71–75, 97–104; U.S. Industrial Commission, *Reports. Volume 10,* 927–28, 275, xviii–xxi.

21. U.S. Senate, *Report of the Country Life Commission,* 41–43. See also Danbom, *The Resisted Revolution;* Thompson and Warber, *Social and Economic Survey,* 11.

22. For descriptions of this process in other regions, see Hahamovitch, *Fruits of Their Labor,* 83–84, 165; and Montejano, *Anglos and Mexicans,* 213–18.

23. Cronon, *Nature's Metropolis,* 18.

24. See Thernstrom, *Poverty and Progress;* Chudacoff, *Mobile Americans.*

25. Leiserson, "The Problem of Unemployment," 11–12; for an alternative view, see Schneider, "Tramping Workers," 212–14.

26. Kusmer, *Down and Out, on the Road;* DePastino, "From Hobohemia to Skid Row"; Schneider, "Tramping Workers"; Adrian, "Organizing the Rootless."

27. Williams, *Keywords,* 65–66. See also Bell and Newby, *Community Studies,* 27.

28. Gordon, Edwards, and Reich, *Segmented Work;* Edwards, *Contested Terrain;* Whipp, "Labour Markets," 768–91.

29. See Hahamovitch, *Fruits of Their Labor;* Peck, *Reinventing Free Labor.*

30. Flynt, *Notes of an Itinerant Policeman,* 19. See also Montgomery, *Citizen Worker,* 83–89; Stanley, "Beggars Can't Be Choosers," 1265–93.

31. Fink, "Looking Backward," 15. See also Roediger, *The Wages of Whiteness,* 95–110. For a European example see Seidman, *Workers against Work.*

32. Deutsch, *No Separate Refuge,* 30–40.

33. Lewis, "Expectations," 31–39; see also Trotter, "Race, Class, and Industrial Change," 60–61; Bodnar, Simon and Weber, *Lives of Their Own,* 31–33.

34. Montgomery, *Fall of the House of Labor,* 109–11; see also Barrett, "Americanization from the Bottom Up," 996–1020.

35. Kessler-Harris, "Treating the Male as 'Other,'" 198–99; see also Baron, *Work Engendered;* Cooper, *Once a Cigar Maker;* Parr, *The Gender of Breadwinners,* 232; Canning, "Gender and the Politics of Class Formation," 766–68.

36. Montgomery, *Workers' Control,* 13–14; see also Cooper, *Once a Cigar Maker,* 124; Blewett, "Masculinity and Mobility," 164–78.

37. Way, "Evil Humors," 1407–8; see also Way, *Common Labour,* 199.

38. Courtwright, *Violent Land,* 9, 3.

39. Ibid., 184, 4.

40. Cockburn, "Forum," 161; See also Gorn, "'Gouge and Bite,'" 18–43; Rediker, *Between the Devil and the Deep Blue Sea,* 205–53; Ownby, *Subduing Satan,* 21–102.

41. Parker, *The Casual Laborer,* 17.

42. Parr, *The Gender of Breadwinners,* 238, 10; see also Faue, *Community of Suffering and Struggle,* 16; Peck, *Reinventing Free Labor,* 129–31.

43. Meyerowitz, *Women Adrift;* Peiss, *Cheap Amusements,* 51–55, 108–14.

44. Jellison, *Entitled to Power,* 9. Courtwright uses these data as a simple explanation as to why the western United States was more "violent" than the East.

45. Danysk, *Hired Hands,* 72, 175. On rural middle-class attitudes toward bachelors and work see Stock, *Main Street in Crisis,* 75.

46. Danysk, *Hired Hands,* 76.

47. Neth, *Preserving the Family Farm;* Schob, *Hired Hands and Plowboys.* See also Hahamovitch, *Fruits of Their Labor,* 30–35; Dublin, *Transforming Women's Work,* 8–9.

48. Barrett, *Work and Community,* 90–107; Bodnar, Simon, and Weber, *Lives of Their Own,* 89–108; Kessler-Harris, "Treating the Male as 'Other,'" 190–204; Baron, *Work Engendered,* 15; Stansell, *City of Women.*

49. Monkkonen, *Walking to Work,* 242.

50. Bederman, *Manliness and Civilization,* 11–15. See also Griffen, "Reconstructing Masculinity"; Kimmel, *Manhood in America,* 101–12; D'Emilio and Freedman, *Intimate Matters,* 171–201; Gorn, *Manly Art,* 185–94, 252.

51. Roediger, *Wages of Whiteness,* 6–11; Scott, *Gender and the Politics of History,* 53–67; Janiewski, "Southern Honor," 70–91; Berlanstein, *Rethinking Labor History.* For a different view see Fields, "Ideology and Race." See also Katznelson, *Working Class Formation;* Sewell, "How Classes Are Made," 50–77.

52. Jones, *Languages of Class,* 90–178; Scott, "The Evidence of Experience," 773–97; Scott, *Gender and the Politics of History,* 53–67; Reid, "Reflections on Labor History and Language," 39–54; Gullickson, "Commentary," 200–14; Hanagan, "Commentary," 182–99; see also Palmer, *Descent into Discourse.*

53. Hall, *Reworking Class,* 1–37; see also Whipp, "Labour Markets," 770–73.

54. Hall, *Reworking Class,* 18.

55. Williams, *Problems in Materialism,* 31–49; Canning, "Feminist History," 386; see also Bourdieu, "Structures," 157, 166; Kelley, "'We Are Not What We Seem'"; Scott, *Weapons of the Weak;* Rose, "Class Formation and the Quintessential Worker," 148–54.

❖

1 "Like the Flock of Swallows That Come in the Springtime": The Uneasy Place of Hobo Workers in Midwestern Economy and Culture

THE YEARLY MOVEMENT of laborers through the harvest fields of the Great Plains often confronted observers as a mystery of nature. As early as 1860 an Illinois farmer newspaper labeled harvest workers "birds of passage," and more than sixty years later, in a testament to a popular agrarian myth, a South Dakota correspondent for *Country Gentleman* magazine wrote of harvest workers, "Like the flock of swallows that come in the springtime, they harvest the wheat and then vanish into the unknown again."[1] Another line of thinking painted the harvest workers as a criminal element invading a normally tranquil rural life. "This scourge of the land," wrote a German-language newspaper in 1876, "numbering in the thousands, comes to the northern towns of Iowa and with them robberies, break-ins, [and] thieving come on the calendar."[2]

Americans liked to think of farm country as a world apart from the conflicts that racked urban life in the Progressive Era. But the farm and the factory, the small town and the metropolis, were very much part of the same world. The coming and going of harvest laborers was not a mystery of nature. Nor were the men who harvested wheat and labored on the railroads and in the mines and forests a migratory flock. And although it may have been true that crime increased in Iowa towns during the summer, it bears stating that local people also committed robbery and even murder. What made seasonal laborers such a useful symbol of social dislocation was the pervasive notion that they were truly out of place: wandering men without homes or communities. But laborers were an integral part of the economy of the Midwest, both urban and rural. As a ready reserve of labor power they made possible the expansion of railroads and the industrialization of agriculture. As members of working-class and farming households they aided in the struggle to survive in a market economy.

One of the best ways to see the intertwining of rural and urban life and work is to follow laborers from job to job. When we map these travels, it is apparent that what observers took to be aimless wandering or unthinking migration was guided significantly by economic structures, family, and individual survival strategies. The three life histories that follow were collected by U.S. Commission on Industrial Relations (USCIR) investigator Peter Speek. They are partial sources designed to highlight the notion of floating labor, but they also demonstrate distinct migration patterns. First, cities acted as hubs for laborers' travels. Railroad connections, job information, and recreation were more often urban, but jobs were more often rural. Second, laborers' job histories show local, national, and (with less detail) international migration patterns. The same worker might hold to a tight geographic pattern for several years (often staying in one town) and then light out across the country to seek better fortunes. And third, life histories demonstrate that men working in seasonal industries were ready, willing, and able to take jobs in a variety of different settings: farm work, logging, construction, factory, service, and even the armed forces.

The life history of Norman Daniel provides a good example of all of these patterns (see figure 2). At age 34, Daniel already had wide work experience when Speek and William Duffus took his life story in a hotel room in Colby, Kansas, in July 1914. Daniel was not a political man. He told Speek and Duffus that he could not "see into [the] IWW" and that although "Socialism might work," he had never voted—"never bothered my head about it," he said. His interviewers worried for him, reporting that he drank alcohol and sometimes got "soused." His hands were sunburned but soft, suggesting he was not a hard worker. "This man appears to be on the verge of falling into the hobo class," they concluded.

Born in New Orleans in 1880, Daniel was the son of a master mechanic for a railroad. By the time Daniel joined the Army in January 1906, however, both his parents were dead, at least one from suicide according to his induction papers. Before signing up at Fort Mackenzie, Wyoming, Daniel was working as a laborer at the Great Western Hotel in Sheriden. He spent four

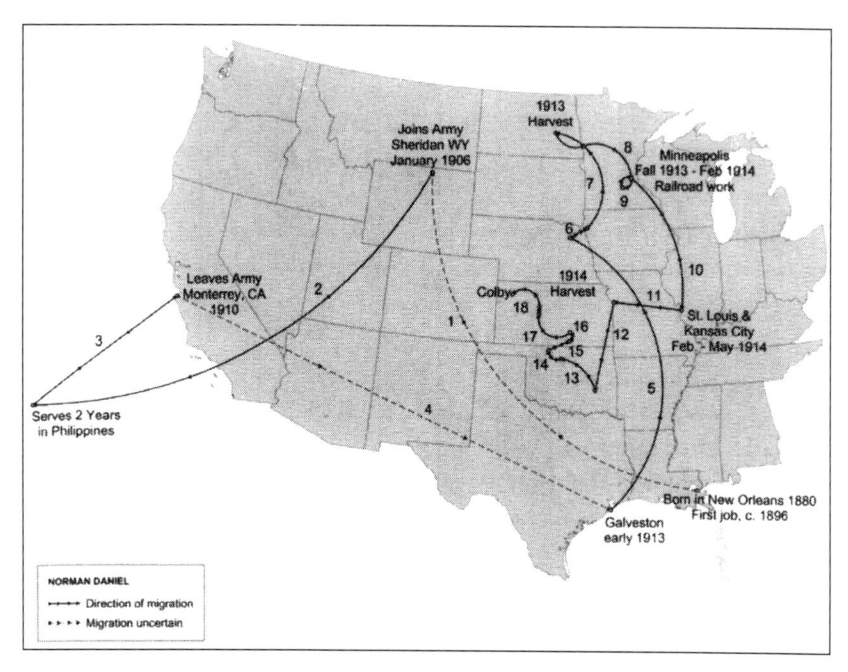

Figure 2. Job history of Norman Daniel, based on data in *U.S. Commission on Industrial Relations, 1912–1915: Unpublished Records of the Division of Research and Investigation* (Frederick, Md.: University Publications of America, 1985). Drawn by Emily Kelley.

years in the Army, part of the time in the Philippines, as he told the investigators, and was discharged in the spring of 1910 at Monterey, California.[3]

We have no information on Daniel's activities between 1910 and 1913, but in the spring of the latter year he left Galveston, Texas and took a series of jobs that took him as far north as the Dakotas, and then south again. He worked railroad construction in Nebraska and western Iowa in June and later in the summer worked for four or five different farmers in the North Dakota wheat harvest. After the harvest, he worked on a "steam shovel outfit" for twenty-seven days and then took a series of short jobs with bad conditions. Hoping to find work elsewhere, he rode freights to St. Louis in freezing weather. He found only odd jobs there, such as shoveling snow. He took "anything to make a few dimes or nickels" and also begged. In March, he moved on to Kansas City, where he found a quarry job outside the city. This job had a mixed crew of whites and blacks, which Daniel objected to despite segregated eating and sleeping facilities. Working "under a Negro boss" was the last straw, and when ordered to perform what he considered a "bad job," Daniel refused and was fired.

In the spring he worked for the Kansas City Terminal Railway Co. The living conditions were terrible: "Shanties, double bunks, one story, blankets dirty, vermin, foul smell all around camp, no toilet. . . . Always sewer gas. Prostitutes soliciting men. Cooking very poor. At times not enough to eat." By mid-June 1914, he was back at wheat harvest work near McAllister, Oklahoma. From there he moved on to Enid, where he joined with a large group of harvesters whom he characterized as the "floating craft." Together they freighted to Alma, where they were met by the U.S. Marshall and employment officer. The officials marched the men uptown, where those with money bought themselves breakfast and farmers waited to hire men for harvest work.

Daniel hired out with a German farmer at "top wages" of $2.50 for a ten-hour day. Conditions on this job were in stark contrast to his previous railroad work: "3 meals (brandy each time) and an afternoon lunch. Work very heavy. Temperature up to 103. Water very good. Slept in a small shack, 2 beds. Sheets. Very clean." Unfortunately, the job was "all but finished" after four and a half days, and Daniel had to move on. From Alma, he freighted to Wellington, where he spent the night. He turned down a harvest job at $2 a day because "no old harvest hand would work for that." He paid passenger fare to Wichita, where he found 200 men already looking for work, so he freighted northwest to La Crosse, Kansas. There he took a job at $4 a day, but the farmer cut his pay to $3 when they got to the farm, so he quit. Moving on to Hays, Daniel had a similar experience. After two hours of work the farmer cut his pay, so he quit. He then worked for three different "Russian farmers" (probably Volga Germans) for $4, good food, and outdoor sleeping. After five days on another job the entire crew quit because they could not get along. In town he waited two days without work for a job paying $4 a day. Finally he got work with another Russian farmer, where board was "nothing extra" and he slept in a wagon. That job ended after two and a half days, and he freighted west, making stops in two small towns before arriving in Colby, where he met the USCIR investigators.

The job history of Sam Gray offers a more compact migration pattern (see figure 3). At thirty-five years old, the Irish-born Gray had been in the United States for twelve years. Apparently more political than Daniel, he told Speek that the IWW was a better organization than the AFL because it was "closer to the laborers." "Horses and cattle," he noted "are kept more cleaner than human beings in the camps in this country." Speek's documentation of Gray's job history began in November 1912 in Milwaukee, where he "'rest-

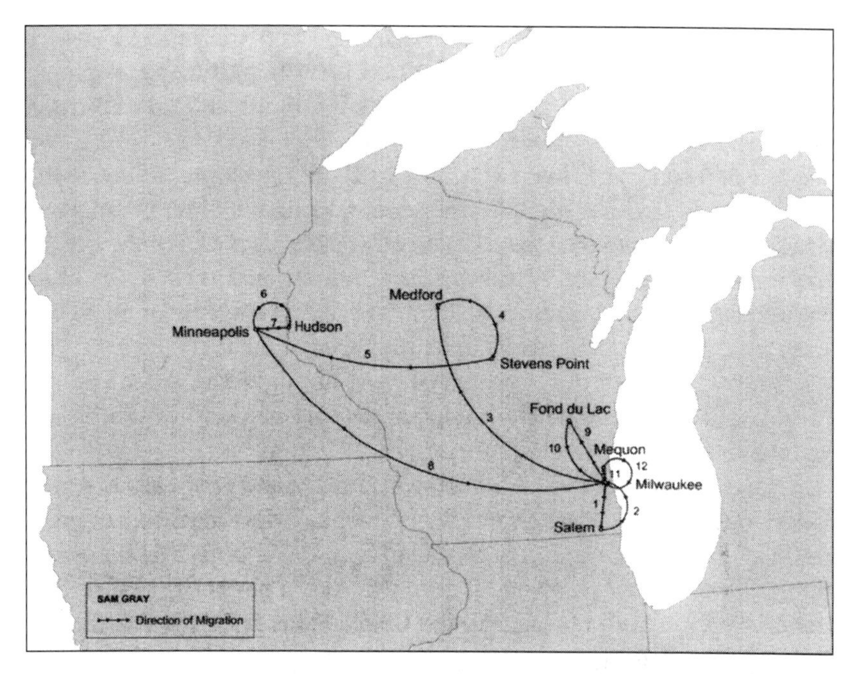

Figure 3. Job history of Sam Gray, based on data in *U.S. Commission on Industrial Relations, 1912–1915: Unpublished Records of the Division of Research and Investigation* (Frederick, Md.: University Publications of America, 1985). Drawn by Emily Kelley.

ed,' drank with other 'floaters' in the saloons—both whiskey and beer; went to shows, and courted the girls." When his money ran out, he was "helped out by temporary friends—other laborers, whom he knew, and who continued to come in from work with money." He also sought out charity from the Catholic church and went hungry.[4]

Gray picked up a construction job in Milwaukee that lasted four weeks, then he worked five weeks at Salem, Wisconsin in the ice harvest. After the ice harvest and a one-week rest in Milwaukee, Gray was in Medford, Wisconsin, working a total of three weeks on a railroad crew. He quit that job because of the foreman, and had to go to Stevens Point to get paid, after which he hopped a freight train to Minneapolis for three days "having a 'little time.'" From there, he walked to Hudson and worked six weeks, quitting "because he could not eat the grub." He rested for two weeks in Minneapolis again, and when his money was gone, he returned to Milwaukee. After three days without work, the State Free Employment Office sent him to a railroad job in Fond du Lac. He worked for five weeks, then he rested again in Milwaukee for a week, at the end of which he picked up work putting up telephone poles just outside of town. He worked that job a month and then returned for several weeks of resting and light work in Milwaukee. Gray's job history reflects a regional migration pattern. He used Milwaukee and Minneapolis as home bases. There he spent his money in saloons and other popular entertainments and made fast friends with other laboring men. For the USCIR Gray represented a typical casual worker without commitment to the labor market, a drinker with questionable moral values, a single man with little desire to settle down and marry, and a supporter of the IWW. Although he held many jobs, it is worth noting that Gray usually worked for about a month straight, probably six days a week at hard physical labor, before quitting and heading to the city for rest and relaxation.

A third laborer, Andrew Hanson, traveled locally and nationally in search of work (see figure 4). Hanson was thirty years old when Speek interviewed him in Olympia, Washington in the fall of 1914, and although he was down and out, Speek concluded that Hanson was still "a physically healthy and decent looking man."[5] He came to the United States from Norway around 1904 and worked first on an Iowa farm belonging to fellow Norwegians. From there Hanson went to Minneapolis and entered the floating labor force. He paid $12 for a construction job high in the Colorado mountains but quickly tired of the vermin-infested straw bedding, high commissary prices, and altitude. He quit after seventeen days, went to Denver, and paid $1 to an employment agent for a job on a dam construction site. Although the food was good at this job, the workers slept in tents on damp ground. After a month Hanson became ill and spent the next three months in a Denver hospital.

While in the hospital, Hanson decided that he preferred the northern climate and resolved to get back to Minnesota. He paid $1 for a railroad job in rural Nebraska but did not take the job once he arrived at the worksite; instead, he rode freight trains into Lincoln, where he picked up short-term work and bought a rail ticket to Minneapolis. In Minneapolis he heard that work was plentiful in Montevideo, Minnesota, so he went there and soon secured a job as a roundhouse laborer. He remained there for seven months, quitting so that he could "see some of his country people in Iowa." After a week's rest, he returned to Minneapolis and paid $2 for a railroad construction job in North Dakota. After one day, he quit and hired out as a farm laborer, spending eight months on the same farm.

With winter coming and almost $200 in savings, he quit the farm job and traveled to northern Minnesota. In a Bemidji saloon he hired out to a

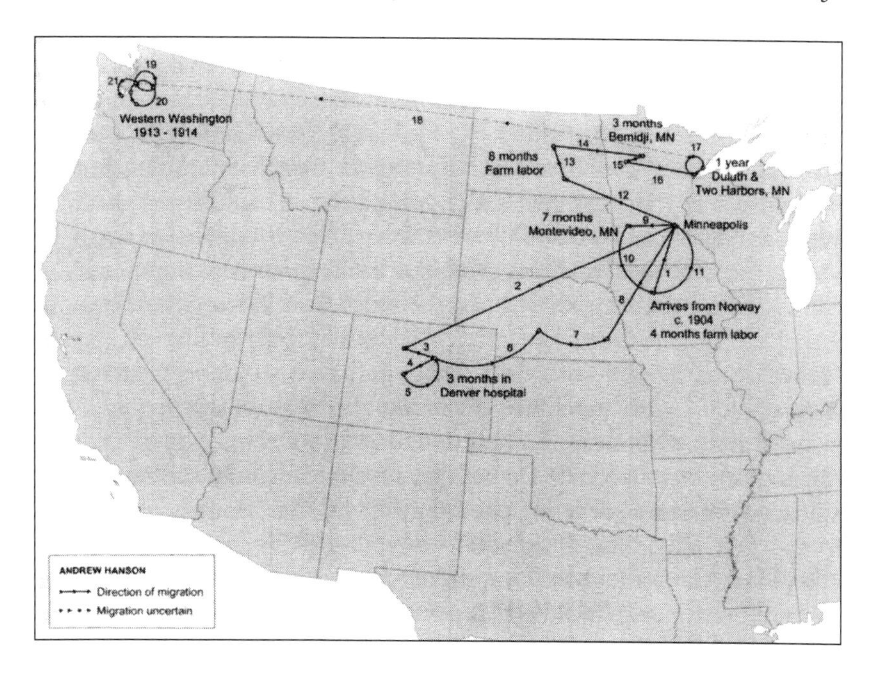

Figure 4. Job history of Andrew Hanson, based on data in *U.S. Commission on Industrial Relations, 1912–1915: Unpublished Records of the Division of Research and Investigation* (Frederick, Md.: University Publications of America, 1985). Drawn by Emily Kelley.

logging camp. The camp had what he considered a good bunkhouse: eighty men sleeping two to a bunk on straw and hay bedding without sheets or pillows. After twenty-seven days on the job he quit, along with sixteen other workers, to protest the firing of two fellow workers. He found another logging job and worked thirty-five days straight, quitting because he was tired. Next he worked in a saw mill until he was laid off at the end of the season. He was unemployed in Duluth for three weeks, then shipped to a railroad construction job on the Northern Pacific. After two weeks he quit because he was ill from the poor food and living conditions. After this job he circulated between Two Harbors and Duluth, working a variety of laboring jobs for about a year.

By 1913 he had moved to western Washington and, based in Seattle and Tacoma, worked a series of logging and construction jobs. He worked for about a month laying ties and rails for a logging railroad thirty miles from Seattle, then was unemployed for six weeks. He paid $1 for work on the Chicago, Milwaukee and St. Paul Railroad but quit after a day because of bad accommodations. Back in Tacoma he paid $1.50 for a job building a logging road, but this job closed down because of heavy snow after seven days. Unemployed for a week, he paid $1.50 for saw mill work that paid $2 a day for ten hours of work. After three weeks he quit because of bad accommodations. Out of work for ten days, he paid $1.50 for another road job but quit after five weeks so he could retrieve his watch from a pawn broker. After two more weeks of unemployment, he secured a job in the mountains but quit after a month because the company reduced the wages. Back in Seattle he got drunk, passed out, and had his money stolen, so he had to pawn his watch again. And so on until Speek interviewed him, and perhaps for years afterward. Hanson's job history combined the local patterns that Sam Gray followed (focused around Minneapolis, Duluth, and Seattle-Tacoma) with the nation-crossing pattern of Norman Daniel's job history. Tragically, the life of intermittent work and poor living conditions had beaten Hanson down when Speek interviewed him. Although he came to the United States because he believed wages were higher in American than in Norway, by 1914 Speek noted, "No future plans; would continue as a common laborer—all he can do. All hope gone—believes that he does not amount to anything. Ambition is gone; will power is weakened. . . . His is sorrowful, even when drunk."[6]

❖ ❖ ❖

Just as Daniel, Gray, and Hanson shuttled back and forth between agricultural and industrial jobs, midwestern and western commerce, politics, and social life reflected complex links between the city and the country. Although the first decades of the twentieth century often are thought of as the period in which cities came to dominate the American culture and economy, the upper Midwest remained overwhelmingly rural in this period. Only Iowa and Minnesota neared majority urban status in 1920, with 46 percent and 44 percent of their population living in towns of 2,500 or more, respectively. North and South Dakota were 86 percent and 84 percent rural in 1920, respectively. Moreover, in 1910 nearly 40 percent of the urban population in the West North Central census region lived in towns with fewer than 25,000 residents.[7] Many of these smaller towns were surrounded by open country, urban islands in a sea of farms, as Robert Wiebe described them in his influential history of the Progressive Era.[8]

The region's rail network provided the vital link between city and country, consumer, commodity, and labor markets. Railroad building itself was a major stimulus to rural economic development, especially on the Great Plains. For instance, track mileage in North Dakota nearly doubled between 1898 and 1915, employing hundreds of thousands of laborers and giving the state the highest ratio of railroads to population in the nation. Emigrant farmers crowded the frequent passenger trains into newly opened territories, and settled residents relied on freight and passenger service to maintain social and economic life in the countryside.[9] Railways also were the largest corporations in the region. Their freight rates often defined the margin between business success and failure for farmers and merchants, just as their wage scales defined the livelihood of many of the region's workers.

Railroads tightly tracked the location of seasonal laborers' jobs, services, and homes, and they were the most common mode of travel until inexpensive automobiles came on the market in the mid-1920s.[10] This close relationship between railroad towns and seasonal work resulted in part from freight trains coursing through the densely populated working-class residential districts. This commonplace of industrial life was a danger to life and property and an enticement to travel. Open boxcars offered easy access to the hinterland, and working men and women regularly availed themselves of the opportunity. Ben Reitman, Chicago's celebrated "clap doctor," claimed to have begun his tramping career at the age of five when he hopped a freight train as it rolled by his home on Chicago's southside.[11]

Larger rail centers also had distinct neighborhoods catering to the needs of traveling laborers, known by hoboes as the *main stem.* The main stem was a neighborhood filled with cheap lodging houses, employment agencies, restaurants, bars, pawn shops, and theaters—and, after 1905, an IWW hall. In Chicago, the main stem was West Madison Street, which Harry Beardlsey of the *Chicago Daily News* described as "the haunt of a great floating population that calls it 'home,' returns to it at the end of each tour, to meet old friends, consider new bookings, and pass golden hours strolling nonchalantly up and down the thoroughfares, or talking in the buffets and booking agencies." It was a neighborhood filled with hoboes and businesses catering to hoboes, so different from the rest of Chicago as to earn the name "Hobohemia."[12] Remembering his first visit to Chicago's main stem in 1921, Len De Caux described the confluence of migrant streams: a trickle of down-and-outers from the East and from the West a "broader stream" of purposeful, hard-working, but poor railroad, harvest, and timber workers.[13] According to Beardsley, West Madison Street was "the Pennsylvania Avenue, the Wilhelmstrasse of the Anarchy of Hobohemia." Across the river to the north was the intellectual and entertainment center of Hobohemia: North Clark Street, a strip of bars, dance halls, brothels, bookstores, and the open-air political forum known as Bughouse Square.[14]

Although Chicago was unquestionably the industrial, railroad, and labor center of the region, other midwestern cities, especially Minneapolis, Milwaukee, and Kansas City, had neighborhoods catering to the needs of mobile laboring men looking to "blow in" their stakes on a little fun. Smaller towns such as Duluth (Minnesota), Superior (Wisconsin), Sioux City (Iowa), and Omaha (Nebraska) served as gateways the timber, iron, and wheat territories and seasonal home to many laborers. As the primarily commercial center to the northern plains and the mines and forests of Minnesota and Wisconsin, the Twin Cities of Minneapolis and St. Paul, Minnesota, arguably exceeded Chicago's importance in the history of upper midwestern laborers. Flour and lumber milling, meatpacking, and railroad car repair were the leading employers in the Twin Cities in the early twentieth century.[15] However, as the Minneapolis Civic and Commerce Association trumpeted, "The farmer of the Northwest customarily looks to Minneapolis for labor to meet the seasonal exigencies of the agricultural cycle."[16] A 1922 study found twenty-six private employment agencies in the lodging house district of Minneapolis that together shipped 100,000 men. Some of these were organized by employers and a few by philanthropic organizations, but most were independent businesses. Public employment agencies shipped an additional 30,000 men the same year. Most were unskilled workers sent to the rural hinterlands of the Twin Cities.[17]

A 1910 study of the Minneapolis lodging house district estimated the city's capacity at 5,800 beds per night, with a total of 45,000 men passing through in a year. No doubt a greater number moved in and out of the city's furnished room apartments on a seasonal basis. For the farmhands and lumberjacks, "Minnie" was part home and part amusement park. Greeting the spring thaw with a winter's worth of earnings, one of the Norwegian immigrant lumberjacks in O. E. Rølvaag's novel *The Boat of Longing* exclaims, "All the drink money could buy! . . . [And] the place was full of pretty girls always on the lookout for a jolly time!"[18] Similarly, Robert Smith recalled learning a lumberjack's song that ended with the lines, "So watch 'em, ketch 'em, the logs are running free / And when we get to Minneapolis, we'll go upon a spree."[19] Along Minneapolis's main stem, as Charles Ashleigh described it in his semi-autobiographical novel, the migratory workers "live in their cheap hotels; eat in their cheap restaurants; and drink in their cheap saloons." Although there were other inexpensive sections in town, Ashleigh wrote, they were for the poor locals, the "home-guards." The main stem was for the floaters alone, a place where a man arriving in town "early in the morning dead broke and chilled from riding on the front end of a passenger train through the cold night" could find shelter, a drink, and a place to wash up in various saloons, with the expectation that he spend some of his stake there once he cashed his check.[20]

In addition to saloons, commercial hotels, and flop houses, Minneapolis and other cities also had lodging houses run by religious charities, and many towns allowed transient workers to sleep in the police lockup. In 1911, Minneapolis ended this latter practice and installed a free Municipal Lodging House on the upper floors of the central police station.[21] Other cities had a similar variety of inexpensive or free lodging, but most laborers found lodging in cheap commercial establishments. The least expensive lodging houses often were converted office buildings or warehouses that provided the bare minimum: a board to sleep on. A common variety consisted of a large room divided into tin-walled cubicles with wire netting draped across the open ceiling of each cubicle. A single iron stove at the end of a long corridor provided heat.[22]

To the southwest of Minneapolis, perched on the low hills along the Missouri River, Sioux City, Iowa, was the southern gateway to the Dakota wheat fields. A meatpacking center with 33,111 residents by 1900, Sioux City grew to 76,411 by 1925, making it Iowa's second largest city. The population of Sioux City reflected the town's industrial profile. Almost one-quarter of Sioux City's employed men worked as laborers of various types. The largest group of laborers worked in meatpacking, but a substantial number also worked for railroad and construction companies. Among the Sioux City residents in more skilled jobs, the building trades employed about 7 percent of the male workers, and railroad crafts employed about 6 percent. By the early twentieth century, Sioux City was an outpost of Chicago-based capital, especially the "Big Five" meatpacking firms. Armour and Cudahy owned the largest plants, and Swift and a lone independent firm had smaller operations. The influence of the Big Five extended to the stockyards, the terminal railroad company, utilities, banks, streetcars, and the local Commercial Club according to a Federal Trade Commission investigation.[23]

Just as Sioux City served the Dakotas, the twin ports of Duluth, Minnesota and Superior, Wisconsin served the mining and logging regions of northern Minnesota and Wisconsin as a transshipment point for goods and a source of labor. Fargo, the largest city in North Dakota, served the Red River Valley and had its own modest packinghouse industry and warehouse businesses. Beyond Duluth, Sioux City, and Fargo, the prairies and forests were dotted with small towns that served as local marketplaces and administrative centers for the rural districts.

❖ ❖ ❖

Before the spread of inexpensive automobiles and the rise of commercial bus lines, the network of urban areas and their rail links structured where and how laborers would go to seek work and rest. However, the changing seasons (and only secondarily the business cycle) determined when laborers moved. Although the system was not a closed one and the movement of workers not constant, it is possible to describe a rough seasonal pattern of migration (see figure 5).[24] In the spring, workers picked up railroad and farm work at the same time that lumber work trailed off. Summer provided steadier work, with the wheat harvesting season beginning in June in Texas and Oklahoma, reaching the Dakotas by late July, and moving north into Canada by September. Threshing began in October and could last until late November depending on weather conditions. Peak demand for farm labor in the upper Midwest came in late July, August, and September. Corn, potatoes, sugar beets, and other crops provided alternative agricultural employment in the fall.

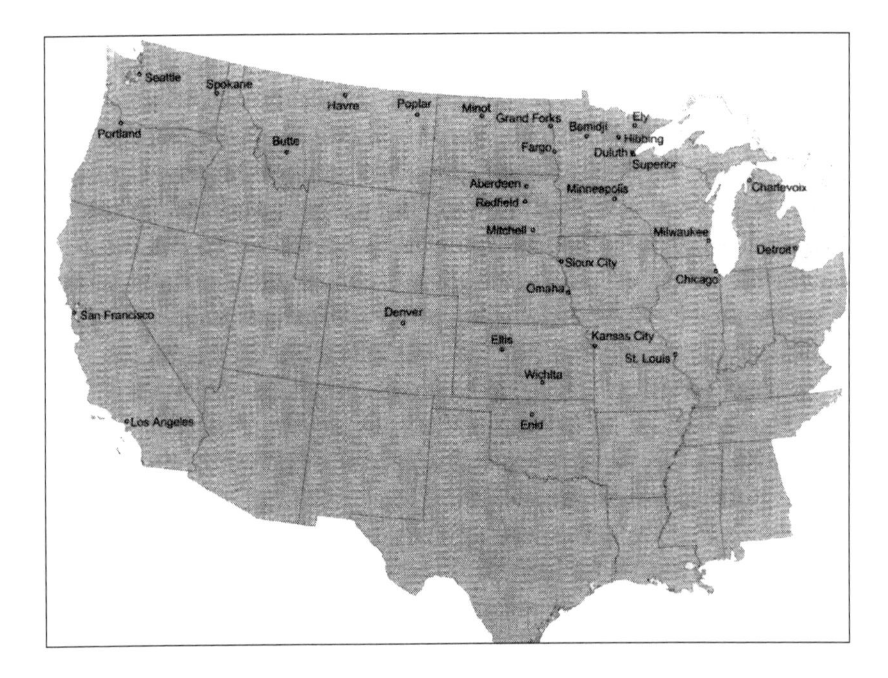

Figure 5. Towns and cities of the Great Plains and upper Midwest mentioned in the text. Map by Emily Kelley.

The volume of work in meatpacking, railroad construction, and other industries followed these agricultural cycles. As an executive of the Northern Pacific Railroad commented with some exaggeration, "Farmers do not have a great deal of work to do on the farms in May, June and July, and we procure a large percentage of our track labor from farms in these months."[25] These extra gangs, as they were called, also consisted of urban laborers and, according to the same executive, were "employed early in the spring and work until harvest time, after which many of them go into the fields and are employed until the harvest is completed, after which they find employment in shops and factories" or, if students, returned to school.[26] In meatpacking, production slowed in the summer both because the heat made refrigeration more difficult and because the tight labor market drove up payroll costs. Slaughtering picked up during the fall as farmers sold off their stock and as other employment opportunities dried up. With the first heavy snows, farm and railroad laborers returned to the cities. Railroad construction and maintenance all but stopped during the coldest months, and farmers who chose to keep their employees over the winter usually offered to pay only room and board. The logging season in the upper Midwest reached its peak in the winter, when frozen roads and lakes made for easier transporting of timber and seasonal unemployment created a ready supply of workers. Those who stayed in the city survived on their winter stake, odd jobs, or, for the lucky few, steady factory work. By January, the brief ice-harvesting season provided extra cash, followed by another lull before the opening of spring work began the cycle again.[27]

As the life stories of Daniel, Gray, and Hanson suggest, laborers could work steadily by shifting between different seasonal industries because logging, mining, construction, and agriculture had complementary slack and busy seasons. However, working in each of the major extractive industries brought laborers face to face with problems ranging from unsanitary bunkhouses to low pay to boredom and loneliness. A closer look at the living and working conditions in each of these industries helps to link the issues of regional economic development with the emergence of laborers' resistance to the floating labor system.

The midwestern logging industry began its long decline after 1900 as the long-log timber was exhausted and the industry shifted to the Pacific Northwest and the South.[28] Still, the state of Minnesota employed 15,886 timber workers in 329 camps during the 1899–1900 season. These workers produced 1.12 billion feet of lumber, enough wood to build a nine-foot-wide sidewalk around the earth, boasted the Minnesota Bureau of Labor.[29] Between 1900 and 1920 midwestern lumbermen shifted to the pulp and paper industry, using the smaller trees that grew in the far North and on the cutover lands. Like the long-log industry, pulpwood was a highly concentrated business, especially in the hands of Edward Backus, who controlled the Minnesota and Ontario Paper Co., which by 1930 was the largest corporation in the state of Minnesota. Smaller timber cutters (known as jobbers) continued to operate, but control of sawmills and pulp processing—the most profitable parts of the industry—was in the hands of large corporations.[30]

Living conditions in lumber camps reflect both the traditional nature of the industry and the fact that lumber companies were shifting their capital to other regions. An exposé of camp conditions by the Minnesota Department of Labor and Industry (MDLI) in 1914 described lumber camps in rough terms. For instance, the headquarters camp of an unnamed company consisted of two bunkhouses, two stables, one warehouse, one commissary, one blacksmith shop, and one cookhouse and dining room, all built out of logs. The bunkhouses were thirty-six feet long by twenty-seven feet wide and eleven feet high. Each housed about one hundred men in twenty-six double deck beds, four feet wide by six feet long. Two, sometimes three men slept in each bunk, and each bunk had three blankets but no pillows or sheets. The bunkhouses were poorly lit by two-foot-square windows at each end and a skylight of the same size. Ventilation was provided by the windows and by a hinged wooden door in the roof. The rough wood floors were scrubbed only once a month. Washbasins and roller towels in each bunkhouse allowed the men to clean up after work, but there were no facilities for washing or drying clothes, and the privies were fouled. However, the foreman, timekeeper, and kitchen crew had a separate, clean privy.

Other investigators discovered similar conditions. Laborers interviewed by the USCIR sometimes told of bedding consisting of pine boughs, hay, or straw.[31] Even at the camps that provided clean sheets, pillows, and blankets, it was difficult to keep bunkhouses clean because "the men have been accustomed to a filthy life in other camps; they do not clean their shoes when they enter the bunkhouse and many, if not all, bring vermin with them."[32] Indeed, the nature of timber work made keeping the bunkhouse clean difficult. The men returned after work soaked in sweat and wet from the snow, and bunkhouses could be drafty and cold. Few employers provided washing facilities or places to dry clothes. They resisted such hygienic innovations for monetary reasons and because they imagined their employees were not worthy of better conditions. As one supervisor told the Minnesota legislature, drying rooms were impractical because the men would steal each other's clothes. In the absence of these innovations, the lumberjacks lived a traditional way, communally in the bunkhouse, smoking pipes and drying clothes over the stove and sharing bunks.[33] The Minnesota report concluded that these conditions "made it impossible for the men to keep their bodies free from vermin."[34]

Food quality was a major issue for lumber workers, and even in camps with inadequate sanitary conditions, investigators sometimes found that meals were plentiful and reasonably healthful. In the camp surveyed by Minnesota officials, the cook and his three helpers cooked in lard cans, had inadequate cleaning facilities (table utensils "were greasy after being washed"), and disposed of kitchen refuse by throwing it on the ground outside the kitchen door. However, investigators concluded that this camp provided healthful meals in a clean setting. The floors were scrubbed regularly, and the men were well fed, with meals including "fresh beef, mutton, salt pork, potatoes, rutabagas, kraut, canned tomatoes and corn." Fruit pies, fresh bread, biscuits, and pastries were regular features, and the "coffee [was] of good quality." A sign posted in the dining room read "No Talking."[35] Judging from other reports and life histories of laborers, good food was not a constant, and bad food was sure to drive lumberjacks away from a job. Even where the food was of good quality, the men had difficulty tolerating the monotonous menu. Problems with food, living conditions, and low wages all contributed to a high turnover rate in the timber industry. For example, one of the largest lumber companies in northern Minnesota hired a total of 23,290 men in 1917 to maintain an average daily payroll of 1,750.[36]

In contrast to the declining timber industry, iron and copper mining in the upper Midwest experienced an enormous influx of capital in the late nineteenth and early twentieth centuries, mostly from Eastern corporations. Mining on the iron ranges of Minnesota began in the 1880s and 1890s, and the Mesabi range in particular quickly became a leading source of iron ore for the nation. By 1900, there were fifty-six iron mines in the state, with an annual output of more than 8 million tons. The population of northeastern Minnesota grew with the mining industry, peaking by 1920 along with the supply of high-grade iron ore. Although a variety of companies operated mines on the Mesabi range, the powerful U.S. Steel corporation exercised disproportionate control of the region's ore and transportation industries.[37] The open-pit mines typical the Mesabi range operated seasonally, shutting down much of their work when winter snows blanketed the area. In addition, Lake Superior was frozen several months a year, and no ore boats could leave the ports at Duluth and Two Harbors. Like iron and copper miners in neighboring Wisconsin and Michigan, mine workers from the Mesabi often found winter work in the forests working as lumberjacks.[38]

The iron range communities were home to a highly diverse population. A 1907 study of the workforce of a large mining company found that nearly 85 percent of the roughly 12,000 employees were foreign-born. Finns made up the largest immigrant group on the range, followed by Slovenians and Croatians, Swedes, and Norwegians. The skilled jobs tended to go to English-speaking workers who had mining experience in Europe or America, and Finnish and Slavic workers dominated the ranks of common labor in the mines. Residential patterns on the Mesabi range reflected the needs of the mining industry, with the population spread across the range in small towns, villages, and company-owned "locations." During the range's first decades, many of the miners were young single men, living in boardinghouses and "bachelor shacks." When Powers Hapgood worked briefly for the Oliver Mining Company in 1920 he stayed in a lodging that consisted of two tin houses, one for the kitchen and dining room and the other a bunkhouse; thirty miners shared fifteen beds.[39] Like other areas popular with single, migrant laboring men, the range had its share of prostitution, gambling, and drinking. As a study of the region noted, "It was not until after 1910 that community life had become sufficiently settled to secure adequate law and order on the Range."[40]

Like the locations and camps in the mining and lumber industries, those in the construction industry usually lacked ventilation, bathing, and sanitary facilities. More often than not employers and commissary companies simply converted boxcars into bunkhouses, kitchens, and dining rooms. This arrangement was typical for "extra gangs," those hired during the busy summer, and had the advantage of being easily moved between various worksites. The more permanent section crew camps that remained in the same location were at times also made of old boxcars placed directly on the ground with their wheels removed.[41] William Leiserson's study of Wisconsin labor camps reported that the typical sleeping car was thirty-four feet long by eight feet wide by six to ten feet high, housing twelve men in six double-deck bunks (one man to a bunk).[42]

The conditions of construction camps were variable. As the MDLI reported of one camp, "At breakfast the potatoes turned black when fried; the sausage was sour and the coffee bitter and unpalatable. . . . There were no sinks or privies for the men. Among the weeds adjacent to the cars the ground was filthy with excrement and old clothes fairly alive with vermin. . . . A number of the men complained of dysentery as a result of the food and the general unsanitary conditions of the camp."[43] However, Minnesota investigators found one model camp that was sanitary and even provided a clinic, nurse, and movie theater for entertainment. But this was certainly the exception rather than the rule. With no state law regulating labor camps, authorities could enforce sanitary codes only when camps were inside city limits. "The owners of the camps have continued their practices for years without let or hindrance," complained the Department of Labor and Industries report, "and often use up the vitality of strong, healthy men in one season and send them back to their homes a menace to the communities."[44]

Conditions had not improved much when the Minnesota Industrial Commission investigated highway construction camps in the summer of 1930. State officials noted that "about half of the sleeping quarters were good, and the other half about equally divided between fair and bad." Although each man generally had his own bed, only half of the bedding was "clean or fairly so," and the other half was "poor," "soiled," dirty," or "very dirty." Although one camp had hot and cold running water and showers, "there appeared to be a scarcity of wash-basins in most of the camps" according to the report. Similarly, although "toilets were provided in most of the camps," conditions continued to be primitive by urban standards. The report also noted that the commission received "numerous complaints . . . that road contractors were taking advantage of the many men out of employment by imposing on their employees long hours of labor, low wages, unreasonable charges for board, poor housing conditions, and compelling them to pay fees to employment agencies for jobs." The same study found that the camps with the highest turnover were those that paid the lowest wages and charged most for board.[45]

As investigators surveying conditions in logging, mining, and construction quickly discovered, laborers often sought agricultural employment when industrial jobs were scarce. Indeed, agriculture was the region's most extensive industry, and wheat farming in particular employed many nonfamily laborers, more than 100,000 harvest workers each year according to a 1924 U.S. Department of Agriculture (USDA) study.[46] The wheat boom of the early twentieth century had its roots in an earlier "bonanza" farming era that set important patterns for wheat farming on the Great Plains. Hoping to sell off their huge land grants and populate the countryside along their lines, the transcontinental railroads set about changing the image of the erstwhile "Great American Desert" by launching an extensive agricultural experiment. Although these bonanza farms of the Red River Valley of North Dakota lingered on in some cases into the 1920s, they reached their peak between 1879 and 1886, according to historian Hiram Drache. "Only the largest feudal estates of Europe or the greatest cotton plantations in the South had anything comparable to the number of men found on the large bonanzas," Drache concluded.[47] During the harvest of 1884, for instance, the largest of the bonanza farms planted 30,000 acres of wheat and hired 1,000 harvest hands who operated 200 reapers and 30 threshers to bring in a total crop of 600,000 bushels. More than thirty years later, the Amenia and Sharon Land Company hired more than 200 farm laborers, as well as a number of grain elevator laborers, carpenters, painters, masons, and hotel and garage workers.[48] The Red River Valley wheat farms developed together with the timber industry of northern Minnesota. Many of the farm workers were off-season lumberjacks, and in the winter farm managers sent their horses to work in the lumber camps.[49]

The location of such huge businesses in farm country made bonanza farms a particularly interesting site of negotiation between industrial and agrarian models. The level of mechanization and the sheer number of workers was a far cry from the typical experience of the hired farmhand. Journalist William Allen White likened the bonanza farm manager to "the superintendent of an important railway division" and the farm laborer to "the mill-hand in the East."[50] John H. Hanson, who worked on the Chaffee farm in the 1880s, added the middle initial "H" to his name because there were so many John Hansons working on the farm that his mail got mixed up. Yet despite the grand scale of production and large numbers of workers, the analogy between farm and factory has its limits. The rural setting and culture of farming meant that relations were as likely to be structured by patronage and paternalism as by strict economics. The subtle balancing act is evident in the diary of Mary Dodge Woodward, who lived on the Dakota bonanza farm managed by her son in the 1880s. She sometimes wrote about the hired hands as if they were part of her own household but at other times made a distinction. "Our family has increased until there are thirty-two," she noted in her diary as the harvest reached its peak. But three days later she wrote that there were "fifteen teams at work and thirty men besides the family." She also criticized hands for spending time in Fargo's saloons.[51] Similarly, the "House Regulations" for workers at Clover Leaf Farms in southeastern North Dakota suggest some of the paternalistic elements of employment on these farms. Among the things laborers could not do on farm property were drink alcohol, use improper language, and keep the lights on after 9 P.M. (see figure 6).[52] Nevertheless, farm employers did not hesitate to fire troublesome hands. Nina Van Ostsand, whose father was the superintendent of a large farm near Wahpeton, North Dakota, remembered a strike by a thresher crew. Her father simply drove into town and hired replacements. The strikers went back to work.[53]

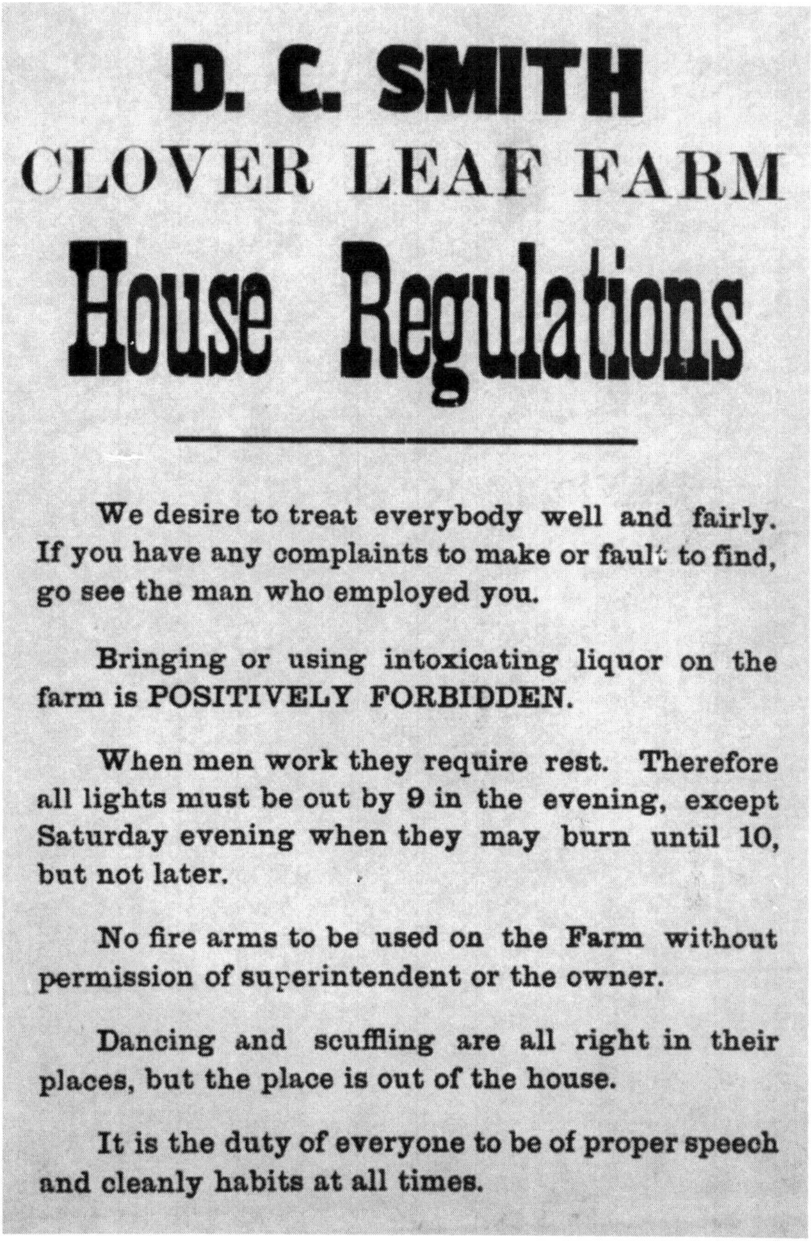

D. C. SMITH

CLOVER LEAF FARM

House Regulations

We desire to treat everybody well and fairly. If you have any complaints to make or fault to find, go see the man who employed you.

Bringing or using intoxicating liquor on the farm is POSITIVELY FORBIDDEN.

When men work they require rest. Therefore all lights must be out by 9 in the evening, except Saturday evening when they may burn until 10, but not later.

No fire arms to be used on the Farm without permission of superintendent or the owner.

Dancing and scuffling are all right in their places, but the place is out of the house.

It is the duty of everyone to be of proper speech and cleanly habits at all times.

Figure 6. Bunk house rules for harvest hands, c. 1885. From the collections of the North Dakota Institute for Regional Studies and the NDSU Archives, North Dakota State University Libraries, Fargo.

By the 1890s, the bonanza system was in decline because of drought, rising land prices and taxes, and the public perception that their great scale hindered the development of healthy rural social relations, according to Drache. But the bonanza farms set the tone for the wheat industry. Their breakup shifted the focus of the industry toward individual farmer-entrepreneurs, who replicated the bonanza's industrial techniques on a smaller scale. Highly mechanized operations, large land holdings, wheat monoculture, and the use of transient labor characterized even family farms on the Great Plains.[54] Production expanded rapidly on the plains in the years after the bonanza boom. Farmers broke new land, and yields were high. The acreage of plowed farm land doubled each decade in North Dakota between 1890 and 1910 and exceeded 9 million acres by 1919. The average value of farm land and buildings in the state more than quadrupled. In 1909, the Dakotas and Minnesota alone produced nearly a third of the nation's wheat. Between 1899 and 1919, the West North Central states produced nearly one-half of the U.S. wheat crop.[55] The southern wheat belt—settled earlier than the Dakotas—did not see such spectacular increases in new farm land, but Kansas farmers returned to the once-drought-ravaged middle and western counties and launched a wheat boom between 1890 and 1920. Wheat acreage in Kansas increased from 1.6 million in 1889 to nearly 6 million in 1909. The most dramatic period of growth was that of World War I, when wheat acreage nearly doubled in the state. By 1919 Kansas was by far the nation's largest producer of wheat, with a crop of 148.5 million bushels.[56]

Wheat production was not spread evenly across the wheat belt; rather, it was concentrated in certain counties with well-suited soil and easy access to markets and labor. Farms in these counties usually were larger than average, more highly capitalized and mechanized, and hired the largest share of harvest labor. For instance, whereas the Kansas farms averaged 275 acres in 1919, half of the farm land in fifteen top wheat-producing counties was in farms larger than 500 acres, and a quarter of the land was in farms larger than 1,000 acres. Important wheat counties in the Dakotas exhibited similar patterns of land concentration. The smaller farms in these regions typically had more diversified crops and harvested with family labor. According to a report by Kansas agricultural officials, a family of four could harvest up to 160 acres of wheat without hired help.[57]

The wheat belt in general was distinguished by a high level of mechanization, and farm machinery costs far outpaced those for farm labor between 1900 and 1930. The most important items of farm machinery were two types of reaper (the binder and the header) and the threshing machine. The binder, whether drawn by horse or tractor, cut the grain stalks near to the ground, scooping them up, mechanically bundling them with twine, and dropping them to one side. A binder crew consisted of one operator (usually the farmer or member of the farm family) and one or two shockers. The shocker walked behind the binder, picked up the bundles, and collected them into shocks by setting them firmly into the stubble left by the reaper. Larger farms used one binder for every 200 acres and three laborers for every two binders. Using the binder, harvesting could begin before the wheat was fully ripe because it continued to ripen in the shock.[58]

Use of the header did away with shocking and often increased the intensity of the harvest. The header, as the name implies, cut the heads off wheat stalks, leaving behind the straw. The wheat heads were then lifted by a conveyor belt into the header barge, a specialized wagon drawn alongside the reaper. When one barge was filled, an empty one was drawn up, and the full barge was taken to unload its wheat onto large stacks. Several stacks usually were placed close together to make threshing more efficient. A typical header crew included seven workers: one header driver, three barge drivers, two pitchers, and one stacker, who built the wheat stacks so as to protect the grain from the weather. The driver and the stacker were skilled workers who earned a dollar or two more a day than the pitchers and barge drivers, who could be less experienced. However, farmers using the header often began the harvest only when the wheat was fully ripened and therefore needed to harvest quickly. The longer a farmer waited to harvest, the greater the chance that something would go wrong and the more intense the work experience. Kansas and Oklahoma farmers used the header more often than did farmers in the Dakotas.[59]

Once the wheat was shocked or stacked, it had to be threshed, or separated, before it could go to market. Between 1900 and 1920, most threshing was done by steam-driven machines, although gasoline-powered threshers appeared after 1915. Once the wheat was sufficiently dry, a threshing machine was set in the midst of several stacks. The steam engine remained some distance away, connected to the thresher by a long belt. Pitchers stood on the stacks and cast wheat into the thresher feeder, while an engineer tended the steam engine. If wheat had been shocked, wagons brought the shocks to the thresher. Most farmers contracted their threshing out to itinerant threshing crews. These were sometimes operated by farmers and sometimes by small-town entrepreneurs. Threshermen regularly hired outside labor, and threshing wages were higher than harvest wages.[60]

After World War I, the combined harvester-thresher became more popular among wheat belt farmers. The combine did the work of reaping and threshing and significantly reduced the overall labor demand in the region. The new technology was heralded as the end of the harvest labor migration, but its adoption was uneven across the wheat belt. For instance, Kansas farmers adopted combines quickly, in part because they worked like headers. Kansas already had nearly 2,800 combines in 1923 and more than 21,000 in 1930. In contrast, North and South Dakota together had only 28 combines in 1925 and fewer than 2,000 in 1928. The damper conditions of wheat growing in the northern states, which encouraged the use of binders rather than headers, also slowed the diffusion of combine technology. As late as 1933, a national survey found that grain harvesting remained an important area of employment for migratory workers, but several laborers declared to investigators that employment conditions had definitely changed for the worse because of the combine.[61]

❖ ❖ ❖

Throughout the rural North farm families carefully negotiated their integration into labor and commodities markets. Few farmers could claim to be self-sufficient, but not all farmers were equally positioned in relation to markets for goods, land, and labor. In older, more stable rural communities, farm families raised a combination of grains, livestock, and garden crops. Often neighbors came together at harvest time to bring in each other's crops in an atmosphere of sociability. In these areas, local men were expected to work as farm laborers to earn capital to buy a farm and start a household, which they often did with the financial help of their families. To be sure, midwestern farms had always been deeply involved in commodity markets. But the vagaries of weather and prices, along with the cash-poor nature of rural economic life, meant that farm families carefully balanced production for home consumption with production for the market.[62]

This balancing act was complicated by the fact that farms were both workplace and household. As Jon Gjerde notes, "Although Americans have tended to romanticize the equality made possible by the family farm, they have remained less cognizant of the disparities within it. Ironically, whether or not free land made people free, it promoted a dependence and reliance within families that tended to trap certain members—such as children—in protracted subservient relationships."[63] Wives and children labored under the authority of the male household head, and the general understanding was that family members ought to work hard for the good of the whole family. Farm women spent their days hauling firewood and water for cooking and washing, tending gardens, and often directing poultry and dairy businesses that fed the family and brought in revenue. Children could be set to simple chores such as weeding fields as soon as they were able.[64]

Farm families also traditionally relied on the labor of neighbors. Threshing rings, barn raising, quilting bees, and other labor-sharing arrangements created opportunities for socializing but also sustained the community as a productive and reproductive unit. Innovations such as cooperative laundries and dairies built on these work-sharing traditions. However, community work patterns were increasingly undermined by a turn to agribusiness according to Mary Neth's study of the farm family.

The increasing proportion of farms operated by renters reflected the complicated nature of these developments. For instance, tenantry in Spink County, South Dakota, increased from 27 percent of all farms in 1900 to 54 percent in 1930. Tenancy in Ward County, North Dakota, exploded from a mere 1 percent of farms in 1900, when land was widely available, to 36 percent in 1930. However, tenant farms in these counties were comparatively large and highly mechanized.[65] In poorer areas tenants and many owner-operators barely survived on small plots and often supplemented their income with seasonal employment on larger farms. Some contemporary observers argued that increasing tenancy rates in wheat-growing areas were a result of small farmers being forced out of ownership by mechanization and rationalization.[66] Others echo the words of Minnesota rural investigators who reported the common perception in that region that "if anybody is making money in farming, it is the renters."[67] The 1929 Agricultural Census found that nearly one-quarter of all farm operators in the West North Central states worked off the farm an average of eighty-one days a year and that full owners—rather than renters—were the largest proportion of farmer-workers. Renting land on shares was less a measure of a tenant's dependence and marginalization and more a measure of participation in the market. Renting was also a typical method of acquiring capital to buy one's own land. It allowed farm operators to take advantage of rising wheat prices by expanding their acreage with little capital. However, renters' unstable tenure in the farm community limited their participation in the informal economic exchanges that sustained less market-oriented farmers, according to Mary Neth. Although tenants themselves often were prosperous, an increasing proportion of tenants in any one area could undermine the community economics of the rural neighborhood.[68]

Within rural communities conflicts arose between farm operators who embraced new agricultural methods and those who resisted change or were too poor to afford modern improvements. So-called progressive farmers looked to state agriculture colleges and county extension agents to learn about fertilizers, new machinery, and crops. Typically the more prosperous and market-oriented farmers, these progressive farmers tended to attribute farm failures to individual ineptitude rather than structural economic causes. Community conflicts grew as progressive farmers turned to mechanization, opted out of labor-sharing arrangements, and hired fewer laborers. Less prosperous farmers suffered doubly from these changes because they relied on community labor to bring in their own crops and on the extra cash from harvest jobs to make ends meet. Nor could they match the productivity of the mechanized farms. Wisconsin farmer Percy Hardiman remembered that the two or three farmers in his neighborhood who sympathized with the IWW were struggling economically and did not have enough food for their children. They were the "type of people who didn't want to follow the progressive things in agriculture to make life better and to earn more money," he told an interviewer.[69] Ultimately, progressives such as Hardiman won out in these community disputes, but in the early twentieth century farm families often were still working through the contradictions of rural modernization.

Laboring work and laboring men intersected this negotiation between households and markets in two ways. First, laboring men were members of families negotiating the tension between self-sufficiency and market orientation. The earnings of farmers' sons and daughters helped sustain the home sphere while their families' reliance on wage labor tied them closer to farming as a business. Second, whether they were from a different ethnic group or simply ill mannered, laborers hired to work on farms represented the incursion of the outside world into the moral and economic structure of the farm household. As Hamlin Garland wrote of the man his father hired to help on the farm for a season, "Jack came from far lands, and possessed . . . unusual powers of dancing and playing the fiddle. He brought also stirring stories of distant forests and strange people and many battles." Whereas the hired man Jack was simply mysterious, the temporary harvest hands were "the wild and lawless element" or "strange nomadic fellows, which the West had not yet learned to call tramps."[70] William Duffus, an investigator for the USCIR, found that farmers were reluctant to house harvest laborers in their homes because they believed laborers were "strange, and often unclean and diseased men."[71]

Laboring men were a living link between the rural household and the market economy that farmers hoped to use to their own advantage but keep at arm's length. Even the farm men who left home to work for wages could become problematic. When Erick Berdahl returned to his family's Iowa farm after winter work in a lumber camp during the 1870s, for instance, his mother was shocked and dismayed by the rough language and manners her son learned among the lumberjacks.[72] Similarly, older siblings told exciting tales of life on the road, enticing younger siblings to leave the farm, as was the case with Nels Anderson, whose interest in hoboing was "fired" by letters from his older brother.[73] To be sure, similar tensions and opportunities arose in working-class families whose children entered the labor market. As Kathy Peiss and others argue, young working-class women struggled with competing expectations to contribute income to family and to spend it on consumer goods. Similarly, working-class sons who hit the road could be a boon to their families when they sent money home from distant jobs or a burden when they returned home unemployed and broke.[74]

Living and working conditions for farm laborers differed from farm to farm depending on the size of the farm, the disposition of the farm employer, and the urgency of the harvest. As Katherine Jellison finds in her study of farm women and technology, midwestern farm families were slow to adopt household technology such as electricity and running water. Instead, they opted to invest in things that would make field work more efficient, such as tractors, or connect them to urban amenities, such as automobiles, telephones, and radios. For instance, almost 70 percent of South Dakota farm families owned an automobile in 1920, but only 12 percent had running water and only 9 percent had electric lights.[75]

Fiske Marbut, a college student turned harvest hand, found a range of conditions all within miles of Hutchinson, Kansas. Arriving there with a friend in late June 1915, Marbut discovered that bad weather was delaying the harvest work. With no cash reserves to fall back on, the two young men walked out of town asking farmers along the way whether they could work for their room and board until the harvest started. Luckily, they found such an arrangement with a prosperous farm family who let them sleep in the barn and set them to work at odd jobs. After a few days, the farmer let his young employees sleep in "nice beds" in the house. When the harvest began, the farmer hired more men, and the crew worked twelve-hour days with a two-hour lunch break. Marbut wrote to his father, "We have a socialist in our gang and he often gives us lectures at noon which forms about my only amusement." After this job ended, Marbut picked up another harvesting job. "I nearly starved to death and slept in a little old shack with a Dutchman, a Swede and a couple of toughs," he wrote his father. The job lasted only two days, although he noted, "If the work had lasted any longer I would have quit." Preparing to leave town, Marbut picked up a third job harvesting and plowing for a farmer who provided tolerable living conditions.[76]

Before the wartime labor crisis, farmers in the wheat belt were less likely to invite their harvest hands to sleep in the farm house, preferring to house them in barns, in granaries, or outside.[77] In his postwar studies of harvest work, Don Lescohier found that 65 percent of harvest hands slept in beds in farmers' houses, but 30 percent slept in barns or granaries. A common complaint among workers was lack of bathing facilities, Lescohier found, because "many of the farms lack bathrooms, or hesitate to allow the harvesters to use them." The farmer who permitted his hands to bathe in horse troughs "is gratefully remembered by his harvest hands," Lescohier noted.[78]

The uneasy place of hired labor within the family farm workplace was particularly clear for women and young boys. Usually women worked for wages on larger operations, where they assisted with household chores such as cooking and washing. At times, they were hired as part of a family group, as in the case of a Nebraska farmer who filed an application for farm help with the U.S. Employment Service, saying he needed a "man, wife and two boys." The wife's wages were "to be included in the husbands and duties as a housewife."[79] Unmarried single women hired out as kitchen workers, especially during the harvest. This work could be more exhausting than harvesting. Lorena Hickok recalled that she had to get up at 3 A.M. to set the stove fire and prepare breakfast for a harvest crew. Then she worked nonstop for three days. "I was a squirrel in a sweltering cage, running frantically round and round in a wheel, never getting anywhere," she wrote in an unpublished memoir.[80] Similarly, young boys often were treated as apprentices, compensated with room, board, and occasionally new clothes or paid half of a "man's wages." For instance, when fifteen-year-old Harvey Raymond ran away from an abusive apprenticeship with a lumber jobber, he felt himself fortunate to find shelter with a farmer who paid him in food and clothing for fifteen hours of work each day.[81]

Adult hired men received better pay than women and children, when the latter were paid at all, but all were expected to labor in the context of the family economy. Itinerant harvester Jack Maloney remembered that it was best to quit a harvest job if you had to work with neighborhood men. "If it was a bunch of home guards there, the smart thing for you to do was get the hell out, you know, because they were working for fame and glory and you were out there to make a payday," he told interviewers.[82] The work hours could be long on farms precisely because laborers were expected to finish working only when all the chores were done, not at a specified quitting time. The practice often was "to work from 'can to can't,' i.e., from the time you can see in the morning, until you can't see in the evening," recalled Robert Saunders. This left little time for leisure and implied that the farmer hired the laborer rather than the laborer's time. Reflecting this legacy, the U.S. Census placed "laborers" in the "domestic and personal service" sector as late as 1900.[83]

Despite these disparate expectations of farmers and their hired workers, it is worth remembering that the categories *farmer* and *worker* were not always so distinct. Instead, we might think of the bulk of the working population of the upper Midwest as orienting themselves to a wide range of opportunities to earn a living for themselves and their families. For instance, farm owners often worked for wages themselves or hired out their teams of horses to construction crews and neighbors with larger farms. Likewise, because employment in most industries was irregular and unreliable, workers often sought to escape wage labor by taking up farming, hunting, fishing, and other subsistence activities. Lacking the capital resources to buy land in agriculturally rich areas, these workers-turned-farmers tilled the rocky soil of the Wisconsin and Minnesota cutover regions. They often found the stumps difficult to clear and the soil good for little more than hay and garden crops, and they rarely hired farm laborers. Therefore, they supplemented their income with wage labor in logging, mining, railroad and road construction, and crop harvesting.[84] For instance, the Immigration Commission reported that Italian immigrant farmers in northern Wisconsin's Barron County regularly supplemented their income with railroad work. The household heads of eleven of twelve farm families highlighted in the report supported their families by railroad wages until their farms became economically viable, for an average period of eight years. Similarly, workers-turned-homesteaders tried to balance residence requirements of the Homestead Act with the need to earn cash to pay for improvements to their land.[85] Another federal investigation, the Joint Commission on U.S.-Canada Fisheries, frequently told of residents in the Lake Superior region combining fishing with farming or work in the forests and mines. During the depression of the mid-1890s, investigators reported that "laborers of the various stone quarries" near Houghton, Michigan survived unemployment by fishing, "catching not only what they ate through the winter, but also supplying the local market" with fish for sale.[86]

Homesteading, fishing, hunting, and other activities on the margins of the extractive economy were opportunities to make do in the context of an irregular, often oppressive wage labor market. Similarly, farmers often took the opportunity to enter the wage labor market when they needed extra money to stabilize their irregular farm income. Instead of seeing distinct classes of farmers and workers, we should view all of these people as part of the same flexible labor force that often found the line between making do and losing out not at the center of commodity and labor markets but at their margins.

❖ ❖ ❖

The varied extractive industries of the upper Midwest provided the context for the movement of laborers across the land. In a sense, this movement was entirely congruent with the seasons and the ways in which different industries arranged production around them. And yet for many who took the time to investigate and write about seasonal laborers, it was anything but natural. The floating labor system became a prime target for reform because it seemed to break down healthy men and send them back to their homes as derelicts. Some noted the danger laborers faced as they "beat" their way on the railroad, riding illegally on freight cars. According to railroad company figures, 156,390 "trespassers" were killed or injured on American railroads between 1888 and 1905. However, one railroad official noted in 1907 that the real figure must be nearly three times the official totals because railroad employees buried the bodies of hoboes in unmarked graves.[87] Similarly, working in mechanized agriculture posed the dangers of swirling blades and gears that often maimed or killed farmers and harvest hands alike.[88]

But the maiming and killing of men drew less attention than the social threat posed by living laborers. In addition to camp conditions, reformers targeted the fee-charging employment agencies that acted as brokers for the labor market. Laborers found their jobs in several different ways. Although the village main street remained an important marketing space for farm labor in the countryside, many laborers found work through private employment agencies. These agencies exercised power over the labor market because large employers such as railroad, lumber, and mining companies used them to find workers. Some employment agents became powerful men by controlling the jobs of whole territories and ethnic groups. But workers often were able to manipulate the system to their own advantage. Between 1900 and 1930, reformers challenged the preeminence of fee-charging agencies in the market, seeking to replace them with state-sponsored free employment bureaus. The roots of their uneven success lay in the fact that the fee-charging system was both exploitive and useful to workers, whereas the free employment bureaus acted essentially as welfare agencies.

For reformers and radicals alike the most galling abuse was also the most basic to the system: laborers literally bought their jobs, often paying extortionate fees. A study of Minneapolis agencies after World War I found that most workers paid about $2 for jobs, although some paid nothing and others paid as much as $6.[89] Other investigators found fees as high as $15.[90] Grace Abbott of Chicago's League for the Protection of Immigrants found that fees usually were highest when the applicant could not speak English. An investigator who "represented himself to be a man who collected 'gangs' was told frankly, 'We charge all we can get'" by a labor agent. The jobs private agents offered rarely lasted more than a month, and workers were paid less than $2 a day.[91] As USCIR investigator Peter Speek argued, given the short duration of many jobs, even a small fee of $1 "may be considered as an exploitation."[92] A report by the Minnesota Department of Labor and Industry revealed a host of abuses including exorbitant fees, misrepresentations of job conditions, sending men to nonexistent jobs, and abuses by "padrones" and "interpreters" for immigrant workers. The state recommended drastic regulation or prohibition of these agencies because of their "record of misrepresentation, duplicity, extortion and corruption."[93]

In addition to charging high fees, a commonly criticized abuse was known as fee splitting. In this practice, agents and crew bosses conspired to place workers on jobs only long enough to pay off their rail fare and other fees, after which they fired them. The jobs would then be filled with new workers, paying new fees. The agent collected the fees and paid a kickback to the crew boss. In one case, an agency held exclusive contract to supply a railroad company with track laborers. The railroad required all employees to pay a $4 fee to the agency, even if they already held jobs. Groups of Greek laborers paid up to $10 for jobs. Sometimes they arrived at their new workplace to find no jobs available. In other cases they were fired on flimsy pretexts within a few days of starting work. Others soon arrived to take their places. According to reformers, the process yielded "one crew coming, one crew going and one crew working."[94] Fee splitting enriched crew bosses and agents while it sustained the floating labor market on which their livelihood depended. Meanwhile, the loss of income and social marginalization laborers endured because of these abuses tied them more tightly to the casual labor market itself.

Other abuses were perhaps less calculated and reflected the confusing nature of the employment agency business and idiosyncrasies of certain foremen. Workers were sent to nonexistent jobs, induced to give gifts to supervisors, charged excessive transportation fees, and paid less than the advertised wage.[95] Similarly, wheat belt commercial clubs routinely published advertisements in papers throughout the Midwest that exaggerated the local demand for labor. The result was a flooded labor market and low wages. Employers often set different pay schedules for short-term and long-term workers. Such a schedule could function either as an incentive for men to stay on the job or as an incentive for employers to maintain high turnover (and thus lower wages). In at least one case, a construction contractor charged workers who quit before the end of the season a higher rate for room and board. Hospital fees of $1 a month were common and were almost never refunded when a worker quit or was fired early.[96]

Another problem stemmed from the shortage of cash at remote worksites. Some employers paid only on specific paydays, forcing workers who quit to wait for payment. Others paid in checks that had to be cashed at a specific bank, usually for a fee. As several farm workers commented, farmers sometimes shortchanged workers on payday because they did not have exact change and refused to give extra. At other times farmers were dissatisfied with a laborer's work and paid less than the agreed-upon rate.[97] Although employers, and especially farmers, faced real difficulties finding cash, many laborers lived on the edge of destitution and needed their pay as soon as they could get it. So shortchanging was not just an annoyance but in most cases a real hardship.

If private employment agents used their gatekeeping role to exploit workers and employers, and employers exploited the desperate need of working people to find work, we should not overlook the range of relationships within the labor market. This was especially true of the social organization of immigrant workers' labor, which ranged from coercive to familial to friendly. As Cindy Hahamovitch and Gunther Peck have shown, immigrant entrepreneurs created profitable businesses of directing members of their own ethnic groups to specific labor markets, be it agricultural work on the Atlantic coast or railroad and mining work in the West.[98] Less powerful but also abusive were men who took advantage of their countrymen's ignorance of English to extract "translator" fees and to intimidate them in other ways. At times, immigrant laborers frustrated the efforts of padrone-like employment recruiters, as Peck argues, often by appealing to government agencies.[99] At other times workers undermined padrone power by securing their own padrone-like power in local settings. Much to the displeasure of the Oriental Trading Company, which contracted with the Great Northern Railway to provide track laborers, two Japanese workers ran their own job brokering business. In return for a $10 fee and a monthly payoff, the two secured their countrymen higher-paying jobs in the Great Northern's roundhouse.[100]

At the other end of the continuum were men who were simply "first among equals": acknowledged leaders among groups of workers with friendship or ethnic affinities. Finnish immigrant John Wiite remembered a group of lumberjacks he worked with in eastern Washington who organized themselves in such a fashion. One of the workers was a Finn named Andy who "spoke good English and was kind of an enterprising young man. He became our leader and spokesman," Wiite recalled. Andy canvassed the various employment agencies in Spokane and returned to his friends with his recommendations.[101] Similarly, laborers in the wheat harvest might find employment through a private or public agency but most often negotiated directly with their farmer-employers. Some developed long-term relationships with farmers, returning to the same jobs year after year. Just as common were groups of friends who hired out together and negotiated a common wage. As the IWW gained influence, groups of Wobblies negotiated with farmers, some of whom had no problem hiring union men.[102]

Laborers also benefited from free transportation passes labor agents distributed to the men they hired. Agents were willing to give passes to any man who paid a fee, regardless of how unlikely he was to actually show up on the job. Laboring men commonly used such passes to get a little bit farther down the road. As a federal employment agent complained in 1918, some laborers had "no intention whatever of working for the Railroads, but for $2.00 they were able to ride the cushions to the harvest fields."[103] This practice became much more difficult during the war-induced labor shortage because employers who were desperate for workers and mindful of government oversight hired guards to travel with laborers and ensure their safe arrival at the job.[104]

The abuses of private employment agents became a staple of Progressive Era social commentary. In government reports, scholarly journals, and charity publications, critics of the system argued for reform or outright state control of the labor market. This public outcry propelled state and federal governments into experiments in labor market regulation, with mixed results. The failure of government intervention had its origin in the contradictory goals that reformers hoped to achieve through free employment agencies. As Udo Sautter argues, the motives behind the creation of free employment bureaus included "humanitarianism, efficiency, and the maintenance of public order."[105] Workers and middle-class reformers recognized the abuses of the private system, but reformers approached the issue from a more paternalistic perspective. As the Wisconsin commissioner of labor wrote, the private agencies "cannot as a rule be safely trusted to deal with the laboring classes."[106]

The conflicting purposes of public employment bureaus were never fully resolved but rather coexisted and even reinforced each other. Most progressives recognized the connection between poverty and crime, a connection that implied that laborers were also potential criminals. Justifying the 1899 Illinois act establishing Free Public Employment Bureaus in that state, the commissioner of labor wrote, "Idleness naturally leads to criminal pursuits, and an idle man belonging to the class who must work in order to live is a menace to the public." The starving man must eat and will steal if he cannot find work, reasoned the commissioner. "That part of the population, however, who have no 'last dollar' to pay for a promise of work, and who are likely to form a dangerous element in a community," are the natural clients of state-sponsored employment bureaus.[107] Only the most hard-pressed workers would be served by such intervention, guaranteeing that public employment bureaus would maintain a paternalistic approach.

Although some reform advocates were perfectly happy with paternalism, arguments focusing on the nature of the modern economy gained prominence in the years before World War I. An early structural focus was the sense that joblessness stemmed from poor communication between workers and employers. As the Wisconsin commissioner of labor argued in 1902, "the vast amount of vagrancy in the United States is due, not so much to a lack of work, as to a lack of knowledge as to where the work can be obtained."[108] Free employment bureaus would act as information clearinghouses, he argued, easing the worker's transition for one job to the next. Reformers would be moral middlemen in the labor market.

Although "connecting the jobless man to the manless job" remained a dominant theme of labor market reform throughout the period, more sophisticated approaches to economic structures soon appeared, along with a growing sense that social scientific investigation gave reformers enough knowledge to address unemployment and vagrancy. Writing in 1916, economist William Leiserson noted a definite shift in reform focus from "the unemployed" to "unemployment," that is "the problem is not personal but economic." Moreover, he wrote, the country's migratory workers were a crucial "reserve army that shifts from city to country . . . in response to a definite demand." Those who are without jobs temporarily "are no more unemployed than are firemen who wait in fire-houses for the alarm to sound." Leiserson called for extensive government intervention in the labor market, including public employment bureaus, regulation of new workers' entrance into the labor market, countercyclical public works programs, decasualization of the labor market, and creation of unemployment insurance.[109]

Although Leiserson envisioned a coordinated approach to the problem of unemployment and casual labor, the actual development of free public employment offices was a state-by-state process. What little interstate cooperation existed before World War I developed in response to the challenge of mobilizing harvest workers in the Great Plains wheat belt. Kansas led the first multistate effort to manage the harvest labor situation in 1904. Dubbed the Western Association of Free Employment Bureaus, this "loose federation" had no great impact and was followed a decade later by the National Farm Labor Exchange, which gathered state officials from the Dakotas, Nebraska, Kansas, and Oklahoma along with representatives of the federal departments of agriculture and labor. The exchange relied on voluntary methods of publicizing labor needs and suffered from cross-purposes. According to a 1924 study of unemployment bureaus, county and state agricultural agents who supplied the exchange with information "consider it their first duty to safeguard the farmers' interests," a euphemism for ensuring a large supply of laborers at low wages.[110]

Greater federal involvement came with the wartime emergency but was short-lived. Between January 1918 and October 1919, the U.S. Employment Service (USES) struggled to implement a national system of free employment bureaus, operating 854 offices at its peak. Congress cut funding to the service in the wake of armistice, and it remained only a weak coordinator and promoter of state activities throughout the 1920s.[111] However, official statistics claimed growing success in directing wheat belt harvest workers. From placing 18,511 harvest hands in Kansas and Oklahoma in its first year, USES figures claimed more than 46,000 placements in the 1919 harvest and 53,072 in 1920. Despite limited federal involvement, the USES counted nearly 100,000 laborers locating work through federal-state employment bureaus in the grain harvest of 1930.[112] These claims may have been exaggerated or counted the same workers multiple times because "word-of-mouth information passed on from one person to another, nicknamed the 'Hobo Gazette,' still remained a favored method" of finding work in the wheat belt in the mid-1920s.[113]

The differentiated and multilayered organization of the labor market served the purposes of employers as well as laborers. Employers and their allies tried to flood the market with surplus workers to keep wages low. In their own efforts to earn a living, private employment agents competed to fill employers' orders. For their part, laborers often manipulated this competition to their own advantage. The abuses of private agents were many and were truly harmful for laborers, but advocates of government intervention misjudged the needs of laboring men. With the appeal for Free Public Employment Bureaus based on charity as well as efficiency, many workers stayed away until they had no other options. The reality was that without an outright ban on private agencies, the "job sharks," as Wobblies called them, retained access to the best jobs.

❖ ❖ ❖

Like many other regions, the Midwest is something of a fiction, its boundaries vague and its residents constantly moving on to some other place. But the Midwest is a useful fiction because it describes a shared experience in time. Immigrants from Europe and Asia came for the same opportunities that brought Canadians, Mexicans, and black and white southerners. These long-distance migrants worked alongside whites, blacks, and Native Americans from the Midwest. The region also shared a common relationship with human society and the natural world, as William Cronon argues. On the fertile plains and around the Great Lakes of mid-continent North America, industrialization transformed both the countryside and the cities, just as the region's forests, mineral wealth, and soil shaped the nature of industry itself. The economy responded to the changing of the seasons as surely as it did the fluctuation of prices. Far from the centers of power—but not isolated—the Midwest was the meeting place of local, national, and international labor and capital markets. Its resources fed the industries at the center of world economic change, and the ready flow of laborers from city to countryside and back again made it all possible.

Looking at this migration from the outside, many equated laborers with migratory birds who returned to the region each year, less out of individual motivation than through instinct. In fact, they were not so much a flock as a grand, disorganized parade. Whatever the metaphor, seasonal laborers were an irresistible focus for social investigation and reform. For many reform-minded middle-class Americans, the abuses of labor agencies, poor conditions in urban lodging houses and rural work camps, the decline of the family farm, and the chronic turnover and underemployment of factory workers signaled the dangers of growing class polarization. In a generally sincere effort to ameliorate these social problems, reformers launched a remarkable array of investigations aimed at justifying and supporting government intervention that would balance the power of corporations and workers on the fulcrum of a scientifically trained and public-minded professional class. For social historians, these investigations are a rich well of documentary evidence on the lives of ordinary people. And yet investigators' confusion over metaphors and explanations suggests that we can also read this documentary legacy as evidence of conflict over the meaning of social division itself. It is to this issue that we turn next.

NOTES

1. *Illinois Farmer* V (11 November 1860), 181, as quoted in Schob, *Hired Hands and Plowboys,* 210; MacDonald, "The Moving Army of Harvest Hands," 15.

2. *Dubuque National Demokrat,* 13 July 1876, 3, as quoted in Gjerde, *The Minds of the West,* note 65, p. 364.

3. Life Story of Norman Daniel, reel 6, *U.S. Commission on Industrial Relations, 1912–1915,* hereafter cited as *USCIR Unpublished Records;* Examination of Recruit: Norman B. Daniel, 16 January 1906; Register of Enlistments, United States Army, 1907, vol. 118, p. 333, NA RG 94.

4. Life History of Sam Gray, reel 6, *USCIR Unpublished Records.*

5. Life Story of Andrew Hanson, reel 6, *USCIR Unpublished Records.*

6. Ibid., pp. 8–9.

7. Department of Commerce, Bureau of the Census, *Fourteenth Census of the U.S., 1920,* vol. 6, pt. 1: *Agriculture, Northern States,* 30; Department of Commerce and Labor, Bureau of the Census, *Thirteenth Census of the United States, 1910, Abstract,* 92. Note that Steve Hahn and Jonathan Prude suggest a population of less than 5,000 as a more appropriate definition of "rural." See "Introduction," in Hahn and Prude, *The Countryside in the Age of Capitalist Transformation,* 7–10.

8. Wiebe, *Search for Order,* 2.

9. Robinson, *History of North Dakota,* 236–37. Railroad construction, and the job boom that went along with it, largely ceased in the state after World War I.

10. Hader, "Honk, Honk Hobo," 453–55. Apparently, the Great Depression undermined this trend toward travel by automobile. A 1938 study found that half of harvest hands were riding freight trains, and most of the rest were traveling on commercial buses. See Cullum, Folsom, and Hay, "Men and Machines in the North Dakota Harvest," as cited in Isern, *Bull Threshers and Bindlestiffs,* 160–61.

11. Stowell, *Streets,* 25–34; see also McGuckin, *Memoirs of a Wobbly,* 9; Bruns, *The Damndest Radical,* 5–6; Reitman, "Life among the Outcasts," unpublished autobiography, Charles H. Kerr Company Archives, Newberry Library.

12. Beardsley, "Along the Main Stem with Red," 1, 4, Ernest W. Burgess Papers, Papers of Students and Collaborators, Nels Anderson, Department of Special Collections, University of Chicago Library (hereafter, Burgess Papers).

13. De Caux, *Labor Radical,* 54–55.

14. Beardsley, "Along the Main Stem with Red," 1, Burgess Papers; Zorbaugh, *The Gold Coast and the Slum,* 105–26.

15. Clark, *Minnesota in a Century of Change,* 224–25; U.S. Bureau of the Census, *Thirteenth U.S. Census, vol. IX, Manufacturers.*

16. Minneapolis Civic and Commerce Association (MCCA), *Minneapolis: Market of the Northwest.*

17. Taylor, "The Labor Market for the Northwest," 1–2, 53, 55. The MCCA report listed thirty-three licensed labor agencies in Minneapolis and fourteen in St. Paul. See also Hartsough, "The Development of the Twin Cities."

18. Rølvaag, *The Boat of Longing,* 164.

19. Smith, "The Minnesota Lumberjack," 3, Robert E. Smith Papers, MHS.

20. Ashleigh, *Rambling Kid,* 90–91.

21. Monkkonen, *Walking to Work,* 11; Brown, *"Broke,"* 28–41, 71–81, 178–82; Johnson, "The Lodging House Problem," 13–14, 25–34; City of Minneapolis, "Annual Report of the Municipal Lodging House," 1; Contrast the descriptions of Kansas City's "Helping Hand Institute" as portrayed in Brown, *"Broke,"* 76–81, and in the fundraising pamphlet "The Lure of the City," State Historical Society of Missouri. See also Wyckoff, *The Workers: An Experiment in Reality, the West,* 38.

22. Minneapolis Civic and Commerce Association, Committee on Housing, *The Housing Problem in Minneapolis;* Groth, *Living Downtown,* 140–51; Solenberger, *One Thousand Homeless Men,* 314–34.

23. U.S. Federal Trade Commission (FTC), *Report on Meat-Packing,* Part I, 102, 42–43, 290–321; Iowa Writers' Program, *Woodbury County History,* 136; Sioux City Commercial Club, *Annual Report, 1915,* 2. See also FTC, *Report on Meat-Packing,* Part III, 139–40. Silag, "The Social Response to Industrialism," 124.

24. Biennial Reports of the Minnesota Department of Labor and Industry (MDLI) and the Minnesota Industrial Commission, 1913–30, published monthly data for laborers placed by the state's free employment bureaus.

25. Rapelje to Donnelly, 15 February 1924, 2. Records of the Northern Pacific Railway (NP Railway), MHS. See also Danysk, *Hired Hands,* 89–101.

26. Rapelje to Clark, 18 December 1924, 3, NP Railway, MHS.

27. Leiserson, "Labor Camps in Wisconsin"; Speek, "U.S. Commission on Industrial Relations, Report on Psychological Aspects of the Problem of Floating Laborers," *USCIR Unpublished Records;* Hiles, *The Ice Crop;* Barrett, *Work and Community in the Jungle,* 28–29; Parnell, "The Broom Corn Industry," 750–51; Engerman and Goldin, "Seasonality in Nineteenth-Century Labor Markets," 125.

28. Clark, *Minnesota in a Century of Change,* 226–27.

29. Minnesota Bureau of Labor, *Seventh Biennial Report,* 238.

30. Clark, *Minnesota in a Century of Change,* 227–28; Searle, *Saving Quetico-Superior,* 34–53; Eichholz, "Virginia and Rainy Lake Logging Company," Iron Range Research Center (IRRC); Engberg, "Collective Bargaining," 205–11; Haynes, "Revolt of the 'Timber Beasts,'" 163–74. On logging in Canada see Radforth, *Bushworkers and Bosses.*

31. Life Histories of Andrew Hanson and P. K. Small, *USCIR Unpublished Records.*

32. Speek, "Report on Conditions in Labor Camps," 64, *USCIR Unpublished Records.*

33. See photographs in Leiserson, "Labor Camps in Wisconsin," 13, 17; MDLI, *Fourteenth Biennial Report,* 196–98; Testimony of Frank Gillmor, House of Representatives, State of Minnesota, "Hearings before Committee on Labor and Labor Legislation, Labor Troubles in Northern Minnesota," 30 January 1917, 264–306, John Lind Papers, MHS, P933, Box 8; Smith, "The Minnesota Lumberjack," 2–4, Robert E. Smith Papers, MHS.

34. MDLI, *Fourteenth Biennial Report,* 198; Boose, "The Lumber Jack," 414–16.

35. MDLI, *Fourteenth Biennial Report,* 197–98.

36. Peter Speek, "Report on Lumber Camps in Charlevoix, Mich., Jan. 1914," reel 5; Life Histories of Andrew Hanson, P. K. Small, Harvey Raymond, W. A. Kinney, and Fred Kiener, *USCIR Unpublished Records;* Boose, "The Lumber Jack," 414–16. See also letter from "D.R." responding that conditions are not as bad in his camp as those described by Boose and that the main problem is that lumberjacks work themselves

into unemployment: *International Socialist Review* 16 (March 1916): 569–70; Leiserson, "Labor Camps in Wisconsin," 14–15; "Remarks for 1917," Yearly Report Binder, Frank Gillmor Papers, MHS.

37. Alanen, "Years of Change," 157–61; Minnesota Bureau of Labor, *Seventh Biennial Report,* 243–44.

38. Syrjamaki, "Mesabi Communities," 464, 101; Alanen, "Years of Change," 155–94. On seasonality in copper mining in Michigan's Upper Peninsula, see Lankton, *Cradle to Grave,* 164; on Montana copper mining, see Emmons, *Butte Irish.*

39. Powers Hapgood Journal, 3, MHS.

40. Syrjamaki, "Mesabi Communities," 101–21, 472.

41. Speek, "Report on Conditions in Labor Camps," *USCIR Unpublished Records,* 3; Speek, "Report on the Preliminary Investigation of the Construction Camps in the States of Dakota and Montana from July 25 to August 10, 1914," *USCIR Unpublished Records,* 3.

42. Leiserson, "Labor Camps in Wisconsin," 7–8; Lohse, "From a Construction Worker," 550–51.

43. Speek, "Report on Conditions in Labor Camps," 63, *USCIR Unpublished Records;* MDLI, *Fourteenth Biennial Report,* 192. For a detailed description of conditions on an Oregon construction project, see Heard, "'Our' Cililo Canal," 483–86. On Canadian railroad construction camps in this period see Bradwin, *The Bunkhouse Man.*

44. MDLI, *Fourteenth Biennial Report,* "Coon Creek Camp," 194, quote on 188; Kansas City Board of Public Welfare, *Seventh Annual Report,* 80–82.

45. Minnesota Industrial Commission, *Fifth Biennial Report,* 257–60.

46. Lescohier, "Sources of Supply," 1.

47. Drache, *The Day of the Bonanza,* 111.

48. Amenia and Sharon Land Co. Papers, Box 83, folder 1, North Dakota Institute for Regional Studies (NDIRS). The company paid more than $17,000 in wages to farm laborers in 1916–17.

49. Woodward, *The Checkered Years,* 182, 197; Interview with Olaus Hanson and John Jensen, p. 6, NDIRS; Interview with Thorfin Jestin, p. 2–3, NDIRS; George W. Tracy, "The Win Tracy Story," 1–2, NDIRS.

50. White, "The Business of a Wheat Farm," 538, 532, 547. See also Coulter, "Industrial History," 569–612; Shannon, *The Farmer's Last Frontier,* 154–61; Cox, "The American Agricultural Wage Earner," 95–114; Taylor, "Origins of Migratory Labor."

51. Interview with John H. Hanson, NDIRS; Woodward, *The Checkered Years,* 184–85.

52. "D. C. Smith, Clover Leaf Farms, House Regulations," Belle Prairie Farm Scrapbook, NDIRS.

53. Nina Carter Van Ostsand to Leonard Sackett, 14 February 1955, 7, James H. Carter Papers, NDIRS.

54. Drache, *Day of the Bonanza,* 215; Shannon, *Farmer's Last Frontier,* 161.

55. Department of Commerce, Bureau of the Census, *Fourteenth Census, 1920, Vol. 5, Agriculture,* 24, 741, 745–46; *Fourteenth Census, 1920, Vol. 6, Part 1, Agriculture, Northern States,* 617; *Thirteenth Census, 1910, Vol. 7, Agriculture,* 272–73; Schoenfeld and Olson, "The Wheat Situation," 99.

56. Department of Commerce, Bureau of the Census, *Fourteenth U.S. Census, 1920, Vol. 5*, 745.

57. Department of Commerce, Bureau of the Census, *Fourteenth U.S. Census, 1920, Vol. 6, Part 1*, 1, 19, 724; *Thirteenth Census, 1910, Vol. 6*, 556; Lescohier, "Conditions Affecting the Demand for Harvest Labor"; Frizell, "About Farm Labor," 145. For a more detailed discussion see Higbie, "Indispensable Outcasts," 69–73.

58. Duffus, "Labor Market Conditions," 4–5, *USCIR Unpublished Records;* Kansas State Board of Agriculture, *Wheat in Kansas*, 89–95. Although state and federal agricultural bulletins provide a wealth of information on farm machinery, a good summary is in Isern, *Bull Threshers and Bindlestiffs.*

59. Isern, *Bull Threshers and Bindle Stiffs*, 97; Lescohier, "Conditions Affecting the Demand for Harvest Labor," 15; Duffus, "Labor Market Conditions in the Harvest Fields of the Middle West, December 1, 1914," 5–6, *USCIR Unpublished Records.*

60. Lescohier, "Conditions Affecting the Demand for Harvest Labor," 24–25; Isern, *Bull Threshers and Bindlestiffs*, 73; Ulonska, "Wheat, Wages—and You!" 205.

61. Allen, "The New Harvest Hand," 279–84; Isern, *Bull Threshers and Bindlestiffs*, 188, 203; Webb, *The Migratory-Casual Worker*, 72–74, 96–97, 99–100.

62. Barron, *Mixed Harvest*, 7–16; Gjerde, *Minds of the West*, 147–52; Jellison, *Entitled to Power*, 108, 119; Neth, *Preserving the Family Farm*, 40–70; Adams, *Transformation of Rural Life*, 49–53; Friedmann, "World Market," 545–86.

63. Gjerde, *Minds of the West*, 150.

64. Jellison, *Entitled to Power*, xx; Fink, *Agrarian Women*, 59–63; Neth, *Preserving the Family Farm*, 17–40; Adams, *Transformation of Rural Life*, 84–89; Gjerde, *Minds of the West*, 152–53; Dublin, *Transforming Women's Work*, 29–75.

65. On the Dakotas see *Thirteenth U.S. Census, 1910, Statistics for South Dakota*, 635, 643; *Thirteenth U.S. Census, 1910, Statistics for North Dakota*, 630, 635; *Fifteenth U.S. Census, 1930, Agriculture*, 1087, 1091–94, 1136–41, 1151. On Kansas see *Thirteenth U.S. Census, 1910, Vol. 6*, 557; *Fourteenth U.S. Census, 1920, Vol. 6, Part 1*, 724. See also Putnam, "Farm Tenancy in Kansas," in *Twentieth Biennial Report of the Kansas State Board of Agriculture*, 1–20; H. R. Walmsley, "Report on Investigation of Farm Labor Conditions in Southwestern Missouri," 20 November 1914, *USCIR Unpublished Records;* Applen, "Migratory Harvest Labor," 91.

66. For statistics on Kansas tenants see *Thirteenth Census of the United States, 1910, Vol. 6*, 557; *Fourteenth Census of the United States, 1920, Vol. 6, Part 1*, 724. See also Applen, "Migratory Harvest Labor," 91; and Putnam, "Farm Tenancy in Kansas," in *Twentieth Biennial Report of the Kansas State Board of Agriculture*, 1–20. See also Walmsley, "Report on Investigation of Farm Labor Conditions in Southwestern Missouri," 20 November 1914, *USCIR Unpublished Records*, which chronicles the miserable conditions among tenants and small holders in western Missouri.

67. Thompson and Warber, *Social and Economic Survey*, 5–7.

68. U.S. Bureau of the Census, *Fifteenth Census of the United States, 1930*, Vol. 4, 430–37; Neth, *Preserving the Family Farm*, 72–73.

69. Percy S. Hardiman, Tape 5, side 1, Wisconsin Agriculturalist Oral History Project, State Historical Society of Wisconsin. See also Neth, *Preserving the Family Farm*, 71–96, 211–13. This distinction may have been less important in the cutover regions, where farming was less profitable. Raymond Wright, who grew up on a small

farmstead in Michigan's upper peninsula, recalled that his parents subscribed to radical Finnish- and English-language magazines as well as mainstream journals such as *Successful Farming* and *Ladies Home Journal.* See Interview with Raymond Wright by Carl Ross, 1992, p. 35, MHS.

70. Garland, *Boy Life on the Prairie,* 44–45, 215, 151; see also Burris, *True Sketches,* 15.

71. Duffus, "Labor Market Conditions," 7, *USCIR Unpublished Records.* Robert Saunders wrote that farmers usually let him sleep in the farmhouse if only one or two hands were employed. If more, the workers slept in the barn. In one case he slept in the house and attended prayer meetings with the family, but he still felt distant from the family because they did not offer to let him take a bath despite his extended stay. See Saunders, "The Road," 131, Robert Saunders Papers, Western Historical Manuscripts.

72. Berdahl, *The Berdahl Family,* 23–24.

73. Anderson, Document 36, Document 40, Burgess Papers.

74. Peiss, *Cheap Amusements,* 68–72; Brown, *Brownie the Boomer,* 15–16, 32–33; Saunders, "The Road," 124A, Robert Saunders Papers, WHMC, St. Louis.

75. Jellison, *Entitled to Power,* 54–55; U.S. Bureau of the Census, *Fifteenth Census of the United States, 1930: Agriculture, Vol. 2, Part 1: Northern States,* 54–56; see also Hahn, "The 'Unmaking' of the Southern Yeomanry," in Hahn and Prude, *The Countryside,* 195–96.

76. Fiske [Marbut] to Papa [Curtis Marbut], 27 June 1915, n.d. [July 1915], and 30 July 1915, Curtis Marbut Papers, WHMC.

77. Duffus, "Labor Market Conditions," 7, *USCIR Unpublished Records.*

78. Lescohier, "Hands and Tools," 412.

79. Application of J. A. Anderson, 3 November 1917, Bureau of Employment Security, Omaha Region, Box 1, RG 183.

80. Lorena Hickok, unfinished autobiography, chapter 2, 15–16, as quoted in Isern, *Bull Threshers and Bindlestiffs,* 99–100.

81. Life History of Harvey Raymond, *USCIR Unpublished Records;* McGuckin, *Memoirs of a Wobbly,* 12–13; see also Brown, *Brownie the Boomer,* 7–13.

82. Interview with Jack Maloney by Sal Salerno and Peter Rachleff, April 21–25, 1988, Radicalism in Minnesota Oral History Project, MHS.

83. Saunders, "The Road," 122, Robert Saunders Papers, WHMC, St. Louis; McGuckin, *Memoirs of a Wobbly,* 12–14; Life Story of Raymond Harvey, *USCIR Unpublished Records;* Woodward, *The Checkered Years;* Brown, *Brownie the Boomer,* 7–13; Nesbit, *Wisconsin, A History,* 299. For a fictional account as life as a young rural laborer see Eaton, *Backfurrow.*

84. This was particularly the case with Finnish miners, many of them blacklisted from mining employment after failed strikes. Syrjamaki, "Mesabi Communities," 218; Tanenhaus, "Gus Hall"; Halonen, "The Role of Finish-Americans," 83. See also U.S. General Land Office records of failed homesteads, MHS; Foster, *Pages from a Worker's Life,* 30–33; Interview with Raymond Wright by Carl Ross, 1992, 34–35, MHS.

85. U.S. Immigration Commission, *Reports of the Immigration Commission, Immigrants in Industries, Vol. 21, Part 24 (Vol. 1), Recent Immigrants in Agriculture,* 426–27, 421–22, 555–61; see also Sixty-First Congress, *Hearings before the Senate Committee on Indian Affairs,* 697–709.

86. U.S. Fish and Wildlife Service, Records of the Joint Commission on U.S.-Canada Fisheries, 1893–95, RG 22: Box 5, Folder 1, Lake Superior Field Notes, 1894, pp. 20–21, 26; see also Interview with William Teddy, July 15, 1894, Box 9, Vol. III, and Interview with C. O. Flynn, Duluth, n.d., Box 7, Vol. I. For similar examples see Gonska, "Cradle of Iron"; Interviews with Robert Lundin (A-88–1027), Cecilia and Arthur Sabattini (A-91–2387), Arvid and Fred Ukura, John Begich (A-84–292), and Richard Graff, Iron Range Research Center; Ames, "Farewell to Wilderness," Floyd V. Ames Papers, Bentley Historical Library.

87. Pangborn, "Discussion on Vagrancy," 73–74. Pangborn estimated that 430,000 trespassers "infest the railroads," and as many as 19,000 were killed and 24,000 injured in 1906 alone.

88. Lescohier, "Work-Accidents and the Farm Hand," 951; Minnesota Bureau of Labor, Industries and Commerce, *Thirteenth Biennial Report, 1911–1912,* chapter 11. Among the frequent newspaper stories on farm accidents, see "Farm Hand Killed by Mowing Machine," *ADN,* 9 August 1916, 1; "Man Escapes Death," *Redfield (South Dakota) Press,* 10 August 1916, 2; "Man Caught in Flywheel," *Redfield (South Dakota) Journal-Observer,* 26 August 1915, 3.

89. Taylor, "The Labor Market for the Northwest," 57.

90. Speek, "A Report on the Preliminary Investigation of the Construction Camps in the States of Dakota and Montana from July 25 to August 10, 1914," *USCIR Unpublished Records,* 3.

91. Abbott, "Chicago Employment Agencies," 296.

92. Speek, "Employment Agencies in South and North Dakota," [9 December 1914], 3, *USCIR Unpublished Records.*

93. MDLI, *Fourteenth Biennial Report, 1913–1914,* 170.

94. Ibid., 171. See also Erickson, *Tenth Biennial Report, 1901,* 764; Abbott, "Chicago Employment Agencies," 297–99; letter to P. L. Prentiss, 13 June 1918, 2, Bureau of Employment Security, Omaha Region, RG 183, National Archives Branch Depository, Kansas City; Kansas City Board of Public Welfare, *Seventh Annual Report,* 84–86.

95. Houk to Beck, 12 December 1912; Cruden to Leiserson 3 January 1913, both Wisconsin Industrial Commission (hereafter WIC), Series 1006, File C1431, Folder 3, State Historical Society of Wisconsin (SHSW); Leiserson to Cruden 7 July 1913, Cruden to Leiserson 10 July 1913, WIC, SHSW; MDLI, *Fourteenth Biennial Report,* 175.

96. O'Carroll to WIC 1911; O'Carroll to Beck 1 November 1910, WIC Series 1006, File 536, SHSW. Duffus, "Labor Market Conditions in the Wheat Harvest," *USCIR Unpublished Records.*

97. Takahashi to Slade, 11 October 1906, Great Northern Railway Company (GN Railway), VP-Operating: General Manager Subject files Box 9; Life history of Norman Daniel, USCIR; MDLI, *Fourteenth Biennial Report;* Minnesota Industrial Commission, *Fifth Biennial Report,* 258.

98. Hahamovitch, *Fruits of Their Labor,* 38–54; Peck, *Reinventing Free Labor,* 15–48.

99. "How the Greek Labor Is Being Exploited Here" clipping, n.d., MHS; George Sfetchys to W. E. McEwen, 25 April 1910; A. Wheelock to McEwen, 8 January 1910; Testimony of Mike Skalas and Santin Hassan, 30 March 1910, Minnesota Labor and Industry Department, House of Labor Correspondence, Railroad Correspondence, 1909–22, MHS.

100. Takahashi to Kennedy, 24 February 1903, GN Railway, VP-Operating: General Manager Subject files Box 9, MHS.

101. Wiite, "My Early Years in the United States," 4, John Wiite Papers, Box 1, Folder 12, Immigration History Research Center (IHRC). See also Speek, "Notes on Investigation in Spokane, Washington, August 10 to August 13, 1914," *USCIR Unpublished Records,* reel 3.

102. "Notes on Harvest Investigation" (n.d., early 1920s), Don D. Lescohier Papers, Box 1, folder 1, SHSW.

103. Letter to P. L. Prentiss, 13 June 1918; see also Acting Examiner in Charge of Railway Division to Assistant Director General, 20 September 1918; Examiner in Charge of Railway Division to Prentis, 24 July 1918, RG 183, Bureau of Employment Security, National Archives Branch Depository, Central Plains Region, Kansas City.

104. Superintendent to Department of Justice, 29 October 1918, RG 183, National Archives, Washington, D.C.

105. Sautter, "North American Government Labor Agencies," 377.

106. Erickson, *Tenth Biennial Report,* 766.

107. As quoted in Erickson, *Tenth Biennial Report,* 770–71.

108. Ibid., 771.

109. William Leiserson, "The Problem of Unemployment Today," 10–12, 17–19. See also U.S. Commission on Industrial Relations, *Final Report;* U.S. Bureau of Labor Statistics, "Unemployment in the United States"; Keyssar, *Out of Work,* 250–98.

110. Harrison et al., *Public Employment Offices,* 539–42; Sautter, "North American Government Labor Agencies"; Speek, "Employment Agencies in South Dakota," *USCIR Unpublished Records.*

111. Harrison et al., *Public Employment Offices,* 128–34.

112. U.S. Department of Labor, Employment Service, *Annual Report of the Director General to the Secretary of Labor for the Fiscal Year Ending June 30, 1918,* 18; U.S. Department of Labor, Employment Service, *Annual Report of the Director General to the Secretary of Labor for the Fiscal Year Ending June 30, 1919,* 50; U.S. Department of Labor, Employment Service, *Annual Report of the Director General to the Secretary of Labor for the Fiscal Year Ending June 30, 1920,* 22; "Report of Farm Labor Division for the Calendar Year 1930," RG 183, Records of the Bureau of Employment Security, USES Early History Files, Box 1.

113. Harrison et al., *Public Employment Offices,* 537. The Minnesota State Division of Employment noted that placements of workers had declined steadily between 1925 and 1930 in all areas except farm labor. See Minnesota Industrial Commission, *Fifth Biennial Report,* 254.

❖

2 Retelling Life Stories: Floating Labor and the Terrain of Progressive Era Social Investigation

ON THE OUTSKIRTS of Redfield, South Dakota, some 500 harvest hands waited impatiently for work. It was July 1914, and the countryside was full of unemployed industrial workers, farmers' sons, homesteaders, and hoboes, each looking to make big wages bringing in the crops. But very few were finding work of any kind. While most spent their idle time washing and mending clothes, playing cards, reading, or discussing politics, F. G. Peterson recounted his life story for 25 cents an hour while Peter Speek took notes.

Speek had been a radical in his native Estonia. He fled in the wake of the failed 1905 revolution against the Russian empire, and eventually he found his way to Wisconsin, where he became a graduate student under John R. Commons and Selig Perlman. Fluent in several eastern European languages, Speek was an ideal investigator for the U.S. Commission on Industrial Relations' study of laborers' working conditions. He visited work camps and hobo jungles, collecting life histories of floating laborers, and he paid the men for their time.

The twenty-four-year-old Peterson was an economic migrant who became a radical in America. Arriving around 1907, he had worked a wide range of jobs: shipyard worker, rubber factory worker, sailor, farmhand, construction laborer, and lumberjack. He became a member of the IWW, and in 1911 fought with fellow Wobblies in the Mexican Revolution. For a brief time he was the elected financial secretary of a town in Baja California. In Redfield, Peterson was an organizer for the IWW. He delivered a rousing speech in favor of industrial unionism that the assembled harvest hands almost unanimously supported, according to Speek's report. Yet despite his wide experience and leadership abilities, Speek chose to focus on Peterson's disappointments. He had given up opportunities to settle down as a farmer in Nebraska and to marry a woman he loved in Los Angeles. He was unemployed and so broke that he could not afford to pay his union dues. Speek concluded that the young man's future looked grim. He would probably go "downward" and become a "hobo and afterwards a tramp of the common type."[1]

And that is all we know about Peterson except that he was back in the wheat belt organizing harvest hands the next summer.[2] Without the life histories, case studies, and autobiographies collected by Speek and other social investigators, our understanding of laboring men's lives would be scant. But these sources, like Peterson's life history, raise as many questions as they answer. Might Peterson have embellished his story in hopes of affecting the reports of the government investigator? Can we really trust Speek's prediction that Peterson would become a tramp? As rich as these sources are for writing history "from the bottom up," we must also recognize that they are not direct representations of life as it was lived. Their creation and circulation through government reports and the popular press were part of a broader conflict over the nature of American society.

Throughout the Progressive Era, middle- and upper-class intellectuals counted, classified, photographed, and otherwise examined the lives of working-class people. Some hoped to bring culture and education to the poor, some sought the assimilation of immigrants; some wanted to support labor organization, and others wanted to increase workers' efficiency. Some inspected lodging houses and working conditions, pored over charity case files, and spoke directly with workers, employers, and other reformers. Others actually disguised themselves as workers to gain a "first-hand experience" of workers' lives. Peter Speek was unusual in that he was himself an immigrant, and his own experiences and political leanings affected the way he reported his findings. But all would-be reformers, including Speek, had one thing in common: They perceived themselves as outsiders, looking in on a class world separate from their own. Whatever their method, investigators mapped out a working-class world that appeared to be a grotesque inversion of middle-class America and yet held the mysterious appeal of a foreign land.[3]

This chapter focuses on how Progressive Era writers made sense of class conflict by telling the life stories of poor working men in a remarkable variety of genres, including undercover investigations, thinly veiled fictions, and more formal social scientific methods. These life stories were both good reading and "enactments of social conflicts and cleavages," as Michael Denning notes of nineteenth-century dime novels. Like dime novels, social investigators' narratives evoked familiar characters—the hopeful immigrant, the hard-working farmer's son, the beguiling agitator—only to place these characters in story lines that inverted readers' expectations. Honesty and thrift were not rewarded. Instead of settling down and starting a family, hard-working laborers fell into an abyss of poverty of dissipation. Playing the part of Virgil leading their middle-class readers through the inferno of industrial society, investigators sought to entertain and instruct. In this way, as Denning argues, ideology is narrative, "a set of stories one tells oneself to situate oneself in the world, to name the characters and map the terrain of the social world."[4] Of course investigators were not writing fiction. They were writing about real people, real life stories. Inevitably, however, questions of investigators' own identities and conflicts of interpretation with worker-subjects muddied the social scientific waters. As historian Kathryn Oberdeck argues, we need to contextualize these narratives within the lives of their authors, the methodological regimes of particular investigations, and the wider social conflicts that engendered them.[5] In this way we get a sense of how different social actors mobilized representations of class division toward particular ends and how these representations took on lives of their own, feeding into a swelling conflict over the nature of social order.

Among the many genres of social investigation literature, the participant-observer investigation, in which writers donned working-class clothes and lived a double life, was among the most popular and most problematic for historians. On one hand, they reveal "first-hand" experiences of the investigator as worker. They take the reader inside factories and lodging houses in ways that other studies do not, and they are full of direct quotations of workers about their jobs and lives. In short, undercover investigations *feel* authentic. On the other hand, these texts are as much about defining differences between investigator and subject as they are about working-class life itself. That is, although the writers appeared to bridge the gap between the classes by temporarily becoming workers, they were in fact portraying for their middle- and upper-class audiences the distance between class cultures. Through text and photographs, investigators naturally called attention to their "real" lives in the course of writing about life as a worker. The sense of otherness upon entering a strange social setting, the economic and physical deprivations they suffered, and the stories of their working-class acquaintances are continually compared with their normal life. Similarly, their readers must have used their own lives as a reference point, just as we today often compare our lives with those of our historical subjects.[6]

Describing workers as dirty, degraded, and vulnerable was a common mode of differentiation between investigator and subject. For instance, Walter Wyckoff, a college graduate turned tramp, opened the second volume of his 1898 narrative *The Workers* with a question that he says faces all down-and-out workers: "Have you the physical and moral qualities which fit you to survive . . . or lacking these does there await for you inevitable wreck under the onward rush of the world's great moving life?"[7] The question is soon answered with the story of a night spent in the company of tramps. Describing his homeless cellmates in a Chicago police lockup, Wyckoff notes, "Their bloated, unwashed flesh and unkempt hair; their hideous ugliness of face, unreclaimed by marks of inner strength and force, but revealing rather, in the relaxation of sleep, a deepening of the lines of weakness, until you read in plainest characters the paralysis of the will. And then there are the stealthy, restless eyes of those who are awake, eyes set in faces which lack utterly the strength of honest labor and even that of criminal wit."[8] Although most were "widely severed from all things human," Wyckoff allows that "there are marked exceptions to the prevailing type . . . sound and strong in flesh, and having about them the signs of habitual decency." However, his thoughts quickly turn from these men to the classical air of his own middle-class community: "Faith and love and high resolve are there, the inspirers of true living, and courage spurs to unflinching effort, and hope lights the way of unsuccess and gives vision through the vale of sorrow and of death. And the common intercourse is the perfect freedom which is bred of high allegiance to inborn courtesy and honor." His own community, he concludes, was "a world of men and women whose plane of life is removed from this by all the distance of the infinite."[9]

Neatly couched in Wyckoff's description of his experience is a juxtaposition of the grotesque bodies of working men with the refined moral and intellectual minds of his middle-class friends. Significantly, Wyckoff presents his middle-class community in a decidedly noncorporeal light, and his logic moves in a subtly genetic fashion. Faith, love, courage, and vision flow not from culture but from "inborn courtesy and honor," whereas the down-and-out working men have no "inner strength and force," and even the homeless men of better character are so only out of "habitual decency."[10]

A further contrast of class images may be found in the photographs that sometimes accompanied the work of authors who investigated tramps in disguise. Perhaps the most striking of these is in Edwin Brown's 1913 book *"Broke": The Man without the Dime.* Here we find two pictures of the author, one captioned "As Himself" and the other simply "Broke" (see figure 7). Edwin Brown "As Himself" appears in a distinguished-looking dark gray suit, well-groomed, with hands behind his back. His coat is unbuttoned but not his vest. The background is undefined and only slightly lighter than Brown's suit, making his head and neck the most visible parts of the photograph. In this representation of the author's official identity, we see no legs, only his upper body. His eyes do not meet the camera. In contrast, Brown appears as "Broke" in a full-body shot. He wears his rumpled pants with suspenders showing. His plain coat is wide open, revealing a slightly bulging stomach. His hands are stuck in his pockets, with his thumbs hanging out. He wears a

Figure 7. Edwin Brown "As Himself" and "Broke." From *"Broke": The Man without the Dime* (Chicago: Browne and Howell Co., 1913). Courtesy of the Newberry Library, Chicago.

hat and a bandanna and appears to have the beginnings of a beard. In contrast to the photograph of the author "As Himself," in which only Brown's face and starched white collar stand out from the gray background, the viewer's eye is first drawn to "Broke's" bulging gut. "Broke" faces the camera directly, his eyes staring into the lens. In addition, barely visible in the background is a nature scene, perhaps suggesting the outdoor life of the hobo.[11]

Photographs contrasting "real" and "worker" identities also appeared in the work of Whiting Williams and Josiah Flynt, and these suggest the complex gender representations involved in disguise investigations. Brown's is a comical tramp, almost a buffoon. In contrast, Whiting Williams always struck a masculine pose when photographed as a worker. His 1920 book provided a refined portrait before the title page and several images of the rough steelworker "Charlie Heitman" (see figures 8 and 9).[12] Josiah Flynt's photographic images reveal another pattern. Flynt's official photo reveals him out of place as an author and respectable citizen with an oversized jacket and reddened cheeks. In contrast, "Cigarette," his tramp alter ego, seems supremely at home before a woodpile, a cigarette in hand (see figures 10 and 11).[13] In their photographs investigators tacked back and forth between class worlds while representing the differences between classes. Their official images established their objectivity, that is, their closeness to their middle- and upper-class readership, whereas their tramp images established the authority of their experience.

Figure 8. Whiting Williams as himself. From his book *What's on the Worker's Mind: By One Who Put on Overalls to Find Out* (New York: Charles Scribner's Sons, 1920). Courtesy of the Newberry Library, Chicago.

Figure 9. Whiting Williams as "Charlie Heitman." From his book *What's on the Worker's Mind: By One Who Put on Overalls to Find Out* (New York: Charles Scribner's Sons, 1920). Courtesy of the Newberry Library, Chicago.

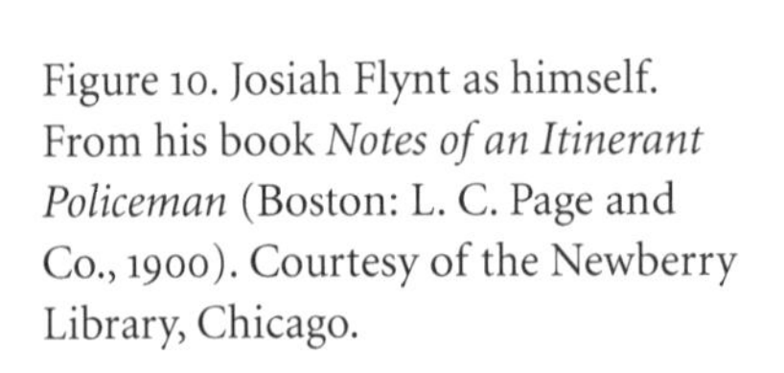

Figure 10. Josiah Flynt as himself. From his book *Notes of an Itinerant Policeman* (Boston: L. C. Page and Co., 1900). Courtesy of the Newberry Library, Chicago.

Figure 11. Josiah Flynt as "Cigarette." From his book *Tramping with Tramps: Studies and Sketches of Vagabond Life* (1899; New York: Century Co., 1907). Courtesy of the Newberry Library, Chicago.

Although participating in the tramp life bolstered the realism of their studies, too much involvement with one's subjects might cancel out the equally powerful authority of objective reasoning. Thus investigators took pains to situate their studies as nonpolitical descriptions of working-class life.[14]

As part of this rhetorical strategy, authors carefully recounted the process of becoming a worker, something that made for good reading as well as explicitly setting off real and undercover identities. Whiting Williams described his descent into the working class as walking "the plank off the good ship 'White Collar' into some seven months of what ought to prove interesting and worth-while adventure on the rough seas of 'Common Labor.'"[15] Edwin Brown wrote that he put on his worker's clothes in a hotel room, covering them with an overcoat to avoid detection as he exited the hotel. Once in the street, he shed the overcoat and "appeared an out-of-work moneyless man seeking assistance in this mighty American industrial center." He spoke in "the language of the army who struggle," asking a man on the street "Say,

Jack, can you tell a fellow where he can find a free flop?"[16] Given the gulf between middle- and working-class experience recounted by these authors, their transformation into workers was surprisingly easy.

Significantly, one of the few investigators who was a seasonal worker *before* becoming an investigator had a different perspective. Nels Anderson worked on road construction crews and in ranching during his youth. After working his way through college in Utah, he was accepted for graduate study in sociology at the University of Chicago. Having personal experience with the hobo world, he chose to write his master's thesis on homeless men in Chicago. Commenting on the vogue of participant observation at the University of Chicago, Anderson later noted that he used the method unlike other investigators. "I did not descend into the pit, assume a role there, and later ascend to brush off the dust. I was in the process of moving out of the hobo world. To use a hobo expression, preparing the book was a way of 'getting by,' earning a living while the exit was under way. The role was familiar before the research began. In the realm of sociology and university life I was moving into a new role."[17]

Even for Anderson, whose identity as a hobo worker did not depend on his experience as an investigator, the task of investigation drew out the class divide. In his case, however, the conventions of the university created a sense of otherness, whereas his return to life among the hoboes—this time to study them—seemed almost natural to him. So although Anderson approached the divide between investigator and subject from a different angle—one is tempted to say "from the bottom up"—his experience still highlighted the cultural gap between the two worlds.

The devices that made investigators' voices authoritative—realistic descriptions of working-class life and workers' bodies, contrasting images of "real" and "worker" selves, and descriptions of their descent into the working class—were both means to an end and ends in themselves. The job of the investigator was to describe and interpret working-class behavior to "the public." But because these texts also elaborated the boundaries between classes, description was interpretation. By retelling the tale of their disguise, by speaking in workers' dialect, even by sincerely admitting their real distance from working-class reality, the tramp ethnographers invoked geographies and social practices that appeared distant from their own. In doing so they firmly positioned themselves and their reading public in opposition to workers. Only middle-class investigators could shift so easily between class identities, and this was the ultimate measure of their power as well as the source of their objectivity.

❖ ❖ ❖

Although investigators' texts drew boundaries between working-class and middle-class worlds, those cultural boundaries simply enticed people to cross over to the other side. On one hand, middle- and upper-class people often defined themselves in opposition to what they considered below them: things "dirty, repulsive, noisy, contaminating." On the other hand, these people, practices, and places became "the object of nostalgia, longing and fascination," as Peter Stallybrass and Allon White argue.[18] So it was with many of the disguise investigators; a note of curiosity very often accompanied their condemnation of workers' social practices. The ways of living investigators labeled as "pathological" marked the boundaries of appropriate class behavior and simultaneously created the desire to transgress those boundaries.

Tramp investigators were deeply ambivalent toward their lives as workers. To be sure, they considered tramps villainous, lazy, dirty, and dangerous to the community because they lured working men into idleness and young boys into homosexuality or crime.[19] They also spread disease and overused relief agencies. For these reasons tramps had to be subjected to the discipline of "work tests" or confined in municipal lodging houses and poor farms. However, investigators often wrote about *tramping*—as opposed to *tramps*—as a liberating experience. As the detective Allan Pinkerton wrote, "No person can ever get a taste of the genuine pleasure of the road and not feel in some reckless way . . . that he would like to become some sort of a tramp."[20] The other side of laziness was freedom from work and social strictures.

The life and work of Josiah Flynt Willard (1869–1907) provide a compelling example.[21] The youngest son of a prominent Chicago family and nephew of temperance advocate Frances E. Willard, he was raised by his mother and older sisters after his father died when he was eight years old. Josiah Flynt (his pen name) claimed to have been born with an urge to wander, and he took to tramping at an early age, remaining on the road for some time. A frequent runaway as a youth, Flynt dropped out of college. He lived as a tramp and occasional worker for about a year until he made his way to Germany, where his mother was living. In the 1890s, he studied at the University of Berlin, tramped widely in Europe, and published popular articles on tramp life.[22] In 1898, Flynt returned to the United States, taking a job as special investigator for the Pennsylvania Railroad. There he put his knowledge of tramp life to the task of keeping trespassers off of the trains.[23] His friends felt that this job and his return to "respectable" society were his undoing. As he struggled with alcoholism and addiction to "stimulants," Flynt's health declined gradually until he died of pneumonia in 1907.

Flynt's posthumously published autobiography contains the reminiscences of several friends that highlight his inner struggle. Tellingly, one friend wrote that he could be at home with any class in any country "if given the *Mask of No Identity.*" It was said that he had a "morbid self-consciousness" that drove him away from the company of middle-class people. However, he was liberated from this affliction by any means to escape his own identity. "Give him a part in a play," a friend wrote, "the disguise of a vagabond, or whisky with which to fortify himself, and the man's spirit sprang out of its prison of flesh, like an uncaged bird." In fact, Flynt is reported to have said, "Whisky makes it possible for me to approach men with a manner which ignores all class barriers. Pass the whisky and it's man to man—hobo, hod-carrier or king!"[24]

Another friend had great respect for Flynt's ability to cross class boundaries. "Where I had dipped," he wrote of his first meeting with Flynt, "he had plunged, and that aim, which I was expressing about then, to 'roam in the sun and air with vagabonds, to haunt the strange corners of cities, to know all the useless, and improper, and amusing people who are alone very much worth knowing,' had been achieved by him."[25] Flynt was quite unlike "other adventurers who have gone about among tramps, and criminals, and other misunderstood or unfortunate people . . . as one might go holiday making to the seaside." Rather, he went among the vagabonds "with a complete abandonment to his surroundings; no tramp has ever known that 'Cigarette' was not really a tramp; he has begged, worked, ridden outside trains, slept in work-houses and gaols, not shirked one of the hardships of his way; and all the time he has been living his own life (whatever that enigma may be!) more perfectly, I am sure, than when he was dining every day at his mother's and sister's table."[26]

So tramping was a liberation from middle-class life dominated by mothers and sisters, an escape into a rough, masculine world of hardship. Yet Flynt's descriptions of fellow tramps suggest little in the way of liberation. Instead, he produced detailed negative portraits of his erstwhile tramp friends, whom he labeled "human parasites." The tramp and the criminal were almost synonymous in Flynt's writing, and there was little sympathy for either. Although all disguise investigators tacked back and forth between "inside" and "outside" class cultures, Flynt had really been on the inside. That is, he had been an unemployed, homeless transient. And yet he still "was not really a tramp" according to his friend. Even the title of his best-known book,

Tramping with Tramps, implies that the author is tramping without becoming a tramp himself. The liberation Flynt found in the guise of a tramp was not open to real tramps. Apparently, only educated people could understand the aesthetic and liberating elements of tramping. So-called uneducated tramps were simply lazy, had to be policed, put into work houses and jails, and generally kept out of sight. The tramping of the middle class could be romanticized only if real tramps were criminalized.

❖ ❖ ❖

Josiah Flynt's friends eulogized him as "not really a tramp," and yet he was more than just a master of disguise. He was in a sense both an actor and a playwright. In the telling of his own life story and those of men with whom he tramped, he wrote and enacted a powerful representation of class division itself. To a large degree both literary and social scientific descriptions of the working class operated similarly. By telling and retelling life stories, writers blurred the line between the fictional and the factual lives. Fictional accounts often reflected real life, and social investigators often fictionalized their "real-life" data. By examining the connections between fiction and social science we can gain insight into how investigators defined class through narrative, that is, through life stories.

Jack London's short story "South of the Slot" is a remarkable literary example of this process.[27] The protagonist is Freddie Drummond, a young sociology professor at the University of California and author of several politically orthodox books on the workers of San Francisco. Drummond is no armchair academic: He collects his data by assuming the identity of a working man. At first, his middle-class values make it hard for his co-workers to accept him. Shocked by the slow pace of work at his cannery job, Drummond finds that he can produce at twice the normal rate. For this achievement, he receives a beating from his co-workers, which "spoiled his pace-making ability" and prompts him to write a chapter titled "The Tyranny of Labor."[28]

With time, however, Drummond becomes "a very good imitation of a genuine worker," speaking the dialect of the working class, sharing their work and leisure-time values, and taking on the persona of Bill Totts, a rough, class-conscious working man. Bill Totts is everything that Freddie Drummond is not. Whereas Drummond is "a very reserved man" with few friends, no vices, and the nickname "Cold-Storage," Bill Totts is a hard-drinking, smoking, and gregarious man. The two are "totally different creatures," London wrote, inhabiting the same body. When Bill Totts beats a scab longshoreman, "Freddie Drummond was somehow able to stand apart"; and once back in the "classic atmosphere of the university," Drummond "sanely and conservatively" generalizes about workers' lives "as a trained sociologist should."[29] Very quickly, Drummond begins to enjoy life as a worker, but a house divided cannot long stand. In one life, Freddie Drummond excels in his academic career and plans his wedding to the upper-class Catherine Van Vorst. In the other life, Bill Totts becomes a union member and develops a fondness for Mary Condon, leader of the glove makers' union. Two personalities, each as real as the other, compete for dominance over the one body.

Soon enough, however, the battle of personalities in "South of the Slot" results in a clear working-class victory. As Freddie Drummond's wedding draws near and Bill Totts's desire for Mary Condon grows stronger, Freddie resolves never to return to his secret life as a worker. Yet at the ultimate moment of decision, Freddie finds that all of his strength has gone into the personality of Bill Totts. Riding through San Francisco in a chauffeured auto, Freddie and his fiancée happen upon a pitched battle between police and protesting workers. As the battle nearly turns in favor of the police, Freddie watches impassively while Bill Totts "heaved and strained in an effort to come to life." Suddenly, the well-dressed Drummond lets out "an unearthly and uncultured yell" and joins the battle on the workers' side as Bill Totts. Bill leaps atop a coal truck and defends it successfully, at the cost of bloodying a few policemen's heads. Then, seeing his sweetheart Mary Condon nearby, he jumps down to the sidewalk and, arm-in-arm with Mary, crosses over the Market Street, disappearing into the "labor ghetto" (see figure 12).[30]

Such a happy ending—at least from labor's perspective—undoubtedly is attributable to London's socialist politics. Yet the story is more than a send-up of Progressive Era academic disguise artists. It is also a gendered representation of class difference. The redemptive violence of the working class is somehow primordial. Bill Totts emerges as if Drummond's experiences as a worker had tapped a deep psychic vein, uncovering the real man buried by the strata of civilized, upper-class life. The victory of the working class therefore was also a victory of a particular style of masculinity.[31]

Other life stories reinforced the very different view that middle-class identity survived working-class experience, that class identity rather than rough manliness was innate rather than environmental. In the midst of his recitation of the living conditions of American workers in the 1880s, for instance, U.S. Department of Labor investigator Lee Meriwether offers the life story of an educated man who triumphs through adversity. The story is merely a supplement to "dry testimony" on the problems of Pacific Coast sailors, Meriwether notes, assuring readers that the story "is thoroughly trustworthy"

JULY, 1914 | The | PRICE TEN CENTS

INTERNATIONAL SOCIALIST REVIEW

SOUTH OF THE SLOT: By JACK LONDON

Figure 12. Jack London's "South of the Slot" was featured in the *International Socialist Review* 15 (July 1914). Courtesy of the Newberry Library, Chicago.

and "is only the counterpart of that of many of the tars who ship from San Francisco after enjoying the hospitality of the boarding-house masters."[32]

The story begins as a narrative of the pioneering self-made man. A young Virginia lawyer goes West to set up his own practice but is unsuccessful. In San Francisco, he is falsely indebted by "Sheeny Isaacs," a sinister boardinghouse master who sells him into virtual slavery under the captain of the ship *Viela*. The protagonist experiences life as a worker as a series of bodily defilements. "The worst thing about poverty is its dirt," he writes, "if poor places could only be kept clean, one wouldn't so much mind. We might get on very well with crusts and plain mush, but when it comes to rooming with unwashed men and sleeping in dirty beds, one's very soul revolts." On the ship his body is further broken by seasickness and the sadistic tortures of the ship's officers.

With his fellow sailors the protagonist tries to stop the abuses of the captain and mates. When they fail the hero resolves to make his escape. He asks his friend, an older sailor named Jack, to help him jump ship, but Jack refuses, signaling that his entrapment in the shipboard working class is partly of his choosing. As the protagonist notes, "I saw that poor Jack had so long lived the life of a sailor-slave that he had come to think that there was no use in trying to do better."[33] The young cabin boy, Mark Tillman, on the other hand, still has enough hope of improving his lot to attempt an escape. He and the hero escape the ship while at anchor off Hawaii. Once on the island, they disappear into the plantation economy disguised as agricultural workers.

This new identity even changes the protagonist's outer appearance and speech. Living with Portuguese workers, he speaks no English. Working in the fields all day, he finds his "skin burned black as a negro's." Yet his new appearance is no problem as long as he is a field hand and he speaks with only field hands. It is only when the protagonist resolves to ask the plantation owner, Colonel Thornton, for a better job that his body transgresses norms of appropriate appearance for an educated white man. As he approaches the planter's house he is suddenly fixed in the gaze of Thornton's beautiful daughter, who is sketching nature scenes. "'Oh, father,'" sighs the fair Miss Thornton, "'he looks exactly like a corsair—a dreadful, wicked, handsome corsair. I want to sketch him, papa. Make him stand still, please." The protagonist stands transfixed as Miss Thornton sketches him.[34]

Suddenly he is intensely aware and ashamed of his field hand's clothing, his unkempt hair and sun-darkened skin. He speaks to the colonel in Portuguese, requesting house duty for his young friend. Thornton agrees to the request and asks the protagonist his name. Recognizing it as a familiar American name, he says, "I knew a lawyer of that name in Virginia. He fought by my side in the Confederate army, and fell in one of the battles before Richmond. Was he a relation of yours?" The protagonist replies, "My father was a lawyer, and was mortally wounded before Richmond, and was buried in the trenches." At which the colonel cries, "He was my friend and comrade."[35] Thus the hero is revealed not to be a cane cutter but the son of a Confederate patriot. The colonel offers him a job appropriate to his real identity, he marries the colonel's daughter, and he takes over management of the plantation.

Meriwether's "Sailor's Story" is a curious one, coming as it does in the midst of a discussion of working-class conditions. More than a romantic aside, the story frames the underlying issue of why working-class conditions are so bad and why the promise of the American West seems to be failing the white male citizenry. When the hero falls on hard times in San Francisco and is "shanghaied" by a sinister, foreign boardinghouse keeper, the story makes the connection between waning prosperity and the twin menaces of immigration and exploitive employers. But through perseverance and personal initiative, the protagonist escapes, leaving behind fellow crew members too beaten down by the system, as well as nonwhite plantation laborers. In the end, however, it is less personal initiative than family connections that save the hero. Unlike London's investigator, whose essential masculine identity develops out of working-class experience, Meriwether's sailor remains essentially white and upper-class. His experience suggests that his class position derives from culture and family more than experience or economics. His new life as a plantation manager is a seamless transition from the imagined world of his dead father, a Confederate patriot.

As the appearance of "The Sailor's Story" within a report on working conditions suggests, fictional and social scientific commentary could share rhetorical strategies. Just as novelists such as London, Upton Sinclair, and Theodore Dreiser wrote in gritty, realistic prose that reflected the muckraking journalism of their day, social scientists used narrative strategies that we might expect to find in literary work. Even statistics at times presented less than objective images of working people. One study treated readers to a tabulation of the "Habits" of 100 inmates of a work house, including categories such as "Wanderlust," "Scandal Monger," and "Lacks Punctuality." A table on "Personality" enumerated those who were "Uninteresting," "Untidy," and had a "Repulsive Face." These variables were significant, the author argued, because "individuals whom nobody likes lose out" and become vagrants. Clearly these are not objective categories; rather, they are like a photographic negative of the investigator's self-image. If vagrants did not work steadily or save their money, one can guess that the author of this study considered himself hard-working and thrifty, not to mention handsome and interesting.[36]

Efforts to classify and enumerate different types of tramps were a hallmark of studies produced by investigators associated with charities and philanthropies. Typically these studies addressed applicants for charity or men arrested for vagrancy or drunkenness.[37] Just as Meriwether supplemented his investigation with the "Sailor's Story," however, other investigators wove the lives and words of their working-class subjects into their analyses. Whether by collecting case histories or quoting directly from their subjects, these methods repackaged workers' experiences within the investigator's own interpretive framework. In other words, they retold workers' stories with a middle-class accent. John J. McCook, a professor at Trinity College in Connecticut, made a long-term study of tramps and published some of the earliest "tramp censuses." Among the more interesting episodes in McCook's investigation was his lengthy correspondence with William "Roving Bill" Aspinwall, a self-styled member of "the fraternity of Haute Beaus."[38] Aspinwall was a pensioned Civil War veteran and an itinerant mechanic. McCook used excerpts from Aspinwall's letters to highlight his broader points about the lifeways of tramps, regularly adding doubting editorial comments and illustrating his articles with photographs of men arrested for drunkenness. Although they were published as Aspinwall's "diary," the dominant voice in these articles was McCook's.

Another striking example of this method are the life stories collected by Peter Speek and other investigators for the U.S. Commission on Industrial Relations. As in the case of Speek's interview with F. G. Peterson, investigators befriended laborers by offering them a cigarette or a meal, told their informant about the commission's work, and assured them that their stories would help improve conditions for laborers. Then investigator and subject went to a hotel room or other quiet place, and the investigator took the worker's life history by means of a uniform set of questions designed to check the veracity of worker's stories. Investigators paid the worker 25 to 35 cents an hour for interviews that might last several hours, very good pay for the mostly unemployed laborers surveyed by the commission.[39] Although the content of the interview was specific to each worker, the questionnaires ensured that all the life histories would generate similar data: a list of jobs, why the worker left jobs, how often he drank or visited prostitutes, and his opinion of the IWW. Variously titled life stories or life histories, the resulting document was a seminarrative set of notes, often jotted down in sentence fragments and usually focusing on the most recent period of the worker's life.

In an effort to synthesize the grim evidence for the commission's final report and make it accessible to a wider public audience, Speek created composite life histories to fit general categories of experience: sons of farmhands and tenants, sons of city laborers and poor people, immigrant laborers, those who formerly had a trade, and those who formerly belonged to the middle class.[40] Although the experiences recounted in most of Speek's field notes were similar, the composites lumped together many of the worst experiences into the life of one fictional laborer. They were at this point truly life "stories," designed as much for emotional impact as for scientific proof. The story of the farm-born youth, for instance, evokes a sense of tragedy, describing as it does the inverse of the American Dream. He begins with the youthful desire to make his fortune, marry, and start a family, but in the end he is just "human wreckage," not even brave enough to take his own life. The hard work and persistence of the laborer lead not to success but to poverty, disease, and a lonely death.[41] Such powerful material quickly found its way into popular and scholarly literature. A reworking of one composite life story and excerpts of several actual life histories appeared in a series of articles in the *Saturday Evening Post* in the summer of 1914.[42] Several years later, the text of Speek's field notes on two interviews appeared as "Autobiographies of Floating Laborers" in a book on labor problems, although they were clearly not autobiographical in the normal sense of the word.[43]

From hobo jungle, to public hearing, to mass media and academic press, the transformation of Peter Speek's field notes into life stories and autobiographies of floating laborers demonstrates how and why data become narrative. The floating laborer was not merely a data point representing the dysfunctional nature of the American economy. Rather, his life story *portrayed* the dysfunctional nature of the American economy by disrupting the cherished narratives of republican commonwealth, upward mobility, and appropriate masculine life course. The floating laborer cannot help himself, cannot get enough money to establish a family, buy a farm, or (if an immigrant) assimilate into American society. The promise that through hard work anyone can make it in America has become a grotesque parody of itself. It is not the inevitable upward mobility of the traditional American narrative that governs the life stories of the migratory workers but its inverse: Floating laborers inevitably go down.

Whether fictional or sociological, narratives about class shared a particular effect. By retelling workers' life stories, authors and investigators communicated to their audience a vivid image of a country divided by class experience. That investigators mingled social science and fiction in no way reduces the usefulness of these sources for historians, although we need to be aware of the context. Indeed, by seeing them as part of a cultural debate about the nature of society, these sources tell a largely untold story. Historians therefore have a role in an ongoing process of retelling life stories, a role we inherit from the social scientists, authors, and workers who came before us.

The encounter with workers, whether real or fictional, simultaneously undermined investigators' class identity and marked the boundaries of different class experiences and cultures. As investigations became more systematic and guided by social science methods, they dropped many of the idiosyncrasies typical of Flynt's generation. However, as the USCIR life stories suggest, more formal social investigations also shared a concern with translating and explaining working-class behaviors for a broadly middle-class public. As laborers' unrest became increasingly associated with the potential threat of revolutionary disruption, investigations became a way not simply to describe workers' conditions but also to identify the causes of workers' protest movements that could be ameliorated without recognizing the legitimacy of those movements. Historians long have noted the shift in Progressive Era reform thinking from an emphasis on poor people's personal moral failings to an emphasis on the systemic problems of the economy. However, investigation of tramps and migrant workers suggests that the moral questions lingered within the economistic focus of the late Progressives.[44]

Regardless of their method, institutional affiliation, or class background, observers of working-class behavior shared a concern over what might loosely be called the work ethic. For reformers, work was a moral imperative, and the fact that others in American society did not share this view was troubling.[45] Many investigators did not understand the implications of irregular employment for workers' attitudes toward work itself. To reformers who failed to see the structural causes of unemployment, an able-bodied man without employment was at once reformable and unworthy of assistance.

But seasonal workers such as the Irishman who spoke with Alice Solenberger viewed work primarily as a means of "getting by." Where investigators thought in terms of careers and saving for the future, laborers spoke of earning a *stake.* In some senses, laborers' use of the term reflected a connection to the West's frontier period, as in *grubstake* and *staking a claim.* However, an older use of the term actually means "to suffice." In this sense laborers' use of the term reflected the rather nonmodern structure of payment common to their line of work and to rural America generally. Payment by the hour (that is, wages) was rare until the late 1920s. Payment was more commonly calculated by the day, month, season, or task. Because they were used to a period of unemployment between jobs, laborers tended to calculate the size of their stake based on the amount that would sustain them until the next job came along. Peter Tamony, who compiled extensive card files on American language, identified many variations on *stake*, suggesting its currency and importance to laborers. A stake man or short-staker was a laborer who moved quickly from job to job, lingering just long enough to earn his stake. In a dictionary of lumber industry jargon Tamony found *stakey* defined as "having a sum of money and apt to quit the job anytime," and a word list for the construction industry added that the stakey worker was "inclined to be independent." This was a kind of independence that was difficult for employers and reformers to understand.[46]

Like the fictional Freddie Drummond, investigators who worked in disguise commented frequently on conflicts between themselves and their co-workers over the speed and intensity of work, conflicts they read as centering on work ethic. Working as a construction laborer at the grounds of the Chicago World's Fair in 1893, Walter Wyckoff found that it "was easy to keep ahead of the men, but it was impossible, apparently, to urge them beyond the languid deliberation with which they shouldered the timber and carried it to the piles." His co-workers instructed, "Go easy with that; there ain't no rush, and you'll make nothing by your pains." But Wyckoff could not understand why young workingmen "with every chance, one would suppose, of winning some preferment through effective, energetic work" would work so slowly.[47] Laborers were akin to "irresponsible school-boys in their feeling of natural hostility to their masters," Wyckoff wrote.[48] Later investigators understood more clearly—as laborers had always known—that what the middle class might call "working up to one's potential" was a major cause of unemployment. For casual laborers, the end of a work task usually was also the end of a job.[49]

Solenberger, Wyckoff, Flynt and others did not grasp this crucial workers' perspective on the problem. For these investigators, the main issue was how to distinguish between reformable and unreformable tramp workers. To that end, they went to lengths to distinguish between temporary and permanent tramps. These efforts reflected the complex nature of the "tramp problem" as one of individuals, communities, and classes. Reformer Edmond Kelly stressed that the principal "danger to the community" posed by vagrants was a result of their influence on other workers. As Kelly wrote, "the few cents he begs, borrows, or steals are spent in the public house side by side with the element of our society most subject to the contagion of vagabondage; there he relates his adventures, brags of his independence, tempts his listeners to drink . . . and diligently undoes what little our compulsory education contributes to good citizenship."[50] Tramps were a threat to social stability and the functioning of the labor market because, as individuals, they were insufficiently committed to wage labor. However, their individual threat implied that all workers were prone to similar indiscipline.

In a sense, therefore, reformers divided the working class into those who were tramps and those who were in danger of becoming tramps. The "tramp problem," as well as the later "crisis of labor turnover," sat at the juncture of individual responsibility and class structure. As individuals, tramps threatened the community by setting a bad example for other workers. The community could protect itself by removing unreformable tramps and subjecting workers who had temporarily become vagrants to the beneficial effects of labor. Those temporarily tramping could be brought back into the community when they regained their habits of industry.[51] However, if the chief "menace of the tramp class" was to lure "the casual working man" into mendicancy, then the tramp problem was particular to the working class. Such an explanation positioned all workers outside the community.

This tension between class and community was present in all social investigations of seasonal and unemployed workers' lives. In the first decades of the twentieth century, however, the focus of social analysis shifted away from individual tramps as the major threat to the community. A growing perception that unemployment was a permanent aspect of industrial society provided part of the incentive for this shift, as did the increasing number of social investigations sponsored by state and federal governments.[52] The new generation of investigators, sometimes affiliated with research universities, believed their knowledge was based on science, not on class interest. As a result, they were confident that their solutions to social problems would serve the "public interest." Concurrent with social scientists' greater emphasis on structural causes of social problems, another current of investigation explored workers' psychological states and their attitudes toward work and management. Ironically, this development meant that tramps—now renamed "casual," "floating," or "migratory" workers—would be portrayed more as passive victims than as agents while unskilled workers were joining unions and going on strike in unprecedented numbers.[53]

The work of Carleton Parker is one of the most compelling examples of this complex engagement with labor's new insurgency and has had a strong influence on histories of the IWW.[54] Parker first wrote about the IWW when he was the director of the California Commission on Immigration and Housing (CIH), producing an important report on the Wheatland hop pickers strike of 1913. He later worked with the USCIR and also as a strike mediator during World War I. Like the fictional Freddie Drummond, Parker was a professor at the University of California; however, as far as we know, he never investigated in disguise.[55] Nevertheless, one obituary characterized him as one of a new group of "frontiersmen" who moved across the class divide in American society: "The new frontiersmen have sought the Hesperides in a new class consciousness, or rather inter-class-consciousness. . . . The elusive and ever-moving frontier-line is now economic rather than geographical."[56]

Like the other "frontiersmen" of class society, Parker interpreted poor workers and the IWW through the lens of his own middle-class experience. Parker developed his ideas about normal family life out of his own experience as an "intellectual migrant," moving with his family fourteen times in ten years. His brief periods of separation from his wife were traumatic and alienating, leaving him with a profound sense that to be a normal man, one had to live in a family.[57] Although Parker shared many assumptions about "normal" life with his middle-class contemporaries, his analysis had the appearance of objectivity. Like other progressive observers of the IWW, Parker openly criticized the autocratic tactics of employers and the atrocious living conditions of migratory workers. As a strike mediator, he cultivated an impartial but hard-headed approach, and like other progressives he championed the public interest amid the competing forces of capital and labor.

Parker was also attracted to the new science of psychology and became convinced that its application to industrial relations offered a way out of the dismal cycle of class war afflicting the West in the World War I era. He goaded economists to jettison the orthodoxy that considered economics a "rational" domain. In contrast, Parker highlighted the profound role of what he considered "instinctual" motives on economic life. The migratory workers, Parker argued, lived under a variety of psychological strains brought on by isolation from family life and women, as well as by dirty and degrading working conditions. Parker argued that poor working conditions were "aggravated by the ability and habituation of this migratory class to read about and appreciate the higher social and economic life enjoyed by the American middle class."[58]

The uncontrolled nature of American industrial development had created a disjuncture between normal life as society deemed it and the kind of life possible for the migratory worker. Having been subjected to the worst elements of capitalism, the IWW migratory worker was not a "mobile and independent agent, exercising free will and moral discretion," Parker argued, but merely "a psychological by-product of the neglected childhood of industrial America."[59] Though condescending, this reasoning allowed Parker to suggest to otherwise unsympathetic middle-class and academic audiences that, however wrong the Wobblies might be in their methods, their critiques of American society were justified. "My main thesis," Parker wrote, "might be stated as a plea to consider the states of conventional 'willfulness,' such as laziness, inefficiency, destructiveness in strikes, etc., as ordinary mental disease of a functional kind, a sort of industrial psychosis."[60] It is likely that such reasoning resonated with conservative labor leaders as well.

Parker's interpretation of the migratory laborers who made up the IWW in the West rested heavily on his perception of normal gender roles for American men. The western economy created a highly mobile pool of labor with neither family ties, nor legal residence (and hence no voting rights), nor "normal sex." As Parker described the typical Wobbly, he was "a neglected and lonely hobo."[61] Separated from the stable family life of the male citizen yet able to read about that life, the migratory laborers revolted as a subconscious reaction to bad conditions. So whereas earlier reform narratives positioned unemployed workers outside the community based on their lack of commitment to wage labor, Parker read workers' indiscipline and revolt as a result of their "abnormal" position in relation to the family and the presumed comforts of family life. Tramps, now called "migratory casual laborers," were no longer even negative agents. They were merely responding unconsciously to bad conditions and the misguided (or cynical) rhetoric of labor radicals.

Parker saw labor's growing radicalism and "bad conditions" as equal threats. Enforced mobility and poor pay and living quarters meant that workers could not act as citizens; indeed, they could not be expected to show the patriotism required of a citizen because they had so little to be thankful for. Undercover investigator C. W. Mills sensed the threat keenly while he posed as an IWW supporter. "I am eating and breathing agitation, agitation that is really anarchy," he wrote in his notes. Workers were frustrated and angered by their joyless, homeless, womanless lives. But the agitation, Mills wrote, was "the workings of the inner circle, the brains of the great army" of migrant workers. Revolution, he sensed, was "boiling and seething on the underside of the thin crust upon which the whole social fabric rests," and the IWW was turning up the heat.[62]

Whether the chosen metaphor was volcanic eruption, tearing of the social fabric, or a revolt of the slaves, the republic was in danger. Parker wrote that the new labor problems were "passive resistance" and "spasmodic waves of unrest and sudden perplexing strikes of unorganized workers."[63] If thirty

Wobblies at Wheatland could "dominate a heterogeneous mass of 2,800 unskilled laborers in 3 days," as Parker had concluded; if, as Mills worried, "the brains of the great army" could "tell this army of its strength," then the nation was indeed in danger of revolution.[64] Bad conditions had brought the nation to this crisis, and only improvements, guided by professional expertise, could save it. Parker took a historical view: "The IWW, like the Grangers, the Knights of Labor, the Farmers' Alliance, [and] the Progressive Party, is but a revolt phenomenon. The cure lies in the care taking of its psychic antecedents, and the stability of our Republic depends on the degree of courage and science with which we move to the task."[65]

Like Parker's California commission, the USCIR was a response to labor violence. In the wake of the bombing of the Los Angeles Times building, Congress convened the tripartite commission with representatives of business, labor, and the public in 1912. Its chair was prolabor attorney Frank Walsh of Kansas City. Academic economists who were colleagues and students of John R. Commons at the University of Wisconsin carried out much of the background investigation. To maximize publicity, Walsh chose to downplay systematic scientific investigation in favor of public hearings. Nevertheless, field investigators carried out a great deal of background study in preparation for the hearings.[66]

Labor economist Selig Perlman wrote the initial research plan for the investigation of the IWW and took a line similar to that of Parker. "The tactics of the unskilled class are nearly always the same," Perlman wrote, whether they are organized by the Knights of Labor or the IWW. Therefore, the commission should investigate "the conditions of the unskilled and floating laborers in general, and not only the small portion of these classes which knew enough to join the IWW."[67] Perlman called for a minimum of statistics and a focus on the qualitative conditions of the workers. The investigators "should mingle with the men, and learn their personal history," as well as study the industrial process. Significantly, Perlman wanted to get at the reasons for the inability of the AFL to organize seasonal workers. He hoped the investigation would find out "whether there is a way of making stable unionism work [among the unskilled], and what are the legislative remedies that would assist the two-thirds of the American laboring class in taking care of their interests in a fashion similar to that which is used by the more fortunate one-third, the skilled and organized."[68] In an unofficial note, Perlman wrote to William Leiserson that "psychology and attitudes are the catchwords" of the impending investigation and report, indicating that workers' opinions would be filtered through an interpretive framework that implicitly discounted their rationality.[69]

The commission's investigations were extensive, providing a rare glimpse into the lives of migratory workers, the attitudes of small-town residents, and the general working conditions in lumber, railroad construction, crop harvesting, and other industries. As Perlman's plan suggested, the investigations had particular public policy goals regarding the roles of the state, industry, and organized labor. A young investigator summed up the social analysis behind the USCIR investigations when he wrote that poor conditions for crop harvesters were "not due to the greed, malice or thoughtlessness of any group of individuals or any single class of society." Rather, these conditions were a result of the failure of society as a whole to meet the "great social needs which can only be met by the state and national governments."[70]

The work of Parker and the USCIR, as well as the wartime President's Mediation Commission, helped focus attention on migratory workers and the problem of seasonal labor markets at a crucial moment in the development of American industrialism. Echoing Parker's analysis, the President's Mediation Commission concluded that migratory laborers were "possessed of a feeling of injustice against [the] lack of continuity of employment, [and] serv[e] as inflammable material for beguiling agitators to work upon."[71] The task of nascent government efforts to bureaucratize the labor market and management efforts to stem the abuses of the "hire and fire" system was to eliminate both "lack of continuity in employment" and "beguiling agitators." As the scale of labor conflict increased during and after World War I, managers and middle-class academics wrestled anew with the dilemma of class and democracy.

Among those who sought a way out of this cycle of conflict was Whiting Williams, a personnel manager who left his job to become a common laborer. The son of an Ohio bank president, Williams attended Oberlin College and trained unsuccessfully for the ministry at the University of Chicago. In 1919, he was on the verge of being fired from his job as the personnel director of a Cleveland steel manufacturer when he decided to go under cover for six months as the worker "Charlie Heitman." Williams wrote in the preface to his 1920 account, "The particular reason for trying to get at the whole matter in this particular way arises from the belief that men's actions spring rather from their feelings than from their thoughts, and that people cannot be interviewed for their feelings."[72] Feelings must be shared rather than observed. As Williams later wrote, the idea for taking on the role of a worker came from a plant superintendent. As they discussed discontent among the steelworkers, the superintendent told Williams that the "right way to study the worker's mind, especially in a time of serious unrest, was to do his job and, so far as possible, live his life." In the months leading up to the great steel strike of 1919, Williams took the superintendent's advice that, "before we discuss with our men their specific demands, we first try to find out *who or what hurt their feelings.*"[73]

Williams made some perceptive observations, but he tended to minimize the importance of economic factors in favor of psychology. He found that American working men drew their self-respect, as well as their livelihood, from their jobs and their jobs alone and had little to say about family, ethnic communities, or working-class women. Williams gave ample space to reporting the words of co-workers, but his conclusions emphasized feelings over thoughts, and his recommendations concerned how management should respond to workers' "hurt feelings" and restore "goodwill." Wages were only part of workers' feelings, he reasoned; the more important part was a worker's "sense of his standing—his comparative standing—in the midst of his particular set or group." According to Williams, workers, managers, and professionals all wanted the same things: to know their place among peers, to be respected by subordinates and valued by superiors.[74]

Williams drew attention to the important role of front-line management in the social life of the factory. The foreman, he wrote, had the power to make a job a "daily heaven of interest and satisfaction or a daily hell of irritation and resentment." It was the foreman's arbitrary power that most bothered Williams and the men with whom he worked and talked. Overbearing bosses decreased workers' personal initiative and brought on needless strikes, he argued. All of this was "extremely expensive to both employer and consumer in the way of lowered output." Repeatedly sent away from plant gates without a job, Williams expressed outrage with a smug plant guard who offered no information on the possibility of work. "How can such a man realize the enormous seriousness of a job to the man who asks for it?" Williams asked his readers, and responding for them he noted that such treatment "makes a real man want to enroll with the upsetters of the system."[75] His anger was not that of an unemployed worker toward an employed worker but that of a manager toward a subordinate whose insensitivity fosters workers' support for unions and Bolsheviks. The threat of revolution loomed so much in Williams's mind that he was actually relieved when one worker "couldn't think of anything better" than steady employment. The utopia of steady jobs could be accomplished without revolution, Williams believed.[76] More humane foremen, guards, and personnel officers, he argued, would reestablish harmony in the factories and dissipate the support for disruptive unions and revolutionary movements.

Initially, Williams planned to share his findings with his employers alone, to secure his job as personnel director. But he soon realized he had fallen into something much more socially and personally profitable. He wrote that the nation needed "somebody to speak up who can speak out of . . . sympathetic knowledge, of both sides of [the] dispute" between labor and management. "If, as we in my company believed, men are square, then something was 'eating them,' so to speak; hunger, hopelessness, injustice; something was wrong. Just what this something was I purposed to find out by getting right in among the workers and looking at things through their eyes."[77] Williams fashioned himself the translator of working people's feelings to both management and the public. And yet, if workers needed to be translated to the public, they were by definition outside the public. After all, he never did an undercover investigation of executives.

Like Josiah Flynt, Williams soon parlayed his fame as an undercover investigator into a consulting career. He traveled to Europe and wrote about conditions there, and during the nationwide railroad shopmen's strike of 1922, he went undercover among both strike supporters and strike breakers, with the blessing of no less than Samuel Gompers.[78] Eventually, Williams consulted for some of America's top industrial firms, and according to his biographer, his "'old shirt and pants' came in handy as he ranged widely about the plants and offices."[79] The "goodwill" and "friendliness" sought by managers could be found in the minds of their workers. But to create the "homogeneous, intelligent, contented body" that managers sought, they first had to get under the workman's cap.[80]

The various modes of social investigation were very much the cultural production of one class trying to come to grips with the realities and politics of another. Alice Solenberger's exasperation with the "philosophy" of seasonal workers was not just a description of those workers' patterns of employment but a moral judgment as well. Likewise, we must view Peter Speek's prediction that the Wobbly Peterson would soon fall into the ranks of the down-and-outers in the context of the USCIR's efforts to weave a particular narrative about the fate of manhood in an industrial society. Despite the growing consensus among social investigators that an uncontrolled economy was the root cause of many social problems, the psychological outcomes of that economy became a major focus of study. Efforts to explain workers' philosophy of life, psychology, attitudes, or lack of friendliness and goodwill toward employers again positioned the workers themselves as the main social problem. In the context of middle-class confusion over workers' attitudes, social investigators' texts provided plausible explanations that also presented clearly separated class worlds. Demarcating class divisions and promoting an image of some workers as "degraded" served many purposes, but perhaps the most significant was to define community in middle-class terms. For workers to be a part of this community they had to *not be tramps,* that is, they had to submit to industrial work discipline.

But this was not the only image of American society in circulation during the Progressive Era. The lively labor and radical press, soapbox speeches in town squares across the country, and innumerable bunkhouse conversations provided alternative images of working-class lives and American society as a whole. A few sons and daughters of the elite actually found radical workers' interpretations more compelling. At the same time Whiting Williams sojourned as "Charlie Heitman," the middle-class radicals Powers Hapgood and Len De Caux crossed over to labor's side on a more permanent basis. After stints as wage laborers, the Harvard-educated Hapgood became an organizer for the Congress of Industrial Organizations while the Harrow-educated De Caux had a career as a labor journalist.[81] What made Williams's style of investigation more "objective" than the exhortations of labor radicals had less to do with his superior methods than with the usefulness of his story in the context of an ongoing conflict.

Tramps and floating laborers were the focus of social investigation because they represented the extreme human manifestation of unregulated industrialization: men without women, workers without bosses, white men "enslaved" by poverty. Investigations were both descriptions of real lives and caricatures, grotesque inversions of what middle-class investigators considered normal. It might be tempting, therefore, to reason that laborers were not so oppressed after all, that investigators embellished the terror of laboring life to serve political ends. But authors' recourse to familiar narratives of worker degradation does not necessarily make their findings useless. Nor should we conclude that none of the social investigators had the interests of workers in mind. In fact, some of those I have criticized were among the most progressive forces in an era known for its reform fervor. Rather, my point is to break down the division between social description and social history so that the sources we use to retell workers' life stories become themselves the subject of analysis. The tension between community and class apparent in the tramp investigations mirrored the experiences of laboring men and residents of towns throughout the upper Midwest. Just as investigators were both repelled by laborers' deviant behavior and attracted to their freewheeling manliness, communities needed unattached male laborers to meet seasonal demand for labor but also saw them as a threat to the social order. The experiences of laboring men and descriptions of those experiences are bound up in the same social history.

NOTES

1. On F. G. Peterson, see Commons, *Trade Unionism and Labor Problems,* 102. For the field notes and typescript report see, *USCIR Unpublished Records,* "Migrant Labor" (reel 6). The *Fourth Census of the State of South Dakota* (1925), 9–13, recorded Redfield's 1915 population as 3,122. On Peterson's Mexican adventure see "To Arms, Ye Braves," *Industrial Worker,* 8 June 1911, 1 (signed by F. G. Peterson and others); "Reds Gain a Great Victory," *Industrial Worker,* 25 May 1911, 4 (signed by "S.G."); "Rebels Are Defeated but Not Conquered," *Industrial Worker,* 6 July 1911, 1 (signed by "Chili-con-Carne"). See also Blaisdell, *The Desert Revolution,* 153, which identifies a Wobbly named Peterson as translator for the Liberal Party Civil Control Commission in Baja California. See also Speek, "Report on Psychological Aspects of the Problem of Floating Laborers (An Analysis of Life Stories)," *USCIR Unpublished Records.*

2. Peterson, "Solidarity Wins All the Time," *Solidarity,* 4 September 1915, 3.

3. For comparison see Mark Pittenger, "A World of Difference," 26–65; De Pastino, "From Hobohemia to Skid Row," 123–79.

4. Denning, *Mechanic Accents,* 77–78. Also see Clifford and Marcus, *Writing Culture;* Clifford, *The Predicament of Culture,* 21–54, 92–113; Stallybrass and White, *The Politics and Poetics of Transgression,* 1–26, 125–70, 191–202; Canning, "Feminist History," 368–404; Brantlinger, *Crusoe's Footprints,* 68–107.

5. Oberdeck, "Popular Narrative," 203.

6. Crapanzano, "Life-Histories," 953–60; Frank, "Finding the Common Denominator," 73.

7. Wyckoff, *The Workers: An Experiment in Reality, the West,* 2. See also Wyckoff, *The Workers: An Experiment in Reality, the East.* An advertisement inside its back cover hails *The Workers* as "one of the most romantic narratives ever written by a scholar, and one of the most valuable to all classes. It is a contribution to the study of humanity."

8. Wyckoff, *The Workers, the West,* 38.

9. Ibid., 39. Stallybrass and White, *Politics and Poetics of Transgression,* 21–23.

10. In another scene, Wyckoff refuses money from a prostitute despite being hungry and homeless, but his working-class partner takes it. Wyckoff, *The Workers, The West,* 32–34.

11. A small oval headshot of Brown as a tramp adorns the cover of *"Broke."*

12. Williams, *What's on the Worker's Mind;* Williams's biographer reiterates the contrast of class images on the title page of his book; see Wren, *White Collar Hobo.* See also the contrasting images in Williams, "The Workers' Speakeasy," 493.

13. See Flynt, *My Life* and *Tramping with Tramps.*

14. Brown, *"Broke,"* xiii; see also Solenberger, *One Thousand Homeless Men,* xi; Clifford, *Predicament of Culture,* 26–32.

15. Williams, *What's on the Worker's Mind,* 3.
16. Brown, *"Broke,"* 28. See also Woirol, *In the Floating Army,* 1.
17. Anderson, *The Hobo,* xiii; Anderson, *American Hobo,* 160–70. Anderson later came to regret his close association with his first book, *The Hobo,* which he believed had limited his chances for academic employment. In a self-described effort to purge this association, he published a humorous analysis of hobo culture under a pen name; see Stiff, *The Milk and Honey Route.* See also Anderson, *Men on the Move,* 1–2; Anderson, *The American Hobo,* xii.
18. Stallybrass and White, *Politics and Poetics,* 191.
19. Flynt, *Tramping with Tramps,* 336–54; Kelly, *The Elimination of the Tramp,* 14.
20. Pinkerton, *Strikers,* 26; see also Wyckoff, *The Workers, the West,* 330–31.
21. Biographical information is from Flynt, *My Life; The National Cyclopaedia of American Biography,* Vol. 13 (1906): 336; Tamony, "Graft, the Underworld, and Josiah Flynt," Peter Tamony Papers, WHMC.
22. These later appeared as *Tramping with Tramps.*
23. The nature of this work can be gleaned from the testimony of an unnamed "Detective" before the Massachusetts Board to Investigate the Subject of the Unemployed, *Report, Part II: Wayfarers and Tramps,* 86–91.
24. Burbank, "Josiah Flynt: An Impression," in Flynt, *My Life,* 349, 352.
25. Symons, "Introduction," in Flynt, *My Life,* xii.
26. Ibid., xvii–xviii.
27. London, "South of the Slot," 34–70. The story also appeared in the *International Socialist Review* 15 (July 1914): 7–17. The "slot" refers to the cable car track that runs the length of San Francisco's Market Street and for London acts as "the metaphor that expressed the class cleavage of Society."
28. London, "Slot," 38–39.
29. Ibid., 40–47.
30. Ibid., 65–69.
31. See also Oberdeck, "Popular Narrative and Working-Class Identity," 204–6.
32. Meriwether, *The Tramp at Home,* 214–33.
33. Ibid., 228.
34. Ibid., 232.
35. Ibid., 233. See Denning, *Mechanic Accents,* for similar dime novel endings. See also Takaki, *Pau Hana,* which notes that Portuguese workers were considered more elite in the plantation hierarchy than Asians.
36. Laubach, "Why There Are Vagrants," 5–6, 13–18, 48.
37. Somewhat more objective than Laubach's study are Solenberger, *One Thousand Homeless Men;* and John J. McCook, "A Tramp Census and Its Revelations," 753–66.
38. McCook, "Leaves from the Diary of a Tramp, I," 2760–67; McCook, "Leaves from the Diary of a Tramp: Train Jumping," 2880–88; McCook, "Leaves, III," 3009–13; McCook, "Leaves, IV," 23–28; McCook, "Leaves, V," 154–60; McCook, "Leaves, VI," 332–37; McCook, "Increase of Tramping," 620–24; McCook, "Leaves, VIII," 873–74. See the full correspondence between McCook and Aspinwall in *The Social Reform Papers of John James McCook.* See also DePastino, "From Hobohemia to Skid Row," chapter 3.
39. Speek sometimes gathered data in disguise, but the life stories seem to have been

taken under more open circumstances. Speek, "Report on Psychological Aspect of the Problem of Floating Laborers," 28–36, *USCIR Unpublished Records.*

40. Ibid., 37–75.

41. Ibid., 37–62.

42. Irwin, "The Floating Laborer: The Case of John Smith," 3–5, 41–51; Irwin, "The Floating Laborer: Some Humble Biographies," 8–9, 61–63; Irwin, "The Floating Laborer: The Need for Teamwork," 14–15, 45–46.

43. Commons, *Trade Unionism and Labor Problems,* 94–103; Speek, "The Psychology of Floating Workers," 72–78.

44. Ringenbach, *Tramps and Reformers;* Keyssar, *Out of Work.*

45. Rodgers, *The Work Ethic,* 17.

46. *Oxford English Dictionary:* "grub-stake: a sum of money earned or saved; a store of provisions or sum of money necessary for survival during a certain period." Note that "to stake" and "to wage" both have the meaning of risking an amount of money on a certain event or contingency, that is to bet (suggesting the long connection between payday and gambling); Peter Tamony Papers, WHMC, Columbia.

47. Wyckoff, *The Workers, The West,* 259.

48. Ibid., 178–79. See also Williams, *What's on the Worker's Mind,* 15–16.

49. See Mathewson, *Restriction of Output.*

50. Kelly, *The Elimination of the Tramp,* 14. See also Flynt, *Notes of an Itinerant Policeman,* 19. Kelly cites Flynt's *Tramping with Tramps* as an authoritative text. On Kelly's role in New York City charity circles, see Ringenbach, *Tramps and Reformers,* 126–29. On the perceived need to compel workers to work, see Montgomery, *Citizen Worker,* 52–89.

51. Björkman, "The New Anti-Vagrancy Campaign," 211.

52. See especially Leiserson, "The Problem of Unemployment Today," 1–24.

53. Ross, *Origins of American Social Science,* 247–50; Edwards, *Strikes in the United States,* 14–15; Montgomery, *Workers' Control;* Foner, *History of the Labor Movement;* Mark Pittenger, "A World of Difference"; Furner, "Knowing Capitalism."

54. Early editions of Melvyn Dubofsky's important history of the IWW quoted uncritically from Parker's negative descriptions of the IWW and especially the union's hobo contingent, but Dubofsky moderated his analysis in subsequent editions. See Dubofsky, *We Shall Be All,* v–vii, 148–49; Preston, "Shall This Be All?," 435–53.

55. Parker employed undercover investigators when he directed the California Commission on Immigration and Housing; Woirol, *In the Floating Army.* Parker had some first-hand knowledge of West Coast working conditions: His college education was interrupted by three years of wage labor, perhaps because of the depression of the 1890s. See *The National Cyclopaedia of American Biography,* Vol. 19 (1926): 321–22. Mitchell, *The Lie of the Land,* 36–57.

56. Parker, *American Idyll,* 22–23. This statement raises the question, If investigators were "frontiersmen," were workers "Indians"?

57. DiGirolamo, "The Women of Wheatland," 242; Parker, *American Idyll,* 137.

58. Parker, *The Casual Laborer,* 17, 125–65. See also Wedge, *Inside the IWW,* another study based on participant-observation that stresses the psychological pathologies of individual Wobblies as the motive force behind the organization. Thanks to Sal Salerno for alerting me to this source.

59. Parker, *The Casual Laborer,* 96, 100.
60. Ibid., 52–53.
61. Ibid., 106.
62. Woirol, *In the Floating Army,* 127–28.
63. Parker, *The Casual Laborer,* 172.
64. Ibid., 189; Woirol, *In the Floating Army,* 128.
65. Parker, *The Casual Laborer,* 124.
66. Furner, "Knowing Capitalism," 274–84; McCartin, *Labor's Great War,* 24–37; Adams, *Age of Industrial Violence.*
67. Perlman, "A Plan of an Investigation of the IWW and of Unskilled and Floating Labor," 1914, 1, *USCIR Unpublished Records.*
68. Ibid., 3–4.
69. Selig [Perlman] to Bill [William Leiserson], n.d. [November 1913], note attached to Speek to Leiserson, 18 November 1913, describing plans for investigating lumber camps in which Speek plans to hire out of the state employment office as a Russian or Finnish immigrant, William Leiserson Papers, Box 38, SHSW.
70. Duffus, "Labor Market Conditions in the Harvest Fields of the Middle West," 14, *USCIR Unpublished Records.*
71. Wilson, *Report of President's Mediation Commission,* 15.
72. Williams, *What's on the Worker's Mind,* vi.
73. Williams, *Mainsprings of Men,* 4.
74. Williams, "What the Worker Thinks," 7 August 1920, 8.
75. Williams, "What the Worker Thinks," 20 March 1920, 9, 49; Williams, "What the Worker Thinks," 21 February 1920, 27.
76. Williams, "The Job and Utopia," 20.
77. Williams, "What the Worker Thinks," 21 February 1920, 9.
78. Wren, *White Collar Hobo,* 55–61; Williams, "Why My Buddies Will Strike Again," 13–14, 32; Williams, "In the Strike Breakers' Camp," 9–10; Williams, "What I Know Now about Railroaders," 13, 29; Williams, "We Were Pals," 11, 28–29. See also Williams, "A Job for Every Man," 9–10, 21–23; Williams, "Hail Columbia," 5, 26–27; Williams, "Who's to Blame," 7–8, 29–30; Williams, "Unsteady Jobs," 18, 28–29; Williams, "Workers' Speakeasy," 493–95, 528.
79. Wren, *White Collar Hobo,* 73–74.
80. Alexander, "Hiring and Firing," 143; Montgomery, *Fall of the House of Labor,* chapter 1.
81. Bussel, *From Harvard to the Ranks of Labor;* De Caux, *Labor Radical;* O'Connor and O'Connor, *Harvey and Jessie.*

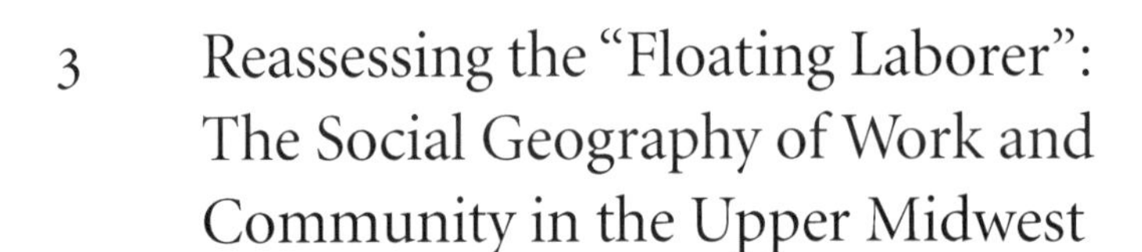

3 Reassessing the "Floating Laborer": The Social Geography of Work and Community in the Upper Midwest

SAM SWANSON AND ANDREW DEVICH were in many respects typical of young laboring men in the upper Midwest in the postfrontier era. Born in Chicago in 1902, Swanson went to live with his uncle on a northern Minnesota homestead after his mother died. His uncle had formerly worked as a carpenter building Pullman railroad cars but left Chicago for a healthier climate after his first wife died of tuberculosis. On the homestead, Swanson grew up as a farm boy, doing typical chores such as milking, splitting wood, and carrying water. When his uncle sold the homestead to retire closer to town, the fifteen-year-old Swanson began his career as a seasonal laborer. He worked for neighboring farmers and then traveled to the Dakotas for the wheat harvest, where he joined the IWW. Some years he followed the wheat into Canada, and others he stayed in the United States working the potato harvest. In winter, he found work in the lumber camps of northern Minnesota. In the early 1920s he took up seasonal work in the iron mines, landing a job with the Oliver mining Company. His farming background convinced the hiring agent that Swanson was not a union man. For several years, he worked the iron mines in summer and the lumber camps in winter, but in 1927, with logging wages low and payments for a new Chevrolet nagging him, Swanson finally settled into permanent mining work.[1]

Another miner, Croatian-born Andrew Devich, had a similar early working life. In Croatia he tended sheep and goats and cut timber with his father and brothers. Devich was the fifth son in his family to emigrate to the United States; he was seventeen years old. Upon his arrival in Duluth in the spring of 1913, his brother greeted him with a new set of work clothes and a job in a lumber camp. His subsequent work and travels revolved around the seasons and a loose network of acquaintances and relatives. During extended periods of unemployment, Devich often lived with a group of Croatian bachelors in Mountain Iron, Minnesota, and he regularly shifted between mining work in the summer and lumber work in the winter. During the 1916 miners' strike, Devich and three friends "bummed" (his word) their way to the North Dakota harvest, where Devich's logging experience served him well. He landed a good job driving a team of horses while his friends labored in the fields. They worked for the same farmer for a month and a half and became friends with another laborer who became a lifelong friend to Devich.

In 1919 Devich went to South Bend, Indiana, after receiving a letter from a friend saying there was plenty of work at the Studebaker plant. The lead turned out to be false, and instead of factory work Devich and another friend from the lumber camps decided to go "on the 'bum'" because "we were bachelors and had no ties, [and] we should see a little of this country of America." After a month-long tour on freight trains to New Orleans, the two men returned to the Midwest, finding jobs in several Illinois coalmines where other "lumberjack" friends worked. When work in the mines gave out, the two went to Chicago and found work in a steel mill through Devich's cousin and boarded with a couple from a neighboring Croatian village. After two years of steady work, Devich quit the steel mill and, on a whim (and the advice of a "gypsy fortune teller"), returned to northern Minnesota. There he began to settle into the Croatian community, living above a pool hall owned by a friend, working the iron mines, meeting his future wife, and, like Swanson, buying a 1927 Chevrolet.[2]

Had contemporary observers met Swanson or Devich before the men settled down, they probably would have considered them both "floating laborers," "homeless men," or "tramps." They seemed to move about without much of a plan, simply following the seasons, moving on when they tired of a particular job, even following the advice of a fortune teller. From the perspective of their lives after 1927, however, their early work experiences take on a different meaning. Like many other young men from farming and working-class communities, Swanson and Devich followed seasonal employment before they settled and established their own households. Their movement between rural and urban work was not a sign of deviance but a reality of the labor market. To put it another way, "floating laborers" did not "float." Their movement across the land was mediated by the changing seasons, their connections to communities, and the institutions and cultural assumptions of the labor market itself.

This chapter explores the social geography of work and community among seasonal laborers during the Progressive Era, mapping out distinctions of race, nationality, occupation, gender, and sexuality. In each case, I have found that familiar social categories are useful but do not explain everything about laborers' experiences. Ethnicity and race affected where laborers would work and what kind of work they did, but very few work camps were starkly segregated. Different lines of work had their own skills, jargon, and clothing, but an enterprising laborer could buy the right clothes and fake the skills long enough to be accepted. And in what seems a quintessentially macho world, men seeking the sexual companionship of other men did not necessarily give up their manliness. This is not to say that the world of seasonal labor was a utopia of equality. Their social betters, skilled workers as much as reformers and employers, looked down on laborers, often considering them parasites, even a quasiracial caste. And laborers had their own distinctions and prejudices. However, the very fluidity of the labor market made absolute exclusions difficult to maintain.

Given this fluidity, it is difficult to define the characteristics of seasonal laborers as a group. The conclusions we draw about laborers depend very much on where we find them in the historical record. Over the course of a working life—even in the course of a few days—a laborer might be a lumberjack, a railroad worker, a farm laborer, a beggar, or a miner. Obviously, this reality defied easy categorization and confused efforts to count and classify seasonal laborers as a group. What little statistical data we have on transient men, such as the "tramp censuses" of the 1890s, police lockup records, and charity case files are scattered and partial. Although tramp censuses often revealed that transient workers were much like the rest of the male population, investigators' accompanying interpretations clearly painted an image of deviance and criminality.[3] Like Progressive Era reformers, historians have sometimes assumed that as single men who were prone to boisterous behavior and arrest, laborers were unattached deviants. "Like the migratories of the West Coast," wrote Melvyn Dubofsky, "those of the plains states lacked wives, families, homes, roots; nothing tied them to society; their alienation, if frequently unconscious, was nevertheless complete."[4]

How might we test these assertions when the census counted neither tramps, hoboes, nor floaters? The answer lies in approaching "floating laborers" not as *floaters* but as *laborers,* a category the census did use. In fact, laboring jobs accounted for a substantial proportion of the occupational structure in the upper Midwest. According to the U.S. Census, laborers in agriculture and the rail and logging industries, along with the numerous "laborers, not otherwise specified," accounted for about 30 percent of all employed men in Iowa, Minnesota, and North and South Dakota in 1900.[5] In the succeeding three decades, the proportion of laborers in the workforce declined. However, in 1930, laborers were still 22 percent of employed men in Minnesota and 30 percent in North Dakota (see tables 1 and 2). Thus, despite their low visibility in historical studies, laborers were a much larger element of the occupational structure than were skilled workers. For instance, although roughly 150,000 men worked as laborers in Minnesota in 1900 and an equal number worked as farmers, only about 28,000 were skilled craftsmen in the building trades.[6]

Table 1. Minnesota Laboring Men, 1900–1940

	1900	1910	1920	1930	1940
Farm laborers, home	53,427	61,026	43,797	38,975	44,898
Farm laborers, wage	38,995	49,928	55,534	76,317	48,498
Unspecified laborers	54,111	54,623	42,129	44,600	19,151
	146,533	165,577	141,460	159,892	112,547

Sources: Bureau of the Census, *Twelfth U.S. Census, 1900, Occupations* (Washington, D.C.: GPO, 1902), 125–33; Bureau of the Census, *Thirteenth U.S. Census, 1910,* vol. 4 (Washington, D.C.: GPO, 1912), 111–23; Bureau of the Census, *Fourteenth U.S. Census, 1920,* vol. 4 (Washington, D.C.: GPO, 1921), 75–91; Bureau of the Census, *Fifteenth U.S. Census, 1930,* vol. 4 (Washington, D.C.: GPO, 1932), 828–36; Bureau of the Census, *Sixteenth Census of the United States, 1940: Population,* vol. 3: *Labor Force,* pt. 3 (Washington, D.C.: GPO, 1943), 701.

Table 2. North Dakota Laboring Men, 1900–1940

	1900	1910	1920	1930	1940
Farm laborers, home	8,988	16,485	13,227	15,025	16,738
Farm laborers, wage	14,748	34,381	22,413	38,463	16,474
Unspecified laborers	6,764	5,699	4,084	5,723	1,181
	30,500	56,565	39,724	59,211	34,393

Sources: Bureau of the Census, *Twelfth U.S. Census, 1900: Occupations* (Washington, D.C.: GPO, 1902), 135–43; Bureau of the Census, *Thirteenth U.S. Census, 1910,* vol. 4 (Washington, D.C.: GPO, 1912), 125–33; Bureau of the Census, *Fourteenth U.S. Census, 1920,* vol. 4 (Washington, D.C.: GPO, 1921), 93–101; Bureau of the Census, *Fifteenth U.S. Census, 1930,* vol. 4 (Washington, D.C.: GPO, 1932), 1222–23; Bureau of the Census, *Sixteenth Census of the United States, 1940: Population,* vol. 3: *Labor Force,* pt. 3 (Washington, D.C.: GPO, 1943).

Certainly this approach also has problems. Census enumerators often were idiosyncratic in their designation of people as different types of laborers. In rural areas, for instance, they sometimes failed to enumerate laborers working on farms as "farm laborers." The enumeration of female laborers presents another problem. More than 95 percent of all laborers counted in the census were men. This was partly because census takers were likely to enumerate women working on farms as nonemployed family members rather than as family farm laborers or as farm wage laborers. The census also counted women employed as cooks and domestic workers separately from laborers, although these were the types of jobs that laborers' sisters, wives, and mothers often held.

A further problem with the census is the highly elastic membership of the seasonal workforce. Down-and-outers mixed with farmers, farm laborers, urban craftsmen, laborers, and even college students. As labor economist William Leiserson noted in 1916, "The vast army of migratory and casual laborers . . . shifts from city to country, from foundry and street work to farm, quarry and construction project in response to a definite demand." Leiserson believed that "practically every wage-earner" passed through the ranks of the floating labor reserve.[7] Inevitably, the census count of laborers includes mistakes, the most significant of which is that they probably undercounted highly mobile workers.

Weighing these considerations, we can still gain further insight into the demographics of laborers using samples of manuscript census data.[8] The laboring men of the West North Central states (Kansas, Missouri, Iowa, Nebraska, South Dakota, North Dakota, and Minnesota) were demographically similar to the general working-age population of that region. According to the 1910 census sample, the region's males over ten years of age were 97 percent white, 80 percent U.S.-born, and 96 percent literate. Laboring men were 95 percent white, 79 percent U.S.-born, and 92 percent literate. In the sample of the 1920 census, a very small number of women were enumerated as farm and nonfarm laborers. Almost all of these women lived in family households: Nearly half lived with parents, more than one-quarter were spouses of household heads, and about 10 percent were household heads themselves. Female laborers tended to be younger than male laborers, they were 84 percent U.S.-born, and they had a slightly lower literacy rate than their male counterparts.

Among the men there were significant differences between farm and nonfarm laborers. With a median age of twenty-one in 1910, farm wage laborers were younger than nonfarm laborers or the population in general.

Only about 12 percent were foreign-born, with Sandinavians and Germans the largest immigrant groups; however, children of immigrants were a significant subsection of this group (see table 3). Interestingly, U.S.-born and immigrant farm wage laborers show different age distributions, with the Americans more tightly grouped at the younger ages and immigrants spread evenly across all ages. This divergence suggests that U.S.-born farm laborers moved more quickly out of laboring occupations than did immigrants. Even among immigrant farm laborers, however, young men were overrepresented, suggesting that farm labor was a young man's occupation. Farm laborers either became farmers in their own right or left farm work for higher-paying industrial jobs.

Nonfarm laborers counted in the 1910 sample were older, more likely to have families, and more likely to be foreign-born. These workers had a median age of thirty (right in line with the general male population of working age). Thirty-six percent of nonfarm laborers were foreign-born, a significantly greater proportion than in the general population of the region. Scandinavians and Germans were most numerous, but foreign-born laborers also included 12 percent Italians, 11 percent Mexicans, 11 percent Eastern Europeans, and 9 percent Greeks. In addition, nonwhite workers were found in much higher proportions (about 10 percent) among nonfarm laborers than

Table 3. Laborers' Country of Birth, 1910

Country of Birth	Laborers Not Elsewhere Classified (n = 1560)		Farm Wage Laborers (n = 2853)	
United States	63.7%	(994)	88.4%	(2523)
Foreign-born	36.3	(566)	11.6	(330)
Germany	4.9	(77)	2.6	(74)
Italy	4.4	(68)	0.1	(2)
Mexico	3.9	(61)	—	
Austria	3.3	(52)	0.7	(21)
Greece	3.3	(51)	—	
Sweden	3.0	(47)	2.0	(57)
Norway	2.3	(36)	2.2	(64)
Russia	2.1	(32)	1.2	(33)
Ireland	2.0	(31)	0.1	(3)
Finland	1.5	(24)	0.2	(5)
Canada	1.2	(18)	0.6	(17)
Hungary	1.0	(16)	0.1	(2)

Source: From the West North Central Census Region IPUMS sample, 1995 Release, for Minnesota, Iowa, Missouri, North Dakota, South Dakota, Nebraska, and Kansas. Prepared with the assistance of Dawn Owens-Nicholson of the University of Illinois Social Science Quantitative Laboratory.

in the region's overall population, reflecting their employment in railroad construction and maintenance.

The census samples also indicate that both farm and nonfarm laborers were closely tied to households, despite their popular image as a menace to communities. Between a fifth and a third of laborers lived away from families over the 1900 to 1920 period. Among farm laborers, census samples indicate that an increasing proportion lived in households with other family members. In 1910 and 1920 more than half of the farm laborers in the sample were young adults living in their parents' home, reflecting the increasing rural population of the region. The proportion of nonfarm laborers living away from family fluctuated between a low of 18 percent in 1920 and a high of 35 percent in 1910. These differences may reflect the different timing of census taking. The 1920 census was taken in January, a slack period for laboring work, and the 1910 census was taken in the spring, when laborers would have been working at distant job sites. Nevertheless, in 1910 40 percent of nonfarm laborers were household heads, 20 percent were children living in parents' homes, and another 6 percent were related in some way to the head of the household in which they resided. Based on samples of the manuscript census, then, a majority of early twentieth-century laboring men lived within the family orbit (see table 4).

A series of studies conducted by U.S. Department of Agriculture (USDA) economist Don D. Lescohier between 1919 and 1921 provides additional perspective on the lives of laborers in seasonal industries. Among the 32,000 harvest hands that the USDA eventually surveyed, Lescohier categorized one-third as farm workers, one-third as skilled workers, and one-third as laborers. Overall, half of the harvest workers were customarily "city" workers, including la-

Table 4. Living Arrangements of Farm and Nonfarm Laborers, 1910

	Laborers Not Elsewhere Classified (*n* = 1560)		Farm Wage Laborers (*n* = 2853)	
Median age (years)	30		21	
Living on farm	3%	(47)	83%	(2368)
Relationship to household of residence				
Household head	40%	(619)	11%	(327)
Child of household head	19	(304)	58	(1658)
Other relative	6	(93)	8	(226)
Not related	35	(544)	23	(642)

Source: From the West North Central Census Region, IPUMS sample, 1995 release, for Minnesota, Iowa, Missouri, North Dakota, South Dakota, Nebraska, and Kansas. Prepared with the assistance of Dawn Owens-Nicholson of the University of Illinois Social Science Quantitative Laboratory.

borers, factory operatives, and craftsmen. The other half were rural, including young farm men working in their home communities, farmers, and migratory laborers.[9] Recent migrants to cities made up a significant proportion of the harvest workforce. Although a majority of the harvesters were raised in rural areas, just over half got their first job in a city. In addition, less than half of harvest hands born on farms normally worked in agriculture. Many of these recent migrants were unskilled laborers, according to Lescohier. Considering the normal image of harvest workers, it is striking that migratory workers without homes amounted to no more than a fifth of the total harvest labor force. Put somewhat differently, 80 percent of the harvest workers surveyed had homes to return to after the harvest. So although the USDA studies did not closely track laborers' household connections, their data support the evidence gleaned from the manuscript census samples.[10]

❖ ❖ ❖

Whether the favored metaphor was a flock of migratory birds or an invading army of unemployed, unskilled workers, most observers considered seasonal laborers to be a homogeneous group. Indeed, roughly 95 percent of the laborers in the upper Midwest were classified as white by the U.S. Census, and an even greater proportion were men. Perhaps paradoxically, or perhaps because of this striking homogeneity, ideas about racial, national, occupational, and gender differences remain central to understanding laborers' experiences and their place in American society. Racial, national, and occupational differences helped to structure where workers would work, what kinds of work they would do, and how they would live in their labor camps. Similarly, laborers' relationships to various types of households and communities facilitated and structured the reach of their mobility. Cultural models of manliness, of familial and fraternal solidarity, and of appropriate roles for men and women helped to define both the labor market and the world to which laborers retreated when they were unemployed or needed a rest.

Broadly speaking, employers and laborers alike considered U.S.-born men of northern European ancestry, Americanized European immigrants, and recent northern European immigrants to be "white men." In turn, white Americans lumped together southern and eastern European immigrants as "foreigners" but usually spoke of African American, Japanese, and sometimes Mexican laborers separately. Clearly, these distinctions were in the eye of the beholder. As a historian of an Idaho timber region noted, people of Norwegian descent described Austrians as "black men" or as being from "a dark race." Similarly, on the Minnesota iron ranges employers classified Montenegrins, Serbs, south Italians, Greeks, and Croatians as "black." Cultural and political differences easily played into these notions of race. For instance, Finnish immigrants sometimes were divided between black and white subgroups, a distinction that overlapped with political and religious affiliations because socialists usually were known as Black Finns.[11]

These broadly held distinctions between laborers in turn affected, but did not dictate, how workers of different racial and ethnic origins interacted. The segregated hiring patterns of large employers, the racism of many white men, and the desire of some immigrants to work with familiar men all separated laborers. But this separation was never complete, in part because labor shortages forced employers to mix men from different origins. Summarizing in 1915 the findings of his investigation for the USCIR, Peter Speek noted that "the term 'white man' (also 'white hobo') . . . applies to native or old-time immigrant laborers, who are boarded by the employers in the camps, or who individually prepare their own meals." In contrast, "'Foreigners' or members of a 'foreign gang' means chiefly newly arrived immigrants organized into their own boarding gang on a cooperative basis, having their own cook, who prepares the meals according to their national customs and tastes." The difference between white men and foreigners was based more on "mode of living than the racial differences underlying these terms," Speek argued. He characterized a white man as "an extreme individualist, busy with himself and looking for himself only." Foreign laborers were "more sociable" and had a "higher sense of comradeship" with those of their own nationality, Speek observed.[12]

Although Speek reported that native and "old-time" immigrants rarely worked with new-immigrant laborers, he did prepare questions for both "foreign-born white men" and U.S.-born members of "foreign" gangs. In fact, many camps mixed "foreign" and "white" boarding styles, as both USCIR and state investigations revealed.[13] Visiting a work camp of the Chicago, Milwaukee, and St. Paul railroad at Great Falls, Montana, in the summer of 1914, Speek found fifty-four men: forty-two foreigners and twelve "natives." However, all the workers lived on a "white man's" basis, with board provided by a commissary company. When he visited a second camp of the same company later in the summer, he found a different arrangement. The twenty-five "white men" (among whom Speek noted three Mexican workers) purchased their board from a commissary company. The forty-six men in the "foreign gang" (forty-three Bulgarians and three Russians) shared the cost of small meals, coffee, soup, bread, and potatoes, but each man provided meats, eggs, and other expensive foods for himself.[14] Visiting what he considered a typical "foreign camp" at Redfield, South Dakota, by contrast, Speek found fourteen immigrant laborers (seven Greeks and seven Romanians) sharing spacious living quarters in "six old box cars, permanently placed on the ground, with windows, doors, floors and chimneys." Many of the regular workers in this camp had left to work in the wheat harvest, and Speek reported that as many as sixty men shared the same quarters during peak work times, sleeping ten to a boxcar. At the time of his visit, the workers received about $1.75 a day for ten hours of labor, as well as free lodging and oil. They prepared their own meals, each contributing about 30 cents a day and buying food in the town. Some of the men had been in the camp as long as five years. The laborers had their own foreman, a Greek, as well as the company's foreman, an American.[15]

Employers had well-developed notions of which ethnic groups provided the most efficient workers for various types of jobs. For instance, an internal telegram between Great Northern Railway managers noted, "We are going to use 57 Japanese extra gang laborers . . . [for] rip-rapping, substituting them for Italians . . . or other labor not fit for rip-rap work. We expect to keep best of gangs now in service [in the] Butte Division, principally Bulgarians, for rip-rap work." These decisions were based on the perception that suitability for particular jobs adhered to particular ethnic groups. Bulgarians and Japanese, in this example, were suitable for "rip-rap work" (spreading stones along track gradings), but Italians were not. Macedonian immigrant Christ Yankoff recalled that Bulgarians, Macedonians, and Greeks often worked together in crews, but Italians were always in their own crews.[16]

Similarly, employers often considered immigrant workers more reliable than their native-born counterparts. In his 1913 report on railroad labor camps in Wisconsin, for instance, William Leiserson noted, "Foremen almost invariably testify that a hobo gang can do four or five times the work of a gang of Greeks or Bulgarians, and that is one of the reasons why the 'white men' get more pay." However, the downside to employing hoboes, or "white men," was their tendency to quit after short periods at work, whereas immigrant laborers tended to stay on for the entire season.[17] Some lumber company officials favored immigrant workers for similar reasons. The general manager of a Michigan lumber operation told a government investigator that "foreigners have a firm purpose to earn money, to save, either to buy land here or to send money to the old country." In contrast, he opposed hiring U.S.-born lumberjacks because "they are the lowest type of natives, the better type do not go to the woods, they are working in the cities, or building up independent small enterprises." In contrast, according to the white clerk at the Lac du Flambeau Reservation in northern Wisconsin, although about

15 percent of the workforce at the local lumber mill were Chippewa, the mill's managers believed "the Indians on this reservation unsteady workers and wherever they can possibly do so they will avoid the hiring of an Indian and employ a white man."[18]

The relative "steadiness" of workers had much to do with the labor market structures that brought them to the worksites across the North American continent. In his study of immigrant labor bosses and workers, Gunther Peck reveals how large mining and railroad employers relied on ethnic intermediaries to provide a steady supply of reliable workers. Known as padrones, these intermediaries connected their countrymen with work, helped them negotiate international borders, and created a network of communication between workers in North America and communities abroad. Peck argues that padrones essentially created the labor market in immigrant workers by recruiting men abroad, financing their travel to North America, and provisioning laborers at the point of production. Although padrones were never able to completely restrict immigrant laborers' ability to quit and seek better pay, Peck argues that they created a form of unfree labor in which workers were beholden to the man who got them their job.[19]

Similar dynamics arose in the efforts of railroad employers in the upper Midwest to recruit Japanese, European, and African American workers. For instance, the Great Northern and the Northern Pacific railroads contracted with the Oriental Trading Company of Seattle to recruit and provision Japanese track laborers. Yet like their "white" counterparts, Japanese workers proved difficult to control. As many as half of the laborers the company shipped in from Hawaii deserted for other jobs once at port in San Francisco.[20] Those who did make it to railroad jobs in the interior regularly left the Great Northern and Northern Pacific for better paying jobs on rival railroads and in cities.[21] Even when working for the same railroad, Japanese laborers took every opportunity to switch to higher-paying roundhouse jobs or issued demands for equal pay with U.S. and European workers.[22] Far from beholden to the Oriental Trading Company, Japanese laborers were leaving the employ of the railroads to take jobs as lumberjacks, saw mill workers, and farmhands, as well as laborers for better-paying railroad lines. As a result, the Great Northern and Northern Pacific raised the wages of Japanese workers and sought an agreement with rival lines to harmonize wage rates and end competition for laborers.[23]

As the railroads began hiring more African American laborers during World War I, they often relied on a combination of white and black recruiters. However, provisioning black workers seemed more problematic to company officials. "Based on experience I have had in handling negro labor [I] think it better to employ negro boarding bosses in preference to white camp outfits," noted the Great Northern's G. H. Emmerson in 1917 in an internal telegram. "Always have found the negro outfits the more effective. Don't think it practical to board negro section laborers except at terminals where a large enough number can be used to justify providing boarding camp," he told subordinates. In contrast, Emmerson advised that Mexican laborers could be housed along with whites.[24]

Of course, black laborers had long intermingled with white and immigrant workers. The company's desire to segregate African American laborers into their own camps should be seen in the context of the company's decision to replace scarce immigrant labor with African Americans. As the trade unionist G. H. Edmunds noted, "There are thousands of laborers of my race who are continually roaming around the country seeking employment, and very frequently, become the victims of unscrupulous labor agents, and thereby become 'strike breakers' or wage reducers." Many of these could be organized, argued R. T. Sims, if only the white working man "would form a clear conception of his own economic interests" and accept black workers into his unions.[25] However, many white workers and government officials simply wanted the migration of southern blacks stopped.[26] So whereas the "racial" divisions between "whites" and "foreigners" had been fluid before the war, race was becoming a more "black versus white" issue. European immigrants considered themselves white, and white workers and government officials increasingly identified African Americans as the dangerous racial other.

Although African Americans traveled as widely as white laborers, in the overwhelmingly white upper Midwest their color drew greater attention to them, often resulting in more intense police harassment. Harry Haywood's first hoboing trip from Chicago to Minneapolis reflected this complex mix of freedom of movement and susceptibility to what we would today call racial profiling. Haywood rode a freight train from Chicago to Beloit, Wisconsin, where he waited overnight in fear of railroad police. "I met a white man, a 'professional' hobo," wrote Haywood, "who took me in tow and told me about the trains leaving in the morning." Together they rode "the blinds" of a passenger train into LaCrosse, Wisconsin, where they and a dozen other hoboes were pulled off the train by railroad police. Standing at the end of a line of hoboes, Haywood was singled out by the police and a watching white fireman. "Say, Jim, let me have that young colored boy over there to slide down coal for me into Minneapolis," called the fireman to the policeman. Haywood spent the rest of the trip shoveling coal. Similarly, after a white harvest hand arrived in Mitchell, South Dakota, bleeding from a gunshot wound he said was inflicted by a black hijacker, "every black man who could be found was searched for weapons," according to a local newspaper.[27] Although antiblack prejudice was perhaps not universal, black workers faced obstacles to their free movement across the region that their white counterparts did not contend with.

Mexican immigrants were also a quickly growing part of the regional workforce. Before 1920, Mexican workers had concentrated in major industrial centers such as Pittsburgh and Chicago, where they worked in foundries, railroad and highway construction, and packinghouses. U.S. Department of Labor investigator George T. Edson found some 1,500 Mexican sugar beet workers in the state of Minnesota in the late 1920s, with a small community of just over 500 living in Minneapolis and St. Paul. Farther south and west, in Nebraska, Colorado, and other states of the Great Plains, Edson estimated that a total of about 50,000 Mexicans worked in the booming sugar beet industry, but only about 3,500 worked in North Dakota, Minnesota, and Iowa. Like other rural workers, these sugar beet laborers found temporary jobs harvesting tomatoes, corn, grain, and hay when their beet fields did not need tending, and as historian Zaragosa Vargas argues, many found their way into more steady industrial employment.[28]

American employers also had their notions about the innate character of Mexican workers. Taking them to be peasants from an undeveloped country, employers praised Mexican workers as docile and fatalistic, "peaceable and healthy persons" who would benefit communities by taking the "place of riff-raff and irresponsible strangers" who formerly worked in seasonal agriculture. Already building tightly knit communities in the early days of their migration to the Midwest, Mexican workers apparently avoided public charities, relying instead on their own benevolent societies. Mexican men also seemed well suited to the harsh conditions of American industry, according to investigator George Edson. "The men, although not muscularly as strong as northern Europeans nor as active and big, show a greater endurance at work in extreme heat, disagreeable odors and nerve-wracking noises than most other races." Whether these assumptions had any basis in fact was less important than the strength of employers' perceptions that Mexican laborers would be a more manageable than the floaters on whom they always had relied.[29]

Native American workers faced different issues as they entered the regional labor force. Like other workers, they often mixed subsistence farming, hunting, and fishing with wage work. Some also had income from logging contracts on their allotment land. The belief of some employers that Native

Americans were unsteady workers derived not only from racism but also from the workers' ability to fall back on these subsistence practices. A study of Wisconsin's Menominee people found "the persistence right into modern times of old forms of exploiting the environment," including maple sugar and berry harvesting, hunting, and fishing.[30] In other words, like the Irish laborer that reformer Alice Solenberger berated for quitting a job just because he had money in his pocket, Native American workers did not always feel compelled to join the labor market. When they did join the workforce, however, they traveled widely and worked in rural as well as urban settings. George C. Peake, an Ojibwa from northern Minnesota who became a successful orator and actor, recalled that after his education in the Carlisle boarding school he returned to Minnesota and became a seasonal laborer. "And so I drifted to the harvest fields of the Dakotas, and from there to the lumber camps of Minnesota. Here I experienced all the hazards and the wild thrill of log-driving down some rushing, turbulent stream," he recalled. After some a time in the migrant workforce, he settled in Minneapolis and "secured employment with the 'pick and shovel brigade,' spending my evenings studying law at a night school."[31] Few Indian workers achieved Peake's level of success, however. In his report on Sioux City, Iowa, George Edson found that Sioux workers sometimes intermarried with Mexicans, but local whites considered Indians "a very inferior class compared to Mexicans and even below negroes in cleanliness."[32]

Like black workers and those from various immigrant groups, Native American laborers might be identified by employers and police with particular negative characteristics but also could move about the countryside and find employment in mines, saw mills, lumber camps, and other industries. Employers and supervisors did not always act on racial and ethnic stereotypes; rather, they used them selectively to make sense of their cosmopolitan workforce and to divide and discipline workers when it suited their purposes.

Being a "white man," whatever the content of that identity, tended to make life a bit easier for laborers. "White" men working in "foreign" gangs often found preferment with foremen and other white workers. For instance, one union official told the Massachusetts Commission on Unemployment that an unemployed union member on the tramp could expect to be "regarded as a white man" as long as he showed his union card.[33] Whiting Williams, a manager who "put on overalls" and worked the steel mills, found himself promoted from laborer to subboss by the gang boss, who was one of the only other English-speaking men in his section, although Williams attributed his promotion to his greater energy as a worker.[34] The New Zealand–born Len

De Caux was more aware of how his language set him apart from the "foreigners" on his gang. "The American bosses barked at the Italians like top sergeants," he noted in his memoir. "If they condescended to relax with them, it was in the manner familiar to me of 'superiors' patronizing 'inferiors,' and would sooner or later include a sharp reminder not to presume." In contrast, the "drifter who came into camp for a meal more than a job, if he was white and spoke American," was treated with "some social equality." De Caux concluded that the message was, "You may be a bum or a dumb punk, but at least you're one of us."[35] Interestingly, similar treatment also could come to immigrants with education and the other markers of middle-class status. Dominic Ciolli immigrated from Italy with his parents as an infant and helped pay his medical school tuition by working on a railroad gang. Having acquired his job through middle-class friends and with an unusual degree of education for a track worker, Ciolli was able to observe his fellow Italian laborers from a distance. He lived and ate with his "white" foreman and was spared the abuse of immigrant padrones and American bosses alike.[36]

The boundary between "white men" and "foreigners" was real but not impermeable. In labor camps, jungles, and boxcars, workers from different backgrounds mingled and shared experiences. Organizers for the IWW realized that "race prejudice," as they referred to both antiblack and anti-immigrant attitudes, could cripple their efforts, so they attempted to bridge the gaps between racial groups.[37] How workers may have pictured this boundary is suggested by the words of an IWW organizer in Aberdeen, South Dakota. Attempting to explain to a reporter the Wobblies' notion of sabotage, the organizer drew a vivid and problematic comparison. Employers would learn to pay workers well, the organizer argued, because underpaid workers would retaliate against their employers by purposefully withholding efficiency, what an IWW slogan celebrated as a "bum day's work for a bum day's pay." Referring to a widely circulating story about Italian laborers who worked with "short shovels," he told the reporter, "We are just like the wop who cut an inch off his shovel when the boss docked his pay two bits."[38] Unfortunately, we do not know the ethnicity of the speaker, but we might assume that he was a so-called white man. Although the widespread use of ethnic slurs certainly was a part of everyday workers' culture, the organizer's embrace of the figurative Italian laborer who cut an inch off his shovel remains problematic. The speaker simultaneously identifies himself with the Italian laborer as a worker while distancing himself from the same laborer as an Italian through the use of the derogatory term *wop*.

Similarly, although the IWW made tenuous advances in organizing African American and white laborers together, the rhetoric of solidarity was not always achieved in practice. Starting in 1916, the number of harvest-related news stories involving African American laborers seemed to be on the increase, and these stories often reported gunplay and violence between white and black workers. On July 26, a black harvester, Newton McAdams, died from injuries he sustained when Wobblies threw him from a train, according to the *Sioux City Journal.*[39] In Redfield, South Dakota, two black men reportedly shot into a crowd of Wobblies who had come to force them off a freight train after they refused to join the union.[40] In Mitchell, three Wobblies went to the police accusing a group of black men of robbing harvest hands. The police promptly arrested and jailed the accused men, but while they were in jail fellow inmates signed them up as IWW members. The next day, when the accused men stood before a judge and pleaded not guilty, their accusers claimed not to recognize them.[41] In another Mitchell incident, a black holdup man working with a white partner shot a white IWW member during a robbery atop a moving freight train.[42] About a week later, in an Aberdeen jungle, Lee Greist, a white "independent" harvester, shot and killed Mac McLean, a black IWW member, after losing a crap game.[43]

Some of the violence between African American laborers and white IWW members may have reflected the latter's belief that farmers were importing black workers to replace IWW members who were making gains in the harvest. As Charles Barr, a representative of North Dakota businessmen, told a Minneapolis newspaper in October 1915, "present labor conditions in North Dakota make the employment of white persons impossible." He planned to visit southern states and arrange special trains to transport some 30,000 black laborers to the harvest. "We are out to remove the Industrial Workers of the World who have made the past season a horror to the North Dakota farmer," Barr added.[44] Officially, the IWW welcomed such a challenge, noting that the union "has some good Negro organizers, just itching for a chance of this kind. Thirty thousand Negroes will come and 30,000 I.W.W.'s will go back. The red card is cherished as much and its objects understood as well by a *black* man as by a white one."[45] Despite the official line and the fact of many African American members, a field delegate wrote to *Solidarity* near the end of the 1916 harvest that some of the newly minted white members did not want to work with black men. In one case, a white IWW crew quit a job after the farmer went to town and hired some black workers who were also IWW members. In another case, on the streets of Bismarck, North Dakota, white union members refused to let a farmer hire a black union member. "We must stop this, if we want the colored man in the One Big Union," warned the writer. "He is easy to get in the union if we treat him right. We find the colored man coming from the South, and we must see that they get into our union. They are trying to take advantage of the opportunities offered them in the North. So let's welcome them to our ranks, and cut out such discrimination against fellow workers."[46] In fact, the IWW was successful enough at organizing African Americans that government agents sent to infiltrate the union in 1919 made special note of the fact. One spy reported with ominous exaggeration that a delegate "known as [the] Jew told these negroes that they should get organized [on] account [of the] race riot" and that the IWW would defend them if they were members.[47]

Although the IWW attempted to organize black workers, at other times they carelessly used racialized language in their propaganda. According to C. F. Mills, undercover investigator for the USCIR, a Sacramento IWW organizer asked how many were married in the crowd of 200 men gathered to listen to his speech. When none raised their hands, he drove home his point. "Well, do you call that living? Even the black chattel slave had a chance to propagate his race. You men don't know what it is to have a home, a wife, a child, and yet you think you live. Think of that the next time you go up to Annie's room to buy yourself a home on the installment plan."[48] Here the Wobbly orator combined race, class, and domesticity, arguing to a presumably white audience that manliness and whiteness would be achieved through marriage and fatherhood. However, by combining a condemnation of prostitution with the notion of the installment plan, this orator may have missed his mark. Many workers surely would have known that they would have to buy their home "on time," with or without a wife. Moreover, suggesting that wage slavery was worse than chattel slavery, as David Roediger argues, was a dubious and problematic tactic that played into popular narratives about contented black slaves.[49]

Such cross-currents of identification and differentiation are evident, though in a less directly political form, in the life history of the laborer Patrick Flynn as recorded in 1914 by Peter Speek. A forty-year-old family man, Flynn lived with his wife in Milwaukee, and his two grown children were attending college with the help of an inheritance from their grandparents. For Speek, Flynn was typical of older white laborers who lost steady work because of injury and labor conflict. In past years, he had been a Great Lakes sailor and watchman in the summer and an iron worker in the winter, and a member of both sailors' and ironworkers' unions. In 1909, he was seriously injured when he was buried under a load of cement in the hold of a ship. He broke his collarbone and ankle and sued the owners of the vessel. After his recovery, he did not return to sailing because the employers' association locked out union members. He refused to join the company union because "his manhood does not allow it."[50]

Unwilling to work on the lakes and unable to find steady iron work, Flynn turned to short-term jobs clearing land and digging ditches in the countryside. Later he rode freight trains to Iowa, where his union card opened the door to a helper's job in the building trades. There were more of these jobs back in Milwaukee, but they were exhausting, the foremen were abusive, and "to keep up his energy he drank beer quite heavily," Speek reported. Finally, he began to rely on the odd jobs he could find through the state's Free Employment Bureau, and at the time of his interview he was digging drainage ditches ten miles outside of town and living at home.

A Democrat and a strong union man, Flynn held opinions on immigration that mixed prejudice with a critique of weak labor laws. He believed that Poles and Italians were taking over Milwaukee and "pressing down the wages" because they would work "for anything they get" in their quest to return to Europe well-off. "Their standard of living is low, they are dirty and live like 'dogs,' all sticking together; they are clannish and trade only with each other," he told Speek. "They exploit each other still worse than the American employers exploit them. The labor laws [in the United States] do not protect them," he concluded, "and they have to protect themselves and this is possible only through strong labor unions." Although Speek did not record that Flynn used the terms "white men" and "foreigners," his analysis evokes this broadly held distinction among laborers. His observations about Polish and Italian immigrants are clichés (clannishness, self-exploitation) as well as observations about the social organization of the labor market. But Flynn's work was as dirty as any performed by immigrants. Indeed, other laborers noted that "white men" were worse off than "foreigners" precisely because "the latter stick together and help each other."[51] Moreover, many middle-class Progressive Era readers would have interpreted Flynn's recourse to drinking beer to fortify himself for hard labor as a sign of alcoholism and degradation.

Flynn may have thought of himself as a "white man," but the same labor laws that failed to protect immigrants had served him poorly, too. The labor market divided laboring men by race and nationality but then set them side by side and subjected them all to the same rules. The fraternal solidarity so evident among immigrant workers seemed to help them survive some of the harsher aspects of the labor market, while promises of independence and social mobility rang increasingly hollow for many U.S.-born white men. This situation did not necessarily result in a breakdown of racial and ethnic identity; rather, a complex negotiation of identity and difference left "white men" feeling superior but somehow cheated out of the spoils of their superiority.

❖ ❖ ❖

In addition to segmenting the labor market, these widely held understandings about racial differences tended to marginalize all seasonal workers regardless of race. As Tomás Almaguer observes in his study of white supremacy in California, European Americans identified racial others not only by their language, skin tone, or other somatic features but also by their association with "various unfree labor systems," such as peonage and contract labor, that seemed to threaten the standing and income of free white labor.[52] For instance, in the eyes of many white trade unionists, blacks and immigrants were dependent races who were predisposed to submit to the authority of their social superiors. Significantly, male trade unionists often thought of white women in the same terms. Many argued that women, African Americans, and immigrants simply were not organizable and therefore were a threat to the organized white male workers.[53] Even radicals such as William Z. Foster dipped into the well of white male superiority when seeking a broader appeal for their arguments. In a 1915 pamphlet titled *Trade Unionism: The Road to Freedom,* in which he praised the inherent revolutionary nature of trade unions, Foster described unorganized workers as "sodden and inert," "human parasites," and "the real enemy of Labor; the true obstacle to liberty."[54]

Who better than Foster to assess the potential of the unorganized? Soon to became celebrated strike leader, in 1915 Foster was just ending his career as a hobo worker. As he knew, laborers were not always free to choose the time and manner of the work, and some found strikebreaking pay hard to refuse. Of course, radicals such as Foster understood that it was capitalism that drove the unorganized to these misdeeds, but in a class struggle everyone has to take sides. For instance, Socialist party leader Victor Berger took the occasion of the 1911 Milwaukee convention of the International Brotherhood Welfare Association (IBWA) to distance his respectable radicalism from the taint of the hobo. Founded by the "millionaire hobo" James Eads How, the IBWA was part philanthropy part political organization, designed to provide education and advocacy to hoboes through "hobo colleges" and the *Hobo News.* "Socialists in all countries have a prejudice against the submerged part of the proletariat," noted Berger. "We are not accustomed to look upon the so-called hobo or casual laborer as a friend of the organized working class. He furnishes strikebreakers and deputy sheriffs in economic struggles and furnishes floating voters at different elections."[55] Thus, impoverished unemployed workers were cast as dependents and hirelings. That their position made them less free in the eyes of Socialist politicians is evident from the comments of Milwaukee's Socialist city attorney to the IBWA convention. "The man who won't work when it is offered him is deserving of no sympathy," he intoned according to a Wobbly delegate. "He should take work even if he only received $1 per day—if he can do no better."[56]

Living on the edge of starvation meant that a laborer might be enticed to sell his vote or sell out his class as a strikebreaker. These harsh realities placed the hobo worker beyond the bounds of community according to these Socialist officials. Much as women, immigrants, and African Americans faced condescension and antipathy from even the most progressive elements of America's white body politic, white laboring men (regardless of where they were born) confronted an ascribed social identity. As E. P. Thompson remarked, class happens when one group of people forms an identity opposed to another group.[57] We can see the comments of Berger, Foster, and other trade unionists as part of "class formation" in which skilled workers, radical intellectuals, and progressive politicians marked off what was "below" them, just as their critiques of employers as parasites marked off those "above." This was how many Socialists envisioned the class divide, or divides, and their place in class struggle.

However, the marginalization of seasonal workers went beyond an ascribed position at the bottom of the economic scale. Through comparison and metaphor, various writers and speakers also positioned migrants as a quasiracial other. Their common plight with immigrant contract workers and their generally "degraded" situation was one element of this positioning. Even by the IWW's reckoning, after all, they were "wage slaves." A second element marked the radicalism associated with migrants as savage. Like the American Southwest, the upper Midwest in the early 1900s was within living memory of its conquest and settlement by European American society. In the overall racial system, "Indian" operated most effectively as a marker of backwardness and savagery as, for instance, when Minnesota Secretary of State Julius Schmahl linked Little Crow, the leader of the 1862 Sioux uprising, with the IWW. "Little Crow hated the whites with a deep, undying, implacable hatred," Schmahl told the citizens of New Ulm, Minnesota in 1919, "not because of any particular wrong they had done them, but because they were white and he was red, because they were civilized and he was a black-hearted barbarian, and skillfully and insidiously he implanted his own hatred into the hearts of his followers until they were ripe for massacre when the opportunity should present itself. . . . He was simply an embryo I.W.W. with an unbridled penchant for destruction."[58]

Similarly, Frank Laubach's study of New York transients opened with a lengthy passage about mob violence during the French Revolution: "Vagabonds, the rebellious of all classes, 'baton-carriers,' mangy, scurfy, emaciated and savage, these were begotten by the abuses of the system, and upon every social sore they multiplied like vermin." These historical savages were a distant echo of the present, Laubach noted in reference to IWW organizing among the unemployed during the winter of 1914: "One cannot read this description without being reminded of the 'Hoboes' Convention,' [and] the mobs directed by I.W.W. leaders."[59] So the equation of savage revolution, whether at the hands of Native Americans or the underclass, often seemed a race war against civilized white middle-class society. That Schmahl and Laubach's comments needed little elaboration for their audiences speaks to the currency that such ideas had in "respectable" society. As Gail Bederman argues, these invocations of "civilization" often linked social and evolutionary supremacy. White men were the pinnacle of the social order because they were also the most advanced from an evolutionary perspective, so the argument ran.[60] For middle-class whites, transient workers were both socially marginal and somehow genetically inferior. Whether they represented vestiges of conquered races, as Schmahl argued, or dysgenic mutations caused by industrialization, as Laubach and others believed, transient workers' bodies, social practices, and politics fell far outside the boundaries of white middle-class community and civilization.

Like the Socialists who saw parasites above and below them on the social scale and the white leaders who equated radicalism with the supposed savagery of Native Americans, laboring men had their hierarchies too. These hierarchies had two primary functions. First, workers used them to distinguish men in different lines of work and especially to distinguish specific skills. The modern-day tendency to see all these men as "unskilled" obscures the fact that driving teams of horses, cutting lumber, or harvesting crops and various types of farm work were distinct occupations that shared a repertoire of skills. The naming system also served a second, less utilitarian function. Wobbly rhetoric about hobo egalitarianism aside, these men, like everyone else, used naming systems as a way to position themselves vis-à-vis other workers. Whiting Williams perceived this as a last-ditch effort to hang on to "self respect." Every "user of the humble shovel," he wrote, "seldom fails to see in even so lowly a tool some scintilla of superiority or standing for his job, and therefore for himself."[61]

Whether or not laborers longed for a sense of superiority over others, as Williams argued, they were familiar with a variety of occupational categories. These could include harvest hand, lumberjack, gandy dancer, snipe, jerry, skinner, mucker, rust eater, dino, and splinter belly, to name a few.[62] To a certain extent, these occupational lines could be identified by special clothing and language. In his novel about a young migrant worker, former IWW official Charles Ashleigh described these different looks as they appeared to his protagonist in the Minneapolis bar where he worked. In general, there was the "atmosphere of recklessness and daring about these fellows who strolled along the streets in their blue overalls, or khaki trousers, with grey or blue shirts, open at the throat, and their black slouch hats." From his bar-back he could see gandy dancers (railroad construction laborers) "with fingers dipped in beer they traced upon the bar the diagrams of new railway branches, which they had been engaged in constructing." Near them were other construction workers, teamsters, who "belonged to a superior breed which looked contemptuously upon those who sweated with pick and shovel." These "teamios" or "skinners" were said to carry razors and attack in groups at the slightest insult. There were also lumberjacks dressed in "heavy, knee-high boots, about which hung their overall trousers, raggedly cut short," and flannel shirts left untucked. Some wore the traditional woolen mackinaw coat. When in need of work laborers would take any job offered, but when offered the choice most stuck to one or two lines of work. Clothing and language were important markers of occupation. Employers questioned the skills of improperly dressed applicants, and workers heading out for a new job often made a point of purchasing appropriate work clothes.[63]

Beyond these occupational categories, the most obvious manifestation of hierarchy within the laborers' subculture was the oft-cited "hobo, tramp, bum" trinity. Middle-class investigators picked up on these distinctions through the writing and speeches of ex-tramps such as Ben Reitman. Although there were many variations on the theme, all posited a hierarchy of character in which "hobo" was at or near the top and "bum" at the bottom. Reitman had it that "the hobo works and wanders, the tramp dreams and wanders and the bum drinks and wanders." A similar version stated, "A hobo is a migratory worker. A tramp is a migratory non-worker. A bum is a stationary non-worker." Nels Anderson offered further refinement, placing the "seasonal worker" above the hobo because the seasonal worker followed a definite pattern, whereas "the hobo, proper, is a transient worker without a program."[64]

Anderson's 1923 sociological study of Chicago's Hobohemia offers vignettes of men he considered seasonal workers, hoboes, tramps, and bums.

The seasonal worker, or "upper class hobo," according to Anderson, tended to have one definite occupation or trade and followed supplementary jobs only during his trade's slack season. Anderson classed "Bill S." as a seasonal worker because he worked a steady job as a practical nurse during the winter but quit every summer to follow short-term migratory jobs out of Chicago and to "loaf" on the main stem. Likewise, "Jack M." worked every summer as a Great Lakes sailor and usually worked as a lumberjack during the winter. In between season he traveled or "loafed" on Chicago's main stem, waiting for his next job to begin.[65]

In contrast to the seasonal worker, the "hobo may have a profession or trade, and also may beg in between jobs," according to Anderson. An English immigrant residing in America for some thirty years, and plasterer by trade, "M.P." was one of Anderson's examples of a hobo. M.P. was a widower with a daughter living in Pennsylvania, and for many years he did not work in his trade but traveled the country, taking "various kinds of work as the notion came to him." Past fifty years old, M.P. confined his work to plastering in Chicago when Anderson interviewed him. "He lives in the Hobohemian areas and is able to get along two or three weeks on a few days' work." He spent his leisure time in the "hobo movement of the city and has been actively engaged in the 'Hobo College.' Recently he won a lot in a raffle. It is located in the suburbs of the city. During the summer (1922) he had a camp out there and he and his friends from Madison Street spent considerable time in his private 'jungle.' "[66]

Perhaps the greatest difference between seasonal workers and hoboes in Anderson's examples was a function of age. One could imagine Bill S. and Jack M. living lives very much like that of M.P. when they got older. In contrast, men Anderson classed as "tramps" rarely worked, and those classed as "bums" were more seriously down-and-out, usually physically injured or alcoholic. The tramp "X" made his living selling pamphlets and copies of the *Hobo News.* He spent his leisure time gambling and writing songs, poetry, and a novel. Similarly, the tramp "C" claimed to have wide experience in traveling by freight train and hoped to promote himself to newspaper men as "the only man who has beat his way on the Pikes Peak Railroad." In contrast to these figures, "A.B."—a "habitual drunkard"—was Anderson's example of a bum. "He migrates a great deal but it seems that his migrations are to escape tedium and monotony rather than to work. He is a little, hollow-chested, under-sized man and he claims to be thirty-two," Anderson wrote. "He picked berries, washed dishes, peddled, but he was also a successful beggar. His success in begging seems to lie in the ability to look pitiful."[67]

Workers themselves were well aware of these boundaries, although not always in the same way that investigators were. For instance, Whiting Williams told a local secretary of an "international hoboes union" that he considered hoboes, tramps, and bums to be all the same. The man's indignant response made clear that he saw a difference and that he was not a tramp but a hobo. The country could not get by without the work of hobo workers, he lectured Williams. "Northwest's gotta have us guys work at lumber in the winter and then Oklahoma's gotta have us work in wheat in summer, and we gotta make quick connections, too, or the crop spoils. So we gotta take the train and we don't believe in spendin' money on fares." The difference was that a tramp just walked from job to job without caring "whether he ever gets there or not—and nobody else does, neither." A bum, this man told Williams, "just bums a drink or a sandwich off people from day to day, 'thout doin' nothin' worth while for it. A tramp is miles above a bum."[68] Such distinctions are also clear from the derogatory hobo terms "stew bum" and "jungle buzzard," used to describe men who too often mooched off their fellows without contributing anything on their own.[69]

Distinctions based on gender and sexuality were another important way in which the hobo community identified its boundaries, both internal and external. Among the generally male hoboes traveled a small number of women who sought employment, adventure, and escape from stifling social expectations. Unlike men whose jobs were in the rural hinterland, transient working women moved from town to town seeking urban employment as clerical workers, domestics, or entertainers.[70] Often dressed in men's clothing, sometimes with short hair, these "sisters of the road" were less noticed than their male counterparts. When they did make news, usually after an arrest, newspapers wrote about them with fascination and a clear sense that they transgressed social norms. "Girl Dressed as Boy Bums Freight Trains with Boys," announced a 1910 *Kansas City Post* headline above a three-photo spread of Elizabeth Carr, a woman tramp, and her male companion. The nineteen-year-old Carr was the daughter of a packinghouse worker from St. Joseph, Missouri, who hoped to ride freight trains all the way to San Francisco to visit her mother and ailing sister. "I don't just know when I first conceived the idea of dressing in boy's clothing and attempting to 'beat' my way across the country on trains. The notion just grew on me, I guess. I didn't have any trouble collecting my 'outfit' and when the time came I dressed, tucked my hair under the cap and started out," wrote Carr for the newspaper.[71] Some of the women who took to the road did so for family reasons, whether it was to reunite with siblings, to stay with their husbands as they sought work in distant cities, or to marry the man of their choosing.[72] Others lived among male hoboes to escape juvenile court authorities or sought out adventure and escape.[73] Still others, such as Eleanora Ryan, dressed in men's clothing and took the road because it seemed to afford more opportunities than the life of a working girl. "It's a tough life, being a man and a bum," Ryan told the *Kansas City Post;* "Still I prefer it to working in shops at small wages."[74]

Male transients' reactions to their "sisters of the road" were mixed. Elizabeth Carr felt that she had been treated "just like I would have been in the parlor of my home" by the men she traveled with. "They acted like perfect gentlemen, and every one of them was kind to me."[75] Similarly, a University of Missouri student and her two friends who crossed the West in 1922 were never harassed by transient men. Much of the time they hitchhiked on the highways. When they hopped a Western Pacific train out of Salt Lake City, "there were four other hoboes aboard who greeted us cordially and surrendered to us the best seats against the coal box." At other times they were assisted by train crews. "For the first time in my life I've found existence absorbingly interesting," the student wrote to her former teacher.[76] Ben Reitman's account of "Boxcar Bertha" and her hoboing life provides additional examples, although it is probably a composite of stories he heard from several women and at least a little imagination. Crossing the country by boxcar with her younger sister, Bertha Thompson found protection from male hoboes. An older hobo acted as their guide until he was kicked off by the train crew. Afterwards, a younger man offered to give Thompson, her sister, and three other women in their boxcar money to bribe the crew if they needed it. When the train arrived in the next big town, the male hobo "fed everybody in the car and insisted on buying overalls and a jacket and cap for each girl," asking nothing in return. "In those days many of the hoboes on the road were like that," Thompson recounted, "they enjoyed beating their way about the country from job to job, making good money and spending it fast."[77] But as Thompson knew in retrospect, this experience was a lucky one. Train crews and male hoboes might just as easily demand sex from women travelers. In a boxcar in Illinois, Thompson met a woman who had been raped on her first hoboing trip. This woman was "pretty cynical about men generally" and at the time traveled with two men who provided her with food, "and in return she had given them what sex expression they wanted."[78]

The stories of these women hoboes point to questions of sexuality, power, and love. Although violence between men and by men against women was an ever-present threat, less destructive relationships were common. Transient men and women negotiated their lives on the margins of society often by forming makeshift households and temporary alliances. As Joanne Meyerowitz writes of Chicago's young working women, "The higher wages of men, plus the social sanction given to a courtship in which a man plied a woman with gifts, encouraged forms of dependence that fell somewhere between professional prostitution and marriage."[79] After a summer of work in isolated camps, seasonal laborers returned to cities such as Chicago and Minneapolis with large bankrolls and equally large appetites for a good time. In the cabarets and dance halls, the hobo with money to burn could easily meet women who were willing to offer their company in return for a meal and a place to sleep. As Thompson recalled of one woman hobo, "She accepted the fact that it was easier for a woman to get along on the road if she was not too particular and she frankly considered her body as her working capital."[80]

Other attachments were more enduring, though not necessarily permanent. Itinerant mechanic Bill Aspinwall told of raucous "Hop Dances" during the hop harvest in upstate New York. The men and women who came to work in the harvest participated with gusto: "One of the main pastimes on Sundays is carousing and drinking, as the numerous surrounding villages are full of saloons. I have seen drunken men and women scattered all over the fields, along Roads, [and] in fences corners." Aspinwall noted that many a working man "gets a wife very suddenly about these times," but the marriages rarely lasted long.[81] Sociologist Nels Anderson documented several of these "transient free unions" among hoboes living in Chicago. As he noted, "There are many women in the larger cities who have no scruples against living with a man during the winter, or for even a year or two, without insisting upon the marriage rite."[82] The case of the hobo M., who lived every winter with one Mrs. S. N., is instructive in this regard. "She worked and usually when she came home very tired he would have the house work done and a meal ready. When she was sick he waited on her. He listened to her troubles and was patient and good natured. In winter he always got up and made the fires." After living together on and off for five years, the couple parted ways but remained friends. Anderson had to admit, in the detached prose of his report, that these relationships "are often more or less sentimental."[83]

Male laborers also established sexual relationships of varying length and intensity with other men. Most social investigators, and perhaps quite a few laborers, disdained homosexuality. As Carleton Parker noted, "There are social dangers which a group of demoralized, womenless men may engender under such conditions [that are a] greater menace than the stereotyped ill effects of insanitation and malnutrition."[84] Although Nels Anderson was less derogatory in his comments, he too questioned the morality of homosexual practices.[85] Many memoirs and oral histories never mention homosexuality, but several mention brief—and quickly rebuffed—encounters with hoboes looking for sex from other men or describe the practice as if observed from a safe distance.[86]

Perhaps one reason for the invisibility of homosexuality was the pervasive relationships between men, especially between older and younger men on the road. At times, these relationships were described in more or less sexual terms. In tramp jargon these men were the "jocker" and the "prushun," respectively. Josiah Flynt defined the "jocker" as "a tramp who travels with a boy and 'jockers' him—trains him as a beggar and protects him from persecution by others." Flynt defined a "prushin" as a tramp boy. "An 'ex-prushun' is one who has served his apprenticeship as a 'kid' and is 'looking for revenge,' i.e., for a lad that he can 'snare' and 'jocker,' as he himself was 'snared' and 'jockered.'" These winkingly circular definitions (a jocker is one who jockers and a prushin is one who gets jockered until he grows up and looks for a boy to jocker himself) point toward sexual relations. And other authors were more direct, defining these roles as "husband" and "wife" or as "wolf" and "lamb."[87]

In *Tramping with Tramps*, Flynt described such a relationship by focusing on sentiment rather than sex.[88] Flynt's narrative recounted his meeting with an old acquaintance, Denver Red, and his "kid" in a San Francisco bar. The older Denver Red was stricken with tuberculosis, and knew he would die soon. He implored Flynt to take the kid back to his home in the East. The relationship of Red and the kid, Jamie, is a stereotypical one between a jocker and his prushun. Red and the kid came together when Red "buys" the kid for a dollar from another tramp. However, the relationship changed when the kid took a liking to Red. "He didn't wanter go home, 'n' I didn't want 'im to," Red told Flynt.[89] Red described his kid as "purty" and "cute." He was proud of Jamie's ability to beg and his handsome appearance. As Flynt and Jamie prepared to board an eastbound freight, Red lectured the kid on how he must forget the ways of the road and live a respectable life. Flynt commented on the scene, "It was the tenderest good-by I have ever seen between a prushun and his jocker. A kiss, a gentle stroke on his shoulder, and he helped him climb into the box car."[90]

As the story of Denver Red and Jamie suggests, sex, sexuality, and normative gender behavior are distinct but interrelated things. So common was the understanding that older men preyed on boys that when recounting their life stories, men felt it necessary to stress that their relationships with an older men were not sexual. Relationships between younger and older working men were an important element of social interaction between laborers, whether or not they were sexual. Older hoboes often taught young men the vital lessons of road life.[91] What did older men get out of these nonsexual relationships? No doubt they sometimes relied on the greater energy of their younger companions to help them survive. However, sharing experiences and teaching the novice were also important ways of defining manliness because they allowed men to display their expertise and, in a sense, to be fatherly.

Therefore, we need not read every relationship between men as a hidden sexual encounter. But for many on the road, sex was definitely on the agenda, and laboring men could expect to encounter other men looking for sexual relations. Nels Anderson's field notes for his study of Chicago's Hobohemia suggest a wide-ranging culture of sexuality among laboring men. Among Anderson's informants who described their early encounters with homosexuality was an eighteen-year-old laborer living on Chicago's main stem. This "Boy Tramp" told Anderson that he had his first experience while working in the wheat harvest. In Kansas he traveled with a man who took a keen interest in his wellbeing. While waiting in a wheat belt town for work to begin, the older man suggested that the two walk out of town to a haystack that would make a good sleeping spot. "When they reached the stack," Anderson's notes recounted, "the man tried to force a union" with the informant, who "opposed him for an hour or so, but finally submitted." Anderson's informant soon parted company with this man but encountered others like him. Over the winter he returned to his home town and had no sexual relations with men. While working in Nebraska and the Dakotas the next year, however, "he met the same types of men, had the same advances, and again yielded. This time he yielded with less coaxing than before. He began to get a certain pleasure out of the practice, and even put himself in the way of men who seemed to be interested." According to Anderson, the "Boy Tramp" had overcome "any scruples he may have had" and strongly argued the merits of homosexuality.[92]

Another of Anderson's informants argued that sex with other men was advantageous for the laborer because it freed him from obligations to women and family that were difficult to maintain economically and emotionally. "Shorty," a middle-aged laborer, had left his child and wife of eight years to live on West Madison Street, but because he and his wife were Catholic they had not divorced. He told Anderson that his wife had taunted that he would soon return home, but he replied that "as long as there were any 'punks' on Madison Street he would be satisfied." According to Shorty, a man was more likely to get sexually transmitted disease from women, and pregnancy would easily hamper his independence. "Give me a clean boy, every time. I'd rather go fifty-fifty with a fellow than to stay with the best woman in town," he told Anderson. Like the laboring men who established seasonal relationships with women, Shorty had lived with another man for two months during the previous winter, but his partner was out of town on a job when Anderson interviewed him. As Anderson noted in his published study, "Homosexual attachments are generally short lived, but they are real while they last."[93]

Whereas Shorty sought mutual satisfaction with his partners, many younger men traded on their sex as yet another temporary job, as a means of "getting by." Boys and young men along West Madison Street solicited men and charged 50 cents to a dollar for their services or received meals and lodging. Anderson's field notes suggest a general competition for the attentions of men arriving on the main stem with money in their pockets. A smaller number of men became professional prostitutes in Grant Park and along the lakeshore, where the "cleaner" and "well dressed" sex workers might earn $6 to $12 a day.[94]

Thus sexual relations between men—like those between women and men—fell on a continuum between rape, commercial exchange, mutual gratification, and love. But what is perhaps most fascinating and perplexing is the way these relationships reflected and transmuted the so-called normal sexual roles affixed to men and women. On one hand, there was the reflection of heterosexuality: the wolf and the lamb, the husband and the wife, the jocker and the prushin, the man and the fairy. As Anderson and others believed, there were two types of so-called perverts. The first type were mostly "men who have developed from childhood feminine traits and tastes, and they may be regarded as predisposed to homosexuality." Some of these men were flamboyantly effeminate, calling each other "ladies" or "miss," going by women's names, wearing makeup, and dressing as women.[95] George Chauncey writes in his study of New York City that the outwardly female traits of the "fairies" and their willingness to play the role ascribed to women in sexual encounters allowed their male partners to retain a sense of heterosexual manliness. In subcultural jargon, these men were "trade," men who had sex with other men but only when they played the "male" role.[96] They constituted what Anderson called the "perverts by conversion," who, "under the pressure of sex isolation, have substituted boy for woman as the object of their desires."[97]

To a large degree this "sexual dyad of fairies and trade," as Chauncey calls it, reiterated the conventions of heterosexuality in an all-male world. As the prostitute "W.B.P." told Anderson, "Some men who play the active role, or male part, in such a union, will not have anything to do with a fag that they think would be guilty of playing the man in such a relation." On the other hand, "men of the feminine type . . . want to think that they are submitting to a man who plays only the active part." But actual sexual practices undermined these boundaries of normal gender relations among male sex partners in several ways. Prostitutes such as W.B.P. had to play both roles to earn a living, and their partners may have implicitly known that this was the case. Meanwhile, men engaging in noncommercial sex seem to have paid less attention to the perceived norms of gender behavior. As Shorty assured Anderson, men "got as much satisfaction out of the passive as the active role." Indeed, he added, "a lot of them big guys in the city are doing it too. There's more people doing it than you think—it's natural." For emphasis Shorty offered, "Say, if you don't tell anybody about it, you can take a crack at me," but Anderson declined.[98]

Despite the wide-ranging subculture of sex between men and their willingness to "justify" their actions, Anderson reported that homosexual practices "are frowned upon by the tramps themselves." According to Lynn Adrian's study of hobo subculture, there were a large number of slang terms for homosexuals, most of them derogatory.[99] Anderson's own evidence tends to complicate his conclusion, instead suggesting a hierarchy of sexual value within the gay subculture. Just as laborers vigorously drew distinctions between hoboes, tramps, and bums, the limited evidence suggests that some in the gay subculture allocated merit along lines of youth, cleanliness, and adherence to gender role norms. For instance, Anderson's prostitute-informant W.B.P. denigrated the sexual relations of men such as Shorty as the last resort of desperate men with no money to pay for sex. W.B.P., a former secretary of the Hobo College, concluded, "The fifty-fifty practice so common on West Madison street and in other areas where the down-and-out hold forth is just a partnership arrangement resorted to so that each party may feel compensated."[100] Like the distinctions between hoboes, tramps, and bums, this one aimed to define an identity and its opposite. However, in the complicated social world of seasonal laborers we can surmise that this boundary of community, like so many others, was both permeable and contested.

❖ ❖ ❖

Relationships between men and between women and men were a stage on which people enacted their social roles. In doing so, they drew from familiar understandings of family life, fraternal solidarity, manhood and womanhood, youth and experience. But because dominant understandings of these roles seemed out of place given the economic realities, the men and women who lived by seasonal labor improvised new roles and different understandings of family and gender. Similarly, the racial, national, and occupational differences between laborers structured who would be included in which community and how far the boundaries of surrogate families might stretch. However, these divisions were rarely hard and fast, in large part because of the fluidity of the labor market.

Surrogate families, real families, notions of manliness, and racial divisions between laborers—as much as camp conditions, employment agents' abuses, and labor supply—were labor market structures. A market cannot exist in a vacuum. Instead, it is the sum of the cultures brought to it by buyers, sellers, and other social actors who try to describe and define its social function. The boundaries of the market, like those of community, were fluid, difficult to trace, and very much contested. The next chapter looks in greater depth at the boundaries of community between migrant laborers and residents of the Great Plains wheat belt. Focusing on the organizing campaigns of the IWW among harvest hands, we can see that the laborers' outsider status was subject to debate among farmers and small-town residents.

NOTES

1. Interview with Sam Swanson by Jack Spiese, 27 October 1967, MHS.

2. Andrew Devich, "My Memoirs," July 1976, Andrew Devich Papers, Immigration History Research Center (IHRC).

3. McCook, "A Tramp Census and Its Revelations," 753–66; Solenberger, *One Thousand Homeless Men,* 129–38; Schneider, "Tramping Workers," 213–17.

4. Dubofsky, *We Shall Be All,* 313.

5. The calculation is based on the following occupational categories: farm laborers (home farm workers and wage workers); lumbermen, raftsmen, and woodchoppers; steam railroad laborers; and general laborers (or laborers, not otherwise specified).

6. U.S. Bureau of the Census, *Twelfth U.S. Census, 1900, Occupations,* 125–33; U.S. Bureau of the Census, *Fifteenth U.S. Census, 1930,* Vol. 4, 828–36.

7. Leiserson, "The Problem of Unemployment Today," 11–12.

8. The following discussion is based on the Integrated Public Use Microdata Series (IPUMS), computerized samples of the manuscript census returns for the West North Central census region for 1900, 1910, and 1920. See <http://www.hist.umn.edu/ipums/>. Data for the following analysis was prepared from the IPUMS 1995 release with the assistance of Dawn Owens-Nicholson of the University of Illinois. To normalize occupational categories over the three censuses, I used the four 1950 occupation categories: farm labor, wage; farm labor, family; lumbermen, raftsmen, and

woodchoppers; and laborers, not elsewhere classified (NEC). This last group is titled slightly differently in the published censuses as "laborers, not otherwise specified" (NOS).

9. Lescohier, "Sources of Supply," 3–5; Lescohier, "Hands and Tools," 412. See also Lescohier, "Harvesters and Hoboes," 482–87, 503–4; Lescohier, "The Farm Hand," 539–40, 606.

10. Lescohier, "Sources of Supply," 5. See also Lescohier, "Harvest Labor Problems"; Lescohier, "Conditions Affecting the Demand for Harvest Labor"; Lescohier, "With the IWW in the Wheat Lands," 380.

11. Schrager, "'The Early Days,'" 163–64. Schrager also notes that Swedish and Norwegian immigrants were more likely to be considered white in part because there were Swedish and Norwegian farmers in the region already. On black and white Finns see Alanen, "Years of Change," 179; Syrjamaki, "Mesabi Communities," 257–75; Powers Hapgood, "Journal," 5, Powers Hapgood Papers, MHS. USCIR investigator Peter Speek also found twenty-five to thirty families from Kentucky working in the northern Michigan timber industry. Significantly, he noted that local "farmers and natives look upon Kentuckians as if they were of an inferior race" because of their drinking and quarreling. Speek, "Report on Investigation of Floating Laborers in Detroit, [and] in the Lumber Camps of Charlevoix County, Mich.," Jan. 1914, p. 14, *USCIR Unpublished Records.* On "white men's camps" in Colorado mining, see Jameson, *All That Glitters,* 140–60.

12. Speek, "Report on Psychological Aspects of the Problem of Floating Laborers," 31, *USCIR Unpublished Records.* See also U.S. Immigration Commission, *Reports of the Immigration Commission, Immigrants in Industries, Vol. 18, Part 22,* 425–31.

13. Speek, "Report on Psychological Aspects of the Problem of Floating Laborers," 31, 34, 36. MDLI, *Fourteenth Biennial Report,* 192–94.

14. Speek, "Notes on the Investigation of a Railway Construction Camp, Number 14, on the Chicago, Milwaukee Road, Great Falls, Montana, July 31, 1914," *USCIR Unpublished Records;* Speek, "Notes on Construction Camp, No. 11, on the Chicago, Milwaukee Railroad, Great Falls, August 1, 1914," *USCIR Unpublished Records.* See also Interview of Christ Yankoff by Frank Ninkovich, 26 February 1971, Roosevelt University Oral History Project.

15. Speek, "Notes on the Investigation of a Railway Construction Camp on the Chicago and North Western Railway at Redfield, South Dakota, 22 July 1914," 1–2, *USCIR Unpublished Records.* See also Vargas, *Proletarians of the North,* 39.

16. H. A. Kennedy to J. M. Gruber, 7 November [1908], GN Railway VP-Operating, General Manager Subject Files, Box 9, file 34–01, MHS. Rip-rap work is construction of embankments with large rocks and stones to prevent undermining of the track bed. Interview of Christ Yankoff by Frank Ninkovich, 26 February 1971, Roosevelt University Oral History Project, p. 12.

17. Leiserson, "Labor Camps in Wisconsin," 4.

18. Speek, "Report on Investigation of Floating Laborers in Detroit, [and] in the Lumber Camps of Charlevoix County, Mich., Jan. 1914," 10, *USCIR Unpublished Records;* U.S. Senate, *Hearings before the Senate Committee on Indian Affairs,* 698.

19. Peck, *Reinventing Free Labor,* 1–9; see also Hahamovitch, *Fruits of Their Labor,* 38–54.

20. General Superintendent to L. W. Hill, 28 February 1906, GN Railway, MHS.

21. Takahashi to Gruber, 21 January 1909; General Manager, NP Railway to Williams, 12 November 1908; Takahashi to Gruber, 9 September 1908; Takahashi to Slade, 8 September 1906, GN Railway, MHS.

22. Assistant General Superintendent to Slade, 29 March 1906; Takahashi to Kennedy, 24 February 1903, MHS. By 1910 the companies made a concerted effort to pay all laborers the same rate regardless of ethnic group. See Assistant General Manager to Takahashi, 21 February 1910, GN Railway, MHS.

23. Assistant General Manager to Takahashi, 27 January 1909; Sewall to Gruber, 7 January 1909, GN Railway Company, VP-Operating: General Manager Subject files Box 9, MHS.

24. Telegram from Emmerson, 21 April 1917; Hess to Godfrey, 18 April 1917, Great Northern Railroad, Vice President, Operating: General Manager Subject Files, Box 9, File 34–13, MHS.

25. G. H. Edmunds to William Wilson, 6 March 1918; R. T. Sims to E. N. Nockels, 19 January 1917, 4; Secretary's General Subject Files, Box 2, Folder 13/65, Records of the U.S. Department of Labor, RG 174, Washington, D.C. On African Americans working in the wheat harvest see Lescohier, "Hands and Tools," 378; Isern, *Bull Threshers and Bindlestiffs,* 139–41.

26. John Lind to Secretary of Labor, 7 July 1917, Secretary's General Subject Files, Box 2, Folder 13/65, Records of the U.S. Department of Labor, RG 174, NA, Washington, D.C.; for background on increased black migration to the North see Grossman, *Land of Hope;* Tuttle, *Race Riot.*

27. Haywood, *Black Bolshevik,* 40–41. "Tramp Gunman Shoots to Kill," *Mitchell (South Dakota) Daily Republican,* 26 July 1916, 4. See also Webb, *The Migratory-Casual Worker,* 88–90.

28. Edson's reports are part of the Paul S. Taylor Papers, The Bancroft Library, University of California, Berkeley; George T. Edson, "Mexicans in Minneapolis and St. Paul" [1927], Box 13, Folder 32; Edson, "Mexicans in the North Central States" [1927], Box 13, Folder 38; Edson, "Mexicans in Sugar Beet Work in the Central West" [1927], Box 13, Folder 39; Edson, "Northern Sugar Beet Mexicans" [1927], Box 13, Folder 40. Vargas, *Proletarians of the North,* 21, 27; Valdés, *Barrios Norteños,* 53. See also Valdés, *Al Norte;* and Mapes, "Defining the Boundaries."

29. George T. Edson, "Mexicans in Sugar Beet Work in the Central West" [1927], Box 13, Folder 39; Edson, "Mexicans in the North Central States" [1927], Box 13, Folder 38, Taylor Papers, Bancroft Library.

30. U.S. Senate, *Hearings before the Senate Committee on Indian Affairs,* 694–709; Felix M. Keesing, *The Menomini Indians,* 184–85, 227–28.

31. Peake, "The Ojibwas Used Firearms," 13; Beaulieu, "A Place among Nations," 403–5.

32. George T. Edson, "Mexicans in Sioux City, Iowa" [1927], Box 13, Folder 30, Taylor Papers, Bancroft Library.

33. "Massachusetts Board to Investigate the Subject of the Unemployed," *Report, Part II: Wayfarers and Tramps,* 54.

34. Williams, *What's on the Workers' Mind,* 23.

35. De Caux, *Labor Radical,* 37.

36. Ciolli, "The 'Wop' in the Track Gang," 61–64.
37. *Solidarity,* 8 October 1910, 2; *Solidarity,* 30 September 1916, 4.
38. "IWW Plans and Aberdeen," *ADN,* 27 July 1916, 5. On the history of "short shovel" tales see Green, *Wobblies, Pile Butts and Other Heroes.*
39. *SCJ,* 26 July 1916, 4.
40. *ADN,* 24 July 1916, 5.
41. *Mitchell (South Dakota) Daily Republican,* 21 July 1916, 1; *Mitchell Gazette,* 22 July 1916, 1.
42. *Mitchell Daily Republican,* 26 July 1916, 4. The wounded man, Charles Summers, was from "somewhere in the south" and was a member of the Odd Fellows as well as the IWW.
43. *ADN,* 1 August 1916, 1. McLean was reportedly from Kansas City. Greist was thirty-three years old, born in Maryland. He was charged with murder but pled guilty to manslaughter. Case #1346, Record of Criminal Cases, Brown County, Aberdeen, South Dakota. He was sentenced to fifteen years in the state penitentiary; see *ADN,* 7 August 1916, 5.
44. As quoted in *Solidarity,* 16 October 1915, 2. The article appeared next to one on the introduction of the combined harvester thresher in Kansas that noted farmers' hope to eliminate the need for transient laborers. See also *Duluth the Labor World,* 16 October 1915, 1.
45. As quoted in Foner, *History of the Labor Movement,* 478 (see *Solidarity,* 30 October 1915, 13 November 1915, and 27 November 1915).
46. *Solidarity,* 30 September 1916, 4. For emphasis, the editor printed the section of the IWW bylaws against discrimination following the letter.
47. Report of Operative 27, 23 July 1919. In the original handwritten notes the phrase "known as the Jew" was rendered as a more direct moniker, "the Jew," offering a better sense of the operative's feelings toward the delegate. See also "The IWW and the IVA," n.d. [1919], p. 5, Report of Operative 61, 26 July 1919, Langer Papers, Box 17, folder 13, University of North Dakota.
48. Woirol, *In the Floating Army,* 125.
49. See Woodruff, *The Advancing Proletariat,* 10; Roediger, *Toward the Abolition of Whiteness,* 127–80.
50. Life History of Patrick Flynn, *USCIR Unpublished Records.* On the lockout of the Great Lakes sailors by the Lake Carriers Association (controlled by U.S. Steel), see memo from Edward Stack, 18 May 1908; "To the Officers and Members of Trades Unions" (n.d.); "To the Officers and Members of the ISUA," 2 April 1909; Casey to Hon. D. S. Alexander, 12 June 1910, Papers of the International Seamen's Union of America, Burton Historical Collection, Detroit Public Library.
51. Life History of Patrick Flynn; Life History of U. B. Martin, *USCIR Unpublished Records.*
52. Almaguer, *Racial Fault Lines,* 13.
53. Kessler-Harris, "Treating The Male as 'Other,'" 190–91.
54. Barrett, *William Z. Foster,* 66–67. Foster later recanted these statements, calling the pamphlet in which they appeared a "sag into right opportunism."
55. *Solidarity,* 18 February 1911, 3, quoting from the *New York Call,* 4 February 1911. The IBWA and the IWW shared members, and the IWW at times tried to take over

the IBWA. See Anderson, *The Hobo,* 235–40; *Solidarity,* 6 March 1915, 1. See also Haywood, *Bill Haywood's Book,* 258.

56. *Solidarity,* 18 February 1911, 1. See also *Solidarity,* 15 July 1911, 2.

57. Thompson, *The Making of the English Working Class,* 9.

58. Schmahl, *Address by Julius Schmahl,* 3–4. See also Mrs. E. J. Hoxie to Governor Burnquist, 3 April 1917, in which a Minnesotan fears local German immigrants will rebel against the United States and should be executed just as the Indians of the Sioux uprising were. Quoted in Chrislock, *Watchdog of Loyalty,* 49. See also Ronning, "Miners on the Warpath."

59. Laubach, "Why There Are Vagrants" 5–6, 13–18, 48. On IWW unemployed organizing in New York City during the winter of 1914, during which the IWW led men into churches to demand food and shelter, see Foner, *History of the Labor Movement,* 442–49.

60. Bederman, *Manliness and Civilization,* 23–31.

61. Williams, *What's on the Workers' Mind,* 225; Williams, *Mainsprings of Men,* 61–62.

62. Anderson, *The Hobo,* 92–93. In contrast, see Montgomery, *Fall of the House of Labor,* 65.

63. Ashleigh, *Rambling Kid,* 93–94; Devich, "My Memoirs," Immigration History Research Center; and Saunders, "The Road," 48, WHMC, St. Louis. On distinct lumberjack clothing and identity, see also Schrager, "'The Early Days,'" 181–82. On skill and Canadian timber workers, see Radforth, *Bushworkers and Bosses,* 55–57.

64. Anderson, *The Hobo,* 87, 90.

65. Ibid., 90.

66. Ibid., 91–93.

67. Ibid., 94–95, 98–99.

68. Williams, *What's on the Workers' Mind,* 225; Schrager, "'The Early Days,'" 186–87.

69. According to Anderson, "The Jungle Buzzard is a tramp who lives in the jungles from what he can beg. He will wash the pots and kettles for the privilege of eating what is left in them." See Anderson, *The Hobo,* 103. According to Saunders, a jungle buzzard was "four degrees below a sonofabitch." Saunders, "The Road," 55, WHMC, St. Louis; Peter Tamony Papers, WHMC, Columbia.

70. Weiner, "Sisters of the Road," 171.

71. *Kansas City Post,* 30 December 1910, 2.

72. "Girl Unravels Box-car Mystery," *San Francisco Chronicle,* 23 November 1913, 56; "Woman Hobo Has Her Feet Frozen" *San Francisco Chronicle,* 1 November 1913, 2; "Hoboes across Country to Wed" *Wenatchee (Washington) Daily World,* 15 April 1913, 1; "$500 for Hobo Girl," *Fargo (North Dakota) Forum,* 3 September 1915, 5; "Jail Girl About to Become Bride," *Spokane (Washington) Spokesman-Review,* 17 November 1915, 10.

73. "Girl Delinquent Lives Hobo Life," *Spokane (Washington) Spokesman-Review,* 16 November 1915, 10; "Girl Returns to Life of Hobo," *Spokane (Washington) Spokesman-Review,* 28 November 1915, 6; "Girl Rides on Engine Tender: Seattle Miss Has Traveled Far without Paying Fare," *Ellensburg (Washington) Evening Record,* 8 July 1913, 2. See also Reitman, *Sister of the Road.*

74. "Arrested in Man's Clothes," *Kansas City Post,* 7 May 1915, 3. See also the fascinating case of "Robert Gaffney," a woman who lived as a man for ten years and was married to another woman for four years. "Lazy 'Husband' Is Woman Disguised," *Spokane (Washington) Spokesman-Review,* 19 February 1916, 1. Jon Gjerde cites two late-nineteenth-century examples of Minnesota women dressing in men's clothing to work as farmhands. See Gjerde, *Minds of the West,* 152; see also Katz, *Gay American History,* 209–79.

75. *Kansas City Post,* December 30, 1910, 2.

76. Helen Broshar to Clarence Alvord, August 10, 1922, f. 466, Clarence W. Alvord Collection, WHMC, Columbia.

77. Reitman, *Boxcar Bertha,* 37–38.

78. Ibid., 55–57.

79. Meyerowitz, *Women Adrift,* 101. See also Peiss, *Cheap Amusements,* 108–13; Reckless, *Vice in Chicago,* 140–62.

80. Reitman, *Boxcar Bertha,* 39.

81. McCook, "Leaves from the Diary of a Tramp, VIII," 873. See also the positive description of camp life at Wheatland, California, in Brown, *Brownie the Boomer,* 209–10.

82. Anderson, *The Hobo,* 141.

83. Ibid., 141. See also Life Story of F. G. Peterson, *USCIR Unpublished Records.*

84. Parker, *The Casual Laborer,* 73–74.

85. Anderson, *The Hobo,* 147; Adrian, "Organizing the Rootless," 226.

86. Hapgood, *The Spirit of Labor,* 49; De Caux, *Labor Radical,* 51, 59; Foster, *Pages from a Worker's Life,* 260–62; Sandburg, *Always the Young Strangers,* 383; Pifer and Sandoz, *Son of Old Jules,* 92–93.

87. Flynt, *Tramping with Tramps,* 395–96; Anderson, *The Hobo,* 147–48; John J. McCook, "Leaves, V," 154; Chauncey, *Gay New York,* 86–91; Katz, *Gay American History,* 48–52.

88. Flynt, *Tramping with Tramps,* 336–54.

89. Ibid., 342.

90. Ibid., 346. For a much darker portrait of a jocker and prushin, see Jack Conroy, *A World to Win,* 58–65.

91. McGuckin, *Memoirs of a Wobbly,* 10; Neufeld, "Portrait of the Labor Historian," 63; Anderson, *The American Hobo.*

92. Anderson, Document 122, Burgess Papers.

93. Anderson, Document 31, Burgess Papers; Anderson, *The Hobo,* 148.

94. Anderson, Document 82, Document 120, Burgess Papers.

95. Anderson, Document 124, Burgess Papers. Conroy, *The Disinherited,* 188.

96. Chauncey, *Gay New York,* 76, 80; Chauncey, "Christian Brotherhood," 189–211; Kimmel, *Manhood in America,* 98–100. See also Fellows, *Farm Boys.*

97. Anderson, *The Hobo,* 144.

98. Anderson, Document 31, Burgess Papers.

99. Anderson, *The Hobo,* 147; Adrian, "Organizing the Rootless," 226.

100. Anderson, Document 120, Burgess Papers.

❖

4 The Hobo, the Wobbly, and the "Battle of Mitchell": Unionization and the Politics of Community in the Wheat Belt

IN THE LAST DAYS of July 1916, armed clashes involving harvest workers, police, and townspeople rocked small towns across the northern Great Plains. Long accustomed to the yearly influx of workers in the wheat harvest, the towns tolerated the usual disruptions. However, when harvest hands organized into opposing groups led by the IWW and the anti-IWW "Yellow-Card Men" exchanged gunfire in the railroad yards outside Mitchell, South Dakota, the police sent out a "riot call" that brought several hundred armed citizens running. As the *Mitchell Clarion* reported it, "All night long the vigilantes held their guns on the rioting hoboes. Banked beside a warehouse, crouched two hundred migrant harvesters. Automobile headlights on cars flanking the mass furnished illumination for the scene. In front of the prisoners stretched a ring of citizens with loaded guns, to see that no man left the gang." In the morning, the "vigilants," led by the sheriff, the state's attorney, and the superintendent of the Anti-Saloon League, forced the harvest hands and their union officials onto the first northbound train.[1]

The so-called battle of Mitchell, along with armed deportations at Redfield and Sioux Falls, South Dakota; Ortonville, Minnesota; and Minot, North Dakota, were typical of wheat belt labor relations. In retrospect they might seem a logical community response to the threat posed by strangers. Indeed, the harvest hands seemed the quintessential outsiders: transient, unattached men with no commitment to the wellbeing of the community. But the stark divide posed by vigilantes on one side and harvesters on the other belies the deep connections between the two. True enough, laborers were transients, but many returned to the wheat belt year after year, some settled into communities, and many residents joined the seasonal labor pool in search of cash wages. Between the headlights and gun barrels of Mitchell's vigilantes and the crouching forms of harvest workers silhouetted against a warehouse we can find the meaning of work, community, and citizenship in Progressive Era America.

This chapter focuses on the struggle between farmers, wheat belt business leaders, governments, and laborers to define community and manage the rural-urban labor market in the upper Midwest. From the early 1900s through the early 1920s, the IWW toiled yearly to build "One Big Union" of harvest laborers in the wheat belt. The community response to harvest hand organizing may be characterized as hostile tolerance. Single male agricultural laborers were both central to the wheat belt economy and socially problematic. Despite the role of bachelor farmers in the rural community, farmers, shopkeepers, and professionals who valued hard work and self-sufficiency tended to see men who remained wage laborers as somehow deficient and probably lazy.[2] But the negative attitude toward laborers was tempered by desires for a harmonious community and the rural economy's need for harvest laborers. Farmers relied on outside labor to bring in their cash crops, and local businesses such as restaurants and hotels did their best business during the harvest. In addition, many recognized that laborers did have a hard life. Not surprisingly, farmers and small-town residents affiliated with the Socialist party and the Non-Partisan League (NPL) supported harvest laborers' efforts to unionize, but even people with less radical views used an antimonopoly rhetoric that saw both farmers and laborers as victims of large industries, especially railroads. In this way, residents could see themselves as the moderating influence standing between "millionaires and mendicants," as a Sioux City trade unionist put it.[3] Deportations, beatings, and arrests were not just a result of laborers' outsider status. Rather, these incidents helped to define the boundaries of community both rhetorically and physically.

The attacks on harvest workers became more intense as a result of IWW organizing, but unionization did not disrupt a harmonious system and bring conflict to the wheat belt for the first time. Instead, the IWW and its Agricultural Workers' Organization (AWO) emerged out of the complex interaction between the culture of rural and urban laboring men and the more consciously political project of labor radicals. Drawing on art, song, cartoons, and open forums, these activists built what Salvatore Salerno calls a "Wobbly sensibility," and this sensibility, rather than the union's institutional structure, formed the basis for organizing.[4] But as we shall see, union activists also consciously developed their loose organizing institutions from within this Wobbly sensibility. Like their adversaries and allies, Wobblies wanted "community" and "stable labor markets." But in contrast to the state-run employment bureaus advocated by progressive reformers, the structures Wobblies created reflected their own lives: seasonal, valuing individual and local initiative, and generally unconcerned with the appearance of respectability.

This chapter approaches the issue of community from two perspectives. First, I follow the development of unionism among wheat belt harvest hands from the early 1900s to early 1920s. Here I am interested in how union tactics and institutions developed in relation to the community of seasonal laboring men. The second strand of the chapter focuses on how unionization spawned debates within settled wheat belt communities as to how laborers ought to be treated. Such arguments reflected internal disagreements over the nature of community and how to fit notions of commonwealth and citizenship with the emerging corporate economic order.

❖ ❖ ❖

Historians have portrayed the IWW as an organization lacking solid structure and clear strategy. True enough, many famous Wobbly-led strikes were actually spontaneous actions to which the organization offered leadership and support. Local unions emerging out of these events usually were ephemeral, collapsing soon after the excitement of the strike subsided.[5] Although membership and local volatility were major problems, the organization also showed a remarkable knack for systematic, if undisciplined, experimentation in organizing, especially with the migratory workers of the West, among whom the union had a substantial base of rank-and-file activists. Moreover, the union set a daunting challenge for itself when it set out to organize laborers in seasonal industries. In addition to the job of creating unions that took in all the workers in a given industry rather than grouping them by craft, the IWW would venture among workers that no other union cared to touch. These workers might have more than a dozen different employers in a given year, spread over an entire continent. The task of keeping track of ardent supporters was difficult enough. As the organization moved from little more than a propaganda league toward something more like a union, the main question was how the IWW would build actual workplace organizations with enough staying power to make the workers' demands stick.

Answers to this question emerged slowly out of years of experimentation, outright failures, and fleeting successes. The organization's thin institutional structure actually eased innovations. With its national leaders playing little more than a loose coordinating and cheerleading role, local branches and small groups of organizers generated much of the early energy, ideas, and action in the drive to unionize migratory workers, as they were coming to be called at the time. New organizing tactics did not simply bubble up from the rank and file, but neither were they dictated in a top-down manner. Instead, an intriguing dialogue developed through the union's publications and open forums held in union halls across the country. The union's primary English-language newspapers, *Solidarity* and the *Industrial Worker*, were open to membership comment, often printing letters and field reports, even on the front page. As a result, organizing ideas and experiences spread rapidly among active members, who like other seasonal laborers had time on their hands and were avid readers.

Although a coordinated organizing drive among harvest laborers did not come until 1915, the IWW recognized the need to organize agricultural laborers much earlier. As General Secretary-Treasurer William Trautmann reported to the 1906 convention, the IWW was having "astonishing success" among lumberjacks, and it was time to push that organization into the harvest fields. Lumberjacks and sawmill workers, Trautmann argued, "should conceive that their own condition will be jeopardized if the I.W.W. fails to organize the workers in the fields in which they seek and secure employment during the remainder of the year; that is mostly in agricultural occupations."[6] For several years, activists debated how to carry out such an organizing drive and experimented with different strategies.[7] Some focused on the urban locals that took in workers of various industries and functioned as educational and social institutions for the unemployed migrants resting on the main stem. In this model, workers organized in the city during the winter would carry the IWW's message to the countryside in the summer. Others advocated a modified form of job or shop organization in which cells of activists at the various railroad, timber, and farm worksites in the countryside tried to enlist their co-workers into the IWW. Theoretically, these "branch locals" would then launch coordinated job actions. Still others sought to coordinate propaganda regionally helping to bring well-known IWW leaders to towns across the Midwest, often with the aid of local Socialist party branches.[8]

These different orientations loosely mapped a brewing internal power struggle that plagued the IWW. At the union's seventh convention, in September 1912, delegates spoke of the need for more systematic organizing as opposed to the "largely chaotic lack of methods that now prevail."[9] In retrospect it is clear that activists drew on various strategies as circumstances demanded. Without urban locals, advocates of job-based organizing had no place to go in the off season. Moreover, confrontational propaganda actions became such a headache for local authorities that some agreed to moderate their harassment of IWW organizers. After 1913, job-based organizing became the union's primary strategy as the Wobblies struggled to translate their theories of industrial unionism into a powerful union of migratory workers.[10]

We can glean the slow and halting development of this union from the pages of the IWW's national newspapers. Ben Williams, editor of *Solidarity,* suggested that the mixed locals be replaced with industrial union locals for the major industries in each local's region, such as a lumber workers' industrial union in Seattle and a construction workers' industrial union in Los Angeles. Each of these locals would then establish branches on job sites that could meet in the camps and send delegates to local meetings.[11] A correspondent to *Solidarity,* W. I. Fisher, replied, "An industrial local that is an absentee one from the job is little or no better" than an urban mixed local.[12] The IWW "must function as a union right where we work and not in some city perhaps a hundred miles away." The union must "colonize" camps and mills, he added, and where possible hold "local business and propaganda meetings and where not possible [hold meetings of] secret job groups."[13]

As the debate filtered through to IWW members at large, comments returned to *Solidarity.* In November 1913, Leroy Crossman of Burley, Idaho, wrote in support of on-the-job organizing. "In the last summer I have seen the group system work out to a nicety in the agricultural districts of southeastern Idaho. Members from the coast and northwest locals along with workers not yet 'lined up' took part in the meetings which were held on the curb or 'labor market,' in the jungles and on the job." Crossman reported that workers won wage increases, a ten-hour day, better sleeping quarters, and rides from work to town at the end of the job. "But nothing was left to the 'hired hand' in the shape of knowledge of the OBU," he lamented. Having briefly been a member of the craft-oriented Sheep Shearers' Union of North America, Crossman pointed to that union's use of corral delegates as a potential model for the IWW. Crossman wondered what special techniques should be used in the construction industry, to which the editor responded that workers should "study the industry, and find out what special formations are needed to secure efficient action and maintain solidarity on the job. Experiences and observations [of job group organizing] should be recorded in our papers . . . for the benefit of all."[14]

As Crossman's letter suggests, job-oriented unionism was developing on its own in the West. However, at the time free speech fights grabbed center stage. These IWW actions had a typical format and aim. Speakers addressed crowds assembled on public street corners and held forth on subjects ranging from the advantages of industrial organization over craft unionism to the evils of "wage slavery" more generally. For a variety of reasons, local authorities decided to break up these meetings and arrest speakers. Knowing they faced arrest, Wobblies sometimes climbed the soapbox and began reading the Declaration of Independence or the U.S. Constitution to dramatize their point. Small-town jails quickly filled to capacity, and Wobblies demanded less crowded quarters. Authorities usually relented after disruptive direct action tactics such as singing, noise-making, hunger strikes, and setting fire to lousy blankets. There were about thirty free speech fights across the country between 1907 and 1916 in towns such as Duluth, Minnesota, Superior, Wisconsin, and Kansas City, Missouri (1911); Minneapolis (1912); Minot, North Dakota and Kansas City (1913); Aberdeen, South Dakota (1914); and Sioux City, Iowa (1915). In addition, the fights at Spokane, Washington (1909–10 and 1915) and Missoula, Montana (1909) drew Wobbly activists from the Midwest.[15]

Many activists became critical of the free speech fights and the union's propagandizing orientation in general. Urban locals that focused on street speaking could never reach workers where it mattered, critics argued. The camp worker only "hears some of it while trying to drown his sorrows and misery by the pickle route in town, it doesn't touch him in the economic sense. He is not working just then and really is not as much interested as many of us used to think."[16] Instead of having expensive halls in big cities, J. S. Biscay argued, local secretaries should set up "a cheap office" in the towns nearest to job sites. Each job would elect delegates to go to the local meetings. Instead of traveling hundreds of miles (and having to quit their jobs), delegates could go to the local on Sunday and be back to work on Monday. So much closer at hand, workers would take a greater interest in union business and "would have something to occupy their minds on lonesome rainy days and holidays. Besides getting on the job," Biscay argued, "the union would fill that aching void of a Sunday solitude of the wild camp."[17]

Wheat harvest organizing drives from 1914 on built upon these ideas. Active locals in the wheat belt discussed on-the-job organizing, took action, and reported their experiences in IWW newspapers. These reports offer an interesting look inside the organizing drive but confirm that on-the-job organizing was at best a rhetorical goal, and town- and jungle-based propagandizing remained the primary Wobbly tactics. As one local reported, "At a meeting of Local 61, Kansas City, it was decided that we travel in small groups instead of in a body, owing to the fact that by doing so we could move quietly and not advertise ourselves, then meet at a given point and do our work after getting on the job." Despite these goals, the men of Local 61 continued "agitating in the jungles" and in town.[18] In mid-June, IWW organizer George Carey wrote from Kansas that large numbers of hands were congregating in small towns and finding going wages to be much less than had been advertised in big-city newspapers. In the town of Hoisington, Carey and fellow workers Christ and Fox set about organizing a mass meeting, advocating that hands not work for less than $4 a day. Apparently most of the prospective harvesters agreed with the demands and joined what Carey called a "Big 4 league": "over 500 men pinned labels on with the B. 4 'trade mark.'"[19]

Other Wobblies were more determined in their efforts at job organizing, and some tension between the camps was evident. James Sullivan reported that when his small group of Local 61 members arrived at Liberal, Kansas, to meet other local members, they had planned to go quietly onto jobs, but "some of the crowd entered with a brass band noise, with the result that in a few hours it was noised about that we were a bunch of IWWs." Sullivan and others advocated hiring out at going wages of $2.50 a day and waiting until the thick of the harvest to make wage and hour demands. "But no," he commented wryly, "some of the fellows wanted to sit around the jungles, philosophize, and fight from there."[20]

Sullivan and five other Wobblies hired out to the owner of the largest wheat farm near Fowler, Kansas, at $2.50. "As his cutting would not start for a week, the six of us went out. We stayed with him the week, eating three squares a day." After harvesting a few days, the Wobblies "were busy trying to line up the other slaves on the job." Having inquired in town and knowing that no unemployed men were available to replace them, they "were ready to act," but the farmer preempted them by firing two of the Wobblies. "Then the other slaves got a lesson in solidarity," Sullivan enthused, "for remembering that an injury to one is an injury to all, the other four walked off leaving the job tied up. . . . Oh yes, he is now willing to pay $3 and not work over ten hours instead of 13 or 14 as he wanted to do." On another job, this group of Wobblies quit after one of their number was fired to make room for a friend of the boss who "was a $2.50 slave and did not object to long hours."[21]

However, even the advocates of job organizing continued with propaganda tactics in 1914. After leaving Kansas, Sullivan and his group soap-boxed their way to South Dakota. In Sioux City, Iowa, they spoke to an enthusiastic crowd that included local workers who wanted to open an IWW hall of their own. In Yankton, South Dakota, they attempted street speaking but were arrested. Sullivan, Fox, and about twenty others disrupted the city jail with songs until the police agreed to let them leave town peacefully. "Owing to the fact that we did not come up this way to start free speech fights, but to carry on agitation," the Wobblies agreed to leave. In Mitchell, their train car stopped in front of the depot, and they used the occasion to deliver a speech. In Aberdeen, they established a "'wobbly' jungle camp" and asked the mayor for a speaking permit, which he denied. "After our meeting in the jungles," Sullivan concluded, "we decided to split up, scatter out and get on the job."[22]

Others were not so quick to leave Aberdeen, and a free speech fight broke out shortly after Sullivan left town. As the harvest neared, some 1,000 to 2,000 laborers congregated in the Brown County seat. The newspaper reported that some housewives along the railway south of town received more than twenty requests for meals each day.[23] The Commercial Club slowly parceled out laborers to smaller towns and directly to farms, but many more job-seekers were on their way from the South and East.[24] A reporter visiting the jungle on the east side of town painted a subdued picture of harvest hands waiting for work and whiling away the hours in card games, music, and cooking.[25] On Friday, July 17, George Carey, W. C. King, and several other Wobblies arrived from Omaha. They held a meeting in the jungles to assess conditions. They found many IWW members and learned that the Commercial Club was urging farmers to pay only $2.50 a day. The city had already refused a street-speaking permit, but as Carey recounted, "everyone present insisted that the agitation be carried to the slaves up-town."[26]

At the appointed hour, 1,500 people gathered by the Aberdeen Fruit Commission Building to watch the spectacle unfold according to the IWW account of the event. Carey mounted the platform, but before he could speak an officer asked for his permit. In typically Wobbly fashion he replied that he had no permit "save the First Amendment to the Constitution." This proved inadequate, and Carey was taken to the police station, where the chief warned that he would be arrested if he began speaking. Carey then returned to the platform, began speaking, and was immediately arrested. Nine other Wobblies tried to speak and met the same fate. At this point, the fight took an unusual turn. Kitty Solomon, nicknamed the "Queen of the Tramps," moved among the crowd telling the men not to work for less than $3 a day. As an officer moved to arrest her, men in the crowd surged forward to protect her but were clubbed back by police. The crowd followed Solomon and the others to the police station, even making a rush for the station door; policemen beat them back with clubs. The crowd dispersed at dinnertime but returned to the jail in the evening to listen to prisoners deliver speeches and lead songs from the barred windows of their cells. When police ordered the prisoners to stop singing, they broke into "My Country, 'Tis of Thee." On Sunday, police cleared the jungles and, according to the IWW, removed some prisoners from the jail, beat them, and ran them out of town.[27]

Despite limited membership gains, the Wobblies declared the 1914 harvest drive a success. "In the face of a numberless army of unemployed," wrote Gabriel Soltis, the IWW was "successful in preventing a fall of wages, as an indirect result of our work in the field." This was done "without any defined plan on the part of the locals."[28] With the end of the harvest, seasonal laborers looked toward a second winter of unemployment. On the strength of the IWW's success of harvest organizing, union leaders urged that attention turn to growing number of winter unemployed in the hub cities of the Midwest, especially Kansas City and Minneapolis but also in smaller centers such as Sioux City, Iowa. The idea was to bring men into Unemployed Leagues, educate them on issues of industrial unionism, and hope that they would become dues-paying members of the IWW when the economy improved.[29] The plan worked well in Minneapolis. As Joseph Gordon reported, "Slaves from North Dakota, Canada, Montana and elsewhere are flocking in by the thousands. Their dream of wealth or an easy winter, made out of the harvest, is shattered, and now they are hopelessly gazing at the empty boards around the employment shark's office and wondering how in hell the snow will taste this winter."[30] On November 1, Local 64 of Minneapolis held a large unemployed rally with speakers from the Socialist party and the AFL as well as the IWW. After the parade, in which "1914 'boes [i.e., resident unemployed workers] actually lined up alongside the floater," a mass meeting resolved to ask the mayor to employ men on public works.[31] Later organizing revolved around more educational issues, especially after the cold weather made parading less practical. Local 64 and the Scandinavian Propaganda League sponsored "open forum" discussions in English and Swedish, as well as frequent dances and "smokers." Activists reported similar tactics in Des Moines and Kansas City.[32]

A variety of local resident and government responses to the IWW's limited success marked the terrain of community between transient workers and their hosts in the wheat belt. As a class, harvest hands could not be welcomed as full community members. In contrast, individual workers could and often did maintain close relationships with residents. Because of these relationships and because many local men worked in the harvest, residents were never automatically or universally hostile to transients. The brief flash of conflict at Aberdeen foreshadowed a pattern that would arise when the IWW began organizing harvest hands more deliberately in 1915 and 1916. First, the police readily used force and deputized citizens to expel "troublemakers." Second, local public opinion was divided on how laborers should be treated. The *Aberdeen Daily News* commended the police for the "determined yet tactful manner in which [they] handled the situation." The crowd could have turned "ugly" at the behest of the "agitators" and "chronic loafers," the *News* editorialized.[33] But the *News* did not portray the "crowd" as a unitary mass. The agitators and loafers "were comparatively few in number," merely "sprinkled" amid the larger group of "harvest hands in search of work." "Much of the trouble seems to have been due to misleading advertisements regarding the number of men needed, and to the men getting here ahead of time," the editors of the *News* concluded.[34] Similar mixed feelings about the IWW and harvest workers even appeared in the column usually reserved for social life. "The hobo question is becoming one of seriousness to all concerned. . . . While there are a good many good men among them, there are hundreds who join the IWW for no other reason than to have a big time at the expense of the people," wrote the *Aberdeen Daily News.*[35]

Brown County residents were not united behind the policy of expelling harvesters en masse, but opposition to the policy was not organized. Part of the problem was that expelling hoboes from one town merely delivered them to the next town up the railroad. Indeed, one reason for the large gathering of hands in Aberdeen was that officials in Mitchell earlier had ordered harvesters to get out of town.[36] But some residents objected to the rough treatment and especially the collusion that occurred between government and railway officials. In Bath, South Dakota, where harvesters congregated after their deportation from Aberdeen, some harvesters found a sympathetic ally. On July 20, a deputized railway detective and the state's attorney ordered some 200 hands to move on. Most complied, but as the *Aberdeen Daily News* told the story, about forty happened onto the property of the local constable, Elwin Stickney. "You are doing no harm," Stickney told the men, "you're on my property and you are welcome to stay here as long as you want to." When the Aberdeen officials attempted to force the men out, Stickney drew two pistols and ordered the officials off his land. "The action of the officers aroused the indignation of Bath people, who are unanimously of the opinion that the men were not given a square deal," noted the *Daily News.* In addition, "the right of Bath people to look after their own affairs was infringed upon without process of law," according the *News.*[37]

Like the state's attorney in Aberdeen, public officials throughout the wheat belt cooperated with railway companies in confronting trespassers in general and the IWW in particular. As the 1914 harvest drew to a close in North Dakota and workers moved on to railway construction, the Great Northern Railway Company worked behind the scenes to gain government cooperation. On October 8, 1914, J. M. Gruber of the Great Northern informed the company of plans to engineer a "coincidental" meeting with North Dakota's governor. "It is to our interest not to have the railroad's hand show in the matter," Gruber wrote; "with elections close at hand, it will also be to the Governor's interest not to have the railroad appear in the matter."[38] After the choreographed chance encounter, the governor obliged the company by dictating a letter to be sent to every county sheriff along the railway line asking them to "disarm" and "disperse" men riding freight cars. "For some time past there has been a large movement of I.W.W.'s and men who perhaps do not belong to that organization, but who are lawless, and a menace to the welfare of our state," the governor's letter stated. "They are a menace to the people of our state, in that they terrorize the people of the towns, are robbing the farmers and the people generally, break into stores and depots, destroy property and do not hesitate to hold up men and commit murder. In farming communities and the smaller towns our women are also in grave danger from this element. In many instances there are more men in these gangs than there are men in the small towns where they congregate," he concluded.[39]

The covert origin of the governor's order indicates that siding with powerful corporations against working people—even against harvest hands—was politically dangerous in the wheat belt. In contrast to the image of a harmonious and homogeneous rural community that many urbanites harbor, the countryside was rife with class, ideological, and ethnic division. The town-based bankers and business leaders who made up the region's Commercial Clubs claimed to represent the farmers' interests in providing a cheap labor force. However, traditional animosities between town and country, as well as the widespread indebtedness of farmers to merchants and bankers, undermined cooperation between these groups. Moreover, many farmers bitterly resented the railroads, which they accused of overcharging on freight. The days of the Populist revolt were well within living memory, some farmers were members of the Socialist party, and a new farmers' organization, the Non-Partisan League, was gaining strength.[40] In the larger cities, skilled workers often were unionized, and railroad workers harbored strong grievances against their employers.

The events surrounding the IWW free speech fights in Minot, North Dakota and Sioux City, Iowa, offer an opportunity to watch some of these divisions in action. Minot (population 6,000 in 1910) was the seat of Ward County, a quickly expanding center of wheat cultivation and an important stop along the Great Northern Railway. It was also the center of power of the North Dakota Socialist party (NDSP), a young organization that in 1909 succeeded in electing one of its leaders, Arthur LeSueur, to the presidency of the newly created city commission government. After two years of successful governing, LeSueur resigned his position in the face of opposition to his program from the non-Socialist commissioners. In 1913, the Socialists again ran a full slate, winning the office of street commissioner and losing each of the other five offices by no more than thirty votes. This kind of electoral strength worried the traditional politicians of Minot, who looked for opportunities to undermine the Socialists' appeal.[41]

That opportunity came in July 1913 when IWW organizers Jack Law and Jack Allen arrived in Minot to help recruit wheat harvest laborers. As in other towns, the Wobblies organized by addressing crowds on open street corners, but this time they were met with heckling and egg-throwing by Minot businessmen. After these incidents, police banned street speaking in the interests of public order, and the free speech fight was on. Minot's Socialists sought to test the ban on speaking while making it clear that they were not affiliated with the IWW. Nevertheless, anyone who tried to speak was quickly arrested by Minot police, including local bankers, politicians, and transient laborers. In addition to the arrests of speakers, police swept the jungles, arresting IWW members. Most of the one hundred people arrested were housed in bull pens and other temporary jails.[42]

The Minot fight ended when all sides met to call a truce. The IWWs and Socialists agreed not to hold street meetings, and the police released all those arrested. In its aftermath, Minot citizens circulated recall petitions for all of the city commissioners, and an election was held in October. Both sides pitched the contest as a referendum on the city's handling of the free speech fight, and the Socialists hoped that their defense of speech rights would be vindicated. Amid high turnout, however, the party's candidates were defeated by more than two to one. The negative fallout for the party continued in the 1914 state primaries. Where once the Socialists seemed to be growing, now they lost by wide margins. The Ward County vote for the Socialist congressional candidate was only half what it had been in 1912. Apparently siding with the IWW in the free speech fight doomed the NDSP. However, much of the party's farm program and many of its best organizers reappeared in the Non-Partisan League, which swept to power in the statewide elections of 1916 by a four-to-one margin.[43]

A similar pattern emerged in Sioux City, Iowa, the scene of the last major IWW free speech fight during April 1915. A much larger city than Minot, Sioux City was a gateway for laborers entering and leaving summer employment in agriculture and construction in the Dakotas. The IWW recognized Sioux City as a strategic town for the harvest-organizing drive and dispatched seasoned organizer Jack Allen in late September 1914. As a wintering spot for seasonal laborers and an important meatpacking center in its own right, Sioux City was ripe for agitation, and within a few weeks Allen established a propaganda league with financial backing from "fellow worker" Laura B. Stretsel, presumably a local Socialist. By November, the league had initiated an Open Forum, or educational night, at the Socialist Party Hall. At the first meeting, "an impromptu address delivered by J. W. Bennett, a prominent trade union man, caused much favorable comment."[44]

What began as small-scale propagandizing grew into a large unemployed movement as cold weather brought seasonal laborers back to Sioux City for the winter. At the Socialist Hall, the Wobblies served a free hot meal daily, with food donated by local merchants. Allen estimated that as many as 3,000 unemployed men congregated in the city by December and reported that more than 800 turned out for an initial meeting of the "Unemployed League of Sioux City."[45] The IWW plan, according to Allen, was to enroll men in the unemployed organization, sustain them and educate them during the winter, "and when they secure a master, have them come into the IWW as members of their class."[46] At its December meeting, the Unemployed League, along with the secretary of the local Associated Charities, discussed more general relief plans such as asking the city council "to employ all comers on street work, sufficiently to enable them to house, clothe and feed themselves."[47] By the end of December, the league claimed 500 members.[48]

Yet despite the apparent sympathy of some residents and the formation by the Commercial Club of a committee to study the issue, conditions for the unemployed remained unchanged. The ice harvest began in the last days of December, and many in the city expected this to reduce unemployment. However, there were not enough ice-harvesting jobs for all the jobless, and Wobblies had already declared wages on the ice harvest inadequate.[49] In early January, as a result of the city's inaction, the IWW staged one of its more colorful actions. As Wobbly J. A. McDonald described it, "about 150 of the unemployed invited themselves to a banquet where the social elect, over a sumptuous repast, were to consider the problem of the hungry and shelterless. The unemployed ate the banquet thus temporarily . . . getting a better solution than the soup line that Commercial Clubs always prescribe after they have themselves banqueted on the product of the toil of the disinherited."[50]

As Sioux City minister Wallace Short recalled, "A few of the more reckless characters picked up slices of bread from the plates on the tables."[51] Outraged by the intrusion, members of the Commercial Club arranged for a loan to the city, which allowed public works projects to begin. City officials issued employment cards to the "worthy" unemployed, put them to work grading roads on four-hour shifts, and ordered an end to free meals at the Socialist Hall. Business leaders hired detectives to identify IWW members, some of whom were subsequently run out of town.[52] Shortly after the incident at the Commercial Club, city officials declared street speaking illegal, setting the stage for a free speech fight. In response, the IWW called on "footloose rebels" from Minneapolis and Kansas City to converge on Sioux City.[53] But when the time came to arrest Wobbly speakers, the police declined to incite a fight, leaving the IWW free to organize.[54]

The direct action tactics of the IWW spurred a variety of responses from Sioux City's resident workers. The *Union Advocate,* newspaper of the trades and labor assembly, at first commented favorably on the city's move to oust Wobblies with "vigorous police methods." The *Advocate* condemned the invasion of the Commercial Club and distanced the AFL and Socialists from the IWW, characterizing the latter as "anarchistic, absolutely no good to anyone, and should not be tolerated for an instant by any community." As far as the *Advocate* was concerned, most of the unemployed were "shiftless" "hangers-on" attracted by IWW agitation and free meals. "At first [the Wobblies] were received with tolerance, even with sympathy. Those who warned against their methods were accused of prejudice. But soon they began to show their hand. Threats of violence were made, demonstrations became boisterous, 'demands' were flaunted, and the culmination came in a march on the Commercial Club rooms at the noon hour," railed the *Advocate.*[55]

IWW organizers recognized this working-class hostility to the organization and to the unemployed in general. "Everywhere we turn, we find that prejudice has laid hold of the minds of the people," wrote Jack Allen to *Solidarity.*[56] Choicer words were reserved for the English-speaking Socialist party members, whom IWW organizer J. A. McDonald characterized as "revolutionists fifty years behind the Progressive Party and 100 years behind their Swedish Branch here."[57] The IWW's request to rent the Socialist Hall for a lecture by the prominent Wobbly leader Vincent St. John revealed dissension among the Socialists themselves. One member recommended donating the hall, but another (whom McDonald identified as a foreman at the Armour meatpacking plant) suggested renting at more than twice the normal price. In the end the Socialists rented the hall for the regular cost of $2.50.[58]

The St. John lectures apparently took place without trouble, and IWW propagandizing carried on openly until the end of March. Then, on March 25, police arrested Tom O'Connor, "a well-known Western rebel," at the IWW Hall on suspicion of burglary. The local secretary and thirteen other men followed O'Connor to the jail, demanding to know what charge he faced. These men were arrested and tried the next day for "interfering with an officer."[59] Once again, the call went out to IWW members to converge on Sioux City, and the free speech fight began in earnest.[60] On March 30, police began arresting IWW street speakers and intensified patrols in the rail yards, where they arrested fourteen "vags," some of whom were IWW members.[61] By April 3 there were sixty Wobblies in the Sioux City jail, a space fit for only thirty according to the jailed unionists. To relieve overcrowding, in anticipation of more arrests, and in hopes of a more public form of punishment, the city built a high wooden fence, or stockade, outside the jail, "into which they are hauling what they claim to be the hardest granite, and they proudly boast that all IWW members will be forced to scab on it," reported the "Rebels in Jail."[62] With typical bravado, the men in jail "elected a committee to present our demands to the bosses. We want and must have $3 and good board for eight hours work, and we will walk back and forth on the bosses time, or else we will not work."[63]

Meanwhile, nightly street demonstrations drew crowds of 600 to 1,000 spectators. On April 3, eleven more Wobblies joined their fellow workers in jail as police broke up yet another street meeting.[64] In the jail, officials herded one group of IWWs after another to the rock pile only to find that they refused to work, even after several were beaten.[65] When the police threatened to withhold food from those who refused to work, the Wobblies declared a hunger strike. Next, the prisoners protested the unhealthy jail conditions by gathering their vermin-infested blankets into a pile and setting them on fire. While firemen put out the blaze, prisoners addressed a crowd gathered outside through their barred windows.[66] Eventually, city officials sought a truce with the eighty-three jailed "rebels." The mayor offered to free the men and give each "a big supper and two big lunches" if they agreed to leave town. If they returned, they faced arrest and prison. The Wobblies declined the deal and countered with demands for open speech in the city and a new suit for each prisoner.[67] Finally, the city agreed to free the prisoners and guarantee free speech rights. In return, the Wobblies agreed to call off further "invasion" of Sioux City by fellow workers. They celebrated their victory with a picnic inside the stockade. As the victorious activists reported in *Solidarity*, "We built our jungles inside the stockade and proceeded to change our would-be prison into a wobbly picnic ground."[68]

The spectacle of the free speech conflict helped to alter the political terrain among Sioux City residents. Trade unionists and their Socialist and liberal allies viewed the heavy-handed police tactics, and especially the stockade, with great concern. Having supported the January plan to resolve the unemployment problem, the *Union Advocate* took a different view of the stockade and rock pile proposed to the city council in early March. In an editorial dripping with sarcasm, the *Advocate* declared that it supported "the rock pile behind the stockade, with an armed guard on every corner." The *Advocate* continued, "And let's not confine its comforts and benefits solely to the underdog in the struggle for existence. Let's include the vagrants who prey upon the community, such as . . . the exploiters of the workers, who are the greatest vagrants of all, always having been non-producers."[69] In addition to denouncing the stockade and rock pile, the editorial critiqued vagrancy laws. "There are some men who wouldn't work if they could," the editor admitted, but "many more who couldn't work if they would, because the work is not to be found; but under the elastic vagrancy laws all may be treated alike, and the policeman or judge isn't even presumed to attempt to make a distinction." If the stockade "is to be used wholly for the further punishment of the unfortunate jobless man, the victim of circumstances and of the numerous class of 'respectable vagrants,' we would advise our fair city to pause a bit and consider. If the idle are to be punished for the crime of idleness," the *Advocate* concluded, "all should be punished alike—the wealthy idler in greater degree, because his sin against humanity is vastly greater."[70] To be sure, such a critique was not an endorsement of the IWW or its tactics, but the tone had changed from condemning the IWW as shiftless hangers-on to defending the rights of "respectable vagrants."

The free speech fight prompted craft unionists to debate the meaning of the events for their city. Their analysis highlighted how the labor market was contested among resident workers and employers and how some resident workers could, rhetorically at least, propose a tentative solidarity with transient workers. The debate over the rock pile taking place within the walls of the Sioux City Labor Temple found its way into the pages of the *Union Advocate,* concisely suggesting the parameters of disagreement. "As far as the IWW are concerned," editorialized the *Advocate,* "there is nothing that can be said in defense of it. Its members are the same sort of irresponsible, lazy, good-for-nothing louts who formerly made an easy living as strikebreakers." Nevertheless, they should be allowed to speak on the streets, the editor concluded, and to deliver the "tirade of abuse characteristic of the organization."[71]

Edward Ashland of the Plumbers' and Steamfitters' Union provided a more sympathetic analysis. The reason the unemployed were in Sioux City at all, Ashland argued, was because local businesses and the Commercial Club had induced them with "exaggerated reports . . . that this section was teeming with prosperity" when in fact there was barely enough work for locals.[72] He found no fault with those who refused to work "[cut] ice for 16 cents an hour while the ice companies boast of paying an 8 per cent dividend!" At times, however, Ashland's representations of the poor resembled those of social scientists: "They are but products of society, the necessary product of conditions under which they have been raised," he noted. "They were taken out of school at a tender age, and all the physical development they got was hanging onto the handles of a plow, and the most inspiring scene before their eyes was the rear end of a mule, and now [they are]reduced to premature old age, with vitality sapped and form bent earthwards, and ambition blasted and hopes blighted."

Yet Ashland showed a greater understanding of and sympathy for the laborers' lot than did most social scientists. Although they had been degraded by their experiences, he thought it unfair that "they are censured and persecuted because they are lacking higher culture and diplomatic methods." Ashland carefully explained the problems of the migrant to his fellow unionists:

> They have not a trade, or profession, or business, and it is harder for a common laborer to get employment than it is for a tradesman. He has to work three times as hard for three times less pay, and when he does land work it is only for a day or two. Steady jobs at laboring are few and far between, and when one is found it is all work and no wages. These fellows, destitute as they are, discouraged as they must be, have a little spark of ambition. They want something more than a mere job. They still have the manhood to say: Hungry as I am, I shall not allow you to take advantage of my impecunious condition and pay me starvation wages for my services.[73]

Ashland called for tolerance of the IWW street speakers. "Whatever our prejudices against their methods," Ashland wrote, striking a religious note, "they must be sincere in the advocacy of their cause when joyously, like the martyrs of old, they will sing on their way to the cell and accept imprisonment for their portion." And evoking a theme from the Populist era but giving it a more Christian spin, Ashland concluded, "Let us admit the frailties of human government and let both millionaires and mendicants realize their necessity of a mediator and adjust their differences according to the love and law of Him who died for all. Let us tolerate the opinions of others and listen to the cry of the oppressed."[74]

Other Sioux Citians agreed with this call to tolerance. One businessman testified on behalf of an arrested soapboxer, for instance. The local Socialist party branch printed a pamphlet titled "Let Us Right This Wrong," which circulated about town before police confiscated it.[75] Perhaps the most noted advocate of tolerance was the Rev. Wallace M. Short, minister of the Central Church in Sioux City. It was his opinion that the Wobblies needed engagement at a moral level rather than jail. In January 1915 he invited the unemployed to attend his church, much to the dismay of the more conventional members of his congregation. Although one IWW leader he spoke to denounced religion, Short found it "surprising . . . how easily these men were influenced by any man who seemed to have a sympathetic understanding of their attitude and condition." Although he was forced out of leadership at his church because of his stand on the IWW, three years later Short led a pro-labor sweep in city elections and remained mayor for six years.[76] Short and his trade union allies avoided the fate of Minot's Socialists in part because Sioux City was a much larger town. Nevertheless, their cautious support of the IWW suggests the range of attitudes toward the union among wheat belt residents. In the face of growing economic inequality, many agreed that a laborers' organization would provide a necessary corrective.

Ironically, victory in the Sioux City free speech fight came just as a strong consensus for job-based organizing grew within the IWW. Sioux City had always been an important urban center for seasonal migrants working in the wheat harvest, and it was now to become one of three farm labor distributing hubs (along with Kansas City and Minneapolis) under a new plan sponsored by several wheat belt state governments.[77] Therefore, although the free speech fight in Sioux City was the last of a passing strategy, securing public speaking rights meant that the IWW would be free to operate in an important gateway city.

Despite these promising signs, the winter of the Sioux City fight had seen the virtual extinction of the IWW at the national level, its membership dipping below 2,500. In this context of national decline and local activism, thirteen delegates arrived in Kansas City in March 1915 to attend a much heralded conference to set up a new Agricultural Workers' Organization (AWO) within the IWW.[78] The AWO's plans reflected the continuing drive toward on-the-job organizing and coordination between locals in the region. Among the suggestions for harvest organizing offered by Local 64 of Minneapolis, for instance, were "that all locals in the grain country co-operate in starting a National Industrial Union of Agricultural Workers, . . . that members stay away from the jungles and get on the job, . . . that the IWW inaugurate a secret information system" and hide their membership from employers, and "that we concentrate forces in Oklahoma, get job control and work our way north as the grain commences to ripen."[79] From the Sioux City local came the comment and suggestion that "one of the great faults with past organization work in the harvest has been that we have not realized the immense task that was confronting us" and therefore relied on a few professional organizers who could reach workers only in big cities and not on the job. To organize on the job, the Sioux City local suggested "furnishing credentials to every capable member of the IWW" and allowing them to sign up new members directly (see figure 13).[80]

The harvest drive of 1915 again was very much a trial-and-error event, but coordination by the AWO created rudimentary institutional structures that spanned the wide-open spaces of the wheat belt. Led by Secretary-Treasurer Walter Nef, the AWO used a two-tiered organizing strategy. Stationary delegates remained in important wheat belt towns such as Enid, Oklahoma; Hutchinson, Kansas; Sioux City, Iowa; and Fargo and Minot, North Dakota. Meanwhile, walking delegates, that is, credentialed member-organizers, traveled the countryside signing up members and receiving a commission for

Figure 13. Wobbly threshermen. From Nils H. Hanson, "Threshing Wheat," *International Socialist Review* 16 (November 1915). Courtesy of the Newberry Library, Chicago.

each new member. These organizers delivered their receipts to stationary delegates and picked up new organizing materials. Initiation fees were set at the high rate of $2.00 on the theory that men would pay good money if they thought the organization was worthwhile.[81]

Although the AWO introduced an unprecedented level of structure and planning into IWW harvest organizing, success and failure were still determined on the ground by small groups of activists. The most dramatic and infamous organizing tactic was the practice of bodily ejecting nonunion workers from freight trains. Known as the 800-mile picket line, the tactic had two goals. First, the AWO hoped to have a "closed shop and an open union," as they often said. That is, they sought to control all the harvest jobs, but unlike the craft unions with restricted membership (which they called "job trusts"), AWO membership was open to all workers. Because it was open to all workers regardless of race, craft, or creed, so the logic went, anyone who refused to join was a scab. The result of this logic was that the line between convincing and coercing laborers to join the union sometimes was thin or nonexistent. However, although Wobblies definitely pressured nonmembers to join, and some physically attacked nonunion men, local authorities regularly exaggerated these threats in their effort to counter IWW influence in the region.[82]

A second goal of the 800-mile picket line was to protect harvest workers from the depredations of holdup men, bootleggers, gamblers, and corrupt railroad workers.[83] This more delicate job was performed by long-time members who traveled in "Flying Squadrons" of two or three men. Retaliation against bootleggers and holdup men (sometimes called hi-jacks) seems to have ranged from destroying liquor and recovering stolen money to beatings, mutilation, and perhaps murder. In his account of several summers on a Flying Squadron, Thomas Bogard tells of recovering money and taking guns from hi-jacks as well as "working over" a few. In addition, he and his partner destroyed the liquor stock of many bootleggers who sold their goods in hobo jungles. In contrast, he claimed never to have bothered bootleggers who let workers come to them and declined requests to "work over" gamblers who had cheated fellow workers (reasoning in both cases that it was the worker's choice to throw away money on booze or gambling).[84] At times, AWO members clashed with corrupt railroad employees who demanded bribes for riding freight trains. In one such case, IWW member James Schmidt was charged with the murder of a railroad brakeman in Aberdeen, South Dakota. Brakeman Ross Farrar confronted Schmidt and a fellow worker in a boxcar and demanded payment for riding. When Schmidt refused, Farrar drew a pistol and fired. Schmidt leapt out of the car and returned fire, killing Farrar. In the opinion of Wobblies, these incidents were organized self-defense.[85]

Another infamous and problematic tactic of the AWO was sabotage, but it is difficult to define exactly what this involved. Although the official IWW line on sabotage was the cause of much debate within the union and the American left generally, individual Wobblies practiced sabotage regularly in two different ways. The first was the conscious withdrawal of effort on the part of the worker. As the slogan went, "little pay, little work." But individuals also performed more direct forms of sabotage against employers' property.[86] Farmers regularly blamed field fires on Wobblies, but the IWW never admitted to setting them.[87] However, they readily embraced other acts. For instance, *Solidarity* reported that farmers who paid less than the union scale "discovered to their extreme dissatisfaction that the bundles were set with the heads upside down, and inside the shocks were found cards bearing the inscriptions: 'Heads down, \$2.50; heads up \$3. Bum pay, bum work.'"[88] Although these tactics were not official AWO policy, neither the union nor *Solidarity* denounced them or dissuaded workers from using them. As J. A. McDonald wrote of the 1915 harvest, the end of the noisy free speech fights heralded quieter tactics: "The IWW's mascot—the cat—is having its tongue amputated and his claws sharpened, as in the past he has done too much meowing and too little scratching."[89] McDonald's article was about nonviolent forms of solidarity, but the metaphor was easily interpreted as a call to sabotage against property. However, despite the attention given to the issue of sabotage, AWO organizers were much more likely to have conflicts with local police over basic organizing issues.[90]

Despite their success during 1915, correspondence printed in *Solidarity* suggests that many in the IWW lacked patience with unorganized laborers, known derisively as "blockheads" and "scissorbills." C. J. O'Donnell's account was typical. When a North Dakota farmer approached a group of harvesters offering \$2.50 per day, O'Donnell and his fellow workers declined the offer because it was below union scale of \$3. Three nonunion men hired out immediately. As they rode out of town on the farmer's wagon, O'Donnell walked alongside and asked loudly enough for the farmer to hear, "Hey, there, IWW, give me a cigarette?" When the worker gave him one, the farmer stopped and fired the three non-IWWs, believing they were Wobblies. He then hired O'Donnell and another man (also a Wobbly) for \$3 per day, thinking they were nonunion. O'Donnell thought that the trick would show the nonunion men that it paid to be in the IWW.[91] Another article ridiculed nonunion workers who wanted to finish up a job after already working ten hours so that they would not have to wait until the next day to go into town: "Both of these men would have been insulted if they had been compared to a mule. [But] it would have been an insult to the mule; as, wise creature, it begins to bray that it is time to quit at five o'clock."[92] In another account, "Radical Red" told of a job with particularly long hours and bad food. When he and his Wobbly companions quit, the other workers asked them to tell the farmer about the bad conditions, but the Wobblies refused. According to this militant, "Some of the yaps, three weeks on the job, suggested we should enlighten the boss as to why we quit, thereby making it better for them. We refused to accommodate them."[93] Such a haughty attitude was common among the Wobblies but tended to limit their appeal to the unorganized. As J. A. McDonald argued, "The man for whom all the unorganized are scissorbills; who makes up for lack of education along the lines of revolutionary unionism by fiery denunciation and bawl-out, should be furnished with a muzzle. . . . We forget that not long ago all of us were what some of us call 'scissorbills.'"[94] These sentiments were echoed by other activists who criticized those who have "persistently dodged the class struggle via the panhandling rout" and the "nickel-grabbing soap-boxer" who gave the IWW a bad name in the eyes of "bonafide wage workers."[95]

The AWO ended 1915 claiming 2,280 new members and money in the bank. It was nearly as big as the rest of the IWW put together. When the wartime economy kicked into high gear during early 1916, the union was in an unusually good position to take advantage of the tightening labor market. The new organization had a coherent strategy well understood by its member-activists and the structure to carry the strategy forward. In addition to its roving organizers, the vital IWW locals in Kansas City, Sioux City, and Minneapolis folded into the AWO, and the organization expanded its network of stationary delegates, adding Wichita and Ellis, Kansas and Aberdeen, South Dakota to Enid, Hutchinson, Fargo, and Minot. In a real sense, the AWO was becoming a regional union for the Great Plains and the upper Midwest.

❖ ❖ ❖

Initially at least, the 1916 IWW harvest campaign received surprisingly favorable and evenhanded press in the wheat belt. A reporter's visit to the Aberdeen local office yielded a picture of the IWW as an efficient, orderly, principled reform group. A Wobbly identified as "Brother Miller" told a reporter, "We want to run out all the hi-jacks, bootleggers and gamblers that would fleece the harvest workers and we want to establish and maintain a proper minimum wage for harvesting."[96] An editorial blurb explained, "The IWW, it appears from the statement, is not so bad as has been reported"; however, the editors considered the union's wage demand unreasonable. "No disorders, traceable to the members of the organization, have yet occurred in South Dakota during the present season."[97] This kind of tolerance was even apparent in some small communities. The Sunday before the infamous "battles" broke out across the wheat belt, IWWs and local men played a game of baseball in the town of Mansfield, south of Aberdeen. The IWW won by two runs.[98]

Recognizing the AWO's potential to disrupt labor relations throughout the West, however, business leaders began to take more coordinated steps against unionization. On July 23, Sioux City officials conferred over the harvest situation, agreeing on the need to deter IWW organizers. Paving contractors and other employers in Sioux City lamented "whispering campaigns" and strikes among their workers, and the *Sioux City Journal* reported that employers expected to "handle the situation themselves through special agents." Sioux City's mayor condemned the Wobblies with typical free-market logic, saying, "These transient workmen are entitled to work at whatever wage they agree to and no community can tolerate the activities of men who would force such laborers to quit." A meeting of businessmen, railroad officials, and the head of the Federal Employment Office in late July suggested fielding "a gang of 'bruisers'" to ride freight trains and counter the IWW.[99] The *Sioux City Journal* reported that a group of fifteen college football players had beaten Wobblies on the freight train from Omaha to Sioux City. Despite a reported dearth of applicants, the Federal Employment Office organized twenty-seven recruits to "fight their way through if necessary" to jobs in South Dakota.[100] Meanwhile, tensions rose in wheat belt towns as a heat wave set in, and newspapers ran stories on violent hoboes.[101] In addition, Wobblies more forcefully and publicly asserted their rights as workers, at times confronting abusive employers on the main streets.[102]

Local officials were uneasy about the presence of large numbers of harvest workers in their towns, tried to restrict migrant workers' movement through their cities, and finally evicted large numbers of workers altogether.[103] Mitchell's mayor planned to meet harvesters as they approached town, pull them off the trains, and search them for weapons before letting them into town. He asked a railroad company official to provide men to augment the town's small police force.[104]

Before Mitchell's officials could put this plan into effect, their counterparts to the north in Redfield were confronted by open "warfare" between rival factions of harvesters. On the morning of July 27, a fight broke out between IWWs and anti-IWW harvesters, dubbed yellow card or yellow ticket men. After shots were fired and a few men wounded, local officials arrived to disarm the men, although many apparently escaped. Later in the day a train arrived carrying a large number of yellow card men into the railyards, where a crowd of Wobblies lingered. Another argument broke out, and according to the *Aberdeen Daily News,* "an IWW on the ground took a shot for luck at the anti's." His shot brought guns out from every direction among the "anti's," who started shooting into the crowd. Several men were injured, and one later died. Armed citizens soon dispersed both groups of harvesters on outgoing freight trains, but not before arresting several men.[105] Two days after the battle, an AWO delegate visited officials at Redfield, and after receiving assurances that a large number of Wobblies waiting to the south could pass through the town unmolested, he led them through on a northbound freight train, "standing on the first car holding the mayor's permit" for protection, as the Sioux City paper reported it.[106] Interestingly, even as the *Redfield Journal-Observer* celebrated the success of what a typographical error called "Ku Klan Klux" methods, the *Redfield Press* blamed the incident on the oversupply of laborers caused by exaggerated predictions of the demand for laborers.[107]

Mitchell's "battle" began soon after Redfield's. According to local newspapers, Wobblies and yellow card men exchanged gunfire in the town's railyards, and a late night alarm whistle brought citizens running, guns in hand. How the incident began is a matter of dispute between sources. The morning after the incident, the *Mitchell Gazette* reported that the trouble began when a black harvester, Frank Henry, failed to produce an IWW card for organizers and was shot by Wobblies. Later reports sounded a bit different. Both the *Mitchell Clarion* and IWW delegate E. N. Osborne's report to *Solidarity* claimed that the wounded man was an African American IWW member (identified as Frank Henry by the *Clarion* and Frank Wells by Osborne).[108] According to Osborne, the trouble began when some yellow card men beat a Wobbly and destroyed his card. "These gunmen, about 15 in number, in company with about fifty unarmed followers, told all our members . . . that they (the IWW) could not ride a train out" without being shot. As a train began pulling out of the yard, the Wobblies moved toward it, and the yellow card men opened fire. One of the injured men, according to Osborne, returned fire as he lay on the ground. The riot call went out, and the townsmen held the hoboes at gunpoint in the open all night. In the middle of the night, police arrived to search the room of AWO delegate Osborne but left without arresting him. In the morning the men were placed on a northbound train, and the police returned to arrest Osborne. He and three other AWO members were taken in separate cars to the outskirts of town "and warned under penalty of the noose if we returned," as Osborne reported it.[109]

As harvest hands continued to arrive in Mitchell from the south, armed citizens met their trains outside town. The "citizens' committees" marched the harvest hands at gunpoint about two miles into the city, held them on the courthouse lawn, and searched them for weapons. Afterwards, they were put on a northbound train. This process continued for several days until the citizens' committees simply turned northbound harvesters back, saying that farmers to the north had enough workers already (see figures 14 and 15).[110]

South Dakotans were divided on the merits of this rough treatment for the IWW. Predictably, there were comments like that of a Yankton editor, who noted that "the incompetents and perverts will always be with us . . . but this question only becomes a menace when these derelicts are permitted to congregate and set to naught the laws and institutions to which the balance of society are required to conform. This country should have no more sympathy for the idle poor class than for the idle rich one."[111] But just as predictably, an Aberdeen Socialist looked at it quite differently. He condemned the suggestions heard about town to call in the state militia to eject Wobblies from South Dakota as an illegal repetition of the 1914 IWW free speech fight in Aberdeen. "So long as present conditions prevail the IWW will grow and thrive and the so-called tramp and hobo who personifies the organization will multiply apace in spite of every opposition," wrote the Socialist. "Today

Figure 14. Mitchell, South Dakota, residents search harvest hands at gunpoint, July 1916. V. H. Masters Collection, Center for Western Studies, Augustana College, Sioux Falls, South Dakota.

Figure 15. Harvest hands leaving Mitchell on a northbound freight train, July 1916. V. H. Masters Collection, Center for Western Studies, Augustana College, Sioux Falls, South Dakota.

he wears a ragged denim overall. Tomorrow, under a better government, he will wear a tuxedo . . . ; or if matters go from bad to worse, some of you, my readers, will be with him and do as he does."[112] In commenting on the conflicts at Mitchell and Redfield, the *Aberdeen Daily News* counseled against driving the IWW out of Aberdeen. Although the paper did not approve of the excessive wages demanded by the union, it did point out that the IWW members "are American citizens [and] they have certain rights as such."[113] In fact, the *News* editorialized that begging, thievery, and drunkenness had decreased with the presence of the IWW in Aberdeen. The paper concluded, with a note of paternalism, that "the men should be treated decently so long as they behave themselves."[114]

In Mitchell, even those who may have favored ejecting harvesters from town worried about the danger posed by an armed citizenry. Far from rallying an orderly defense of the town, as was implied by news reports outside Mitchell, hundreds of people had no clue what the riot alarm meant, and others were less than careful with their weapons.[115] "Wild rumors" of armed bands roaming the countryside frightened residents to such an extent that some were shooting at strangers passing in the town's alleyways. The *Mitchell Gazette* even suggested the need for an "injunction on the possession of arms" not for harvesters, but for residents.[116] In response, the city council selected a group of fifteen men to deal with harvesters. The *Gazette* editorialized that "the situation in the past 10 days when from three to five hundred men responded to the sound of the fire alarm whistle has been rather tense. . . . Guns were carried by men and boys out to meet the oncoming harvesters, and it put the whole town in a furore [*sic*]."[117]

Other residents were more directly opposed to the deportations. Harry Stacy, owner of a restaurant called The Jungles catering to harvest hands and used as the headquarters of the AWO, condemned the expulsion of the harvesters. According to Stacy, "the patrons of my place of business during the past 10 days have conducted themselves in a law abiding and orderly manner." Stacy reported that he fed fifteen to twenty men each day at his own expense in an effort keep the penniless men from begging in the downtown and residential areas. However, most of his patrons were paying customers. The IWW delegate had rented desk space and a room like any other patron. "A square deal should be had by all," concluded Stacy, echoing a common refrain among farmers, workers, and merchants who sympathized with the harvest workers.[118]

The remainder of the 1916 harvest season continued in a similar manner. Police and residents in several towns including Lechter, North Dakota; Ortonville, Minnesota; and Minot, North Dakota clashed with Wobblies and ejected them from town. Headlines screaming of battles involving hundreds of men on either side were often exaggerated. Newspapers in Sioux City and Aberdeen reported that a gang of 300 Wobblies had been "hammered into submission with clubs and baseball bats" in the hands of some 400 residents of Ortonville, Minnesota. The local paper, in contrast, reported that about twenty armed citizens had deported a group of only fifty IWW members.[119]

Despite these setbacks at the hands of local law enforcement—whether exaggerated or not—the AWO grew by leaps and bounds, ending the year claiming about 20,000 members.[120] It had succeeded in convincing a significant proportion of the total labor pool that unionization offered real advantages. No doubt, some portion of this new membership joined simply for protection or with little intention of maintaining membership. But the AWO's reputation, along with the tightening wartime labor market, helped to improve wages for harvest hands. The AWO's financial power and aura of success also made the upstart organization the center of gravity within the IWW. With help from the AWO, new organizing drives were launched in the lumber, oil, construction, and mining industries.[121]

Rank-and-file organizers moved from the wheat harvest into logging and mining work. Iron miners on northern Minnesota's Mesabi range went on strike in December 1916, followed shortly by mill workers and lumberjacks striking the Virginia and Rainy Lake Company in January 1917 (the company operated the largest white pine mill in the world).[122] In response to these troubles, the Minnesota House of Representatives held a remarkable set of hearings in which both the IWW and employers called, questioned, and cross-examined witnesses. Widely reported in the press, the hearings briefly softened the image of the IWW because its representative, Joseph Ettor, "showed himself to be a keen, shrewd, good natured and intelligent gentleman," according to a historian of Minnesota. In contrast, one of the employers' representatives was forced to apologize for an outburst before the House. Such positive public perception of the IWW was short-lived. By April, the legislature had passed acts banning "criminal syndicalism," that is, advocating industrial changes by means of violence, and interference with the draft. A third bill created the Minnesota Commission of Public Safety. In the hands of the state's open shop employers, the commission became a powerful weapon against all unions, radicals, and immigrants. Its first act was to close all saloons, pool halls, and theaters in the Bridge Square district of Minneapolis, the city's main stem.[123]

The limited tolerance shown by certain wheat belt communities such as Aberdeen, South Dakota, in 1916 disappeared completely with the U.S. entry into the European war as the IWW became a major target of a national red scare. But as AWO organizer E. N. Osborne noted in the fall of 1916, much of the coming repression was already being planned before the U.S. declaration of war. Osborne wrote that "the commercial clubs, the farmers' unions, and state, county, municipal and even U.S. government officials, are now devising ways and means of destroying the IWW in the harvest belt next year."[124] In fact, Wobblies faced severe attacks throughout the country, including the lynching of Executive Board member Frank Little in Butte, Montana, and the arrest of almost all of the IWW leadership by federal officials in the fall of 1917. In Sioux City, members of the Commercial Club discussed the formation of a "Civilian Unit" to counter the IWW in town and countryside during the harvest, and business leaders formed vigilance committees throughout the wheat belt.[125] In contrast to previous years, moderate voices were caught in the war hysteria, and few residents dared to stand up for the Wobblies' rights.

Events in Aberdeen, South Dakota, suggest how the changed national climate could easily tip the balance from tolerance to repression. An IWW hall opened there on July 9, over the opposition of the Commercial Club and police.[126] Violence began on July 23, according to Wobblies who wrote to *Solidarity.* The Aberdeen city council passed a resolution declaring the IWW hall a nuisance and ordered it shut. The council justified the closure by asserting that the hall was directing "assaults upon laboring men seeking employment," threatening officers of the law, and threatening to burn crops.[127] Some fifty Wobblies were jailed that evening without charges. At midnight they were removed from the jail, taken out of town in small groups, and beaten. Branch Secretary G. J. Bourg was picked up after closing the hall and received similar treatment. As described by C. E. Lundburg and Chester Micklan, Bourg was taken to a remote location outside town where three carloads of vigilantes met. The vigilantes stripped him of his clothes, held him to the ground, and gave him "thirty or forty unmerciful blows with a pick-handle." Finally, Bourg was made to run a gauntlet of vigilantes, each "taking a kick at him." On the same night, the IWW hall was raided and most of the organizing materials destroyed.[128]

The press in Aberdeen applauded the success of vigilante methods and the cooperation of the police and sheriff in the attacks. "Axehandles are the effective emergency weapons of the home guard," reported the *Daily News,* "breaking up and dispersing in different directions large bands of IWWs is the work, which, cooperating with the sheriff and police they are carrying out with success."[129] The editors of the *Daily News* threatened a local attorney whom they believed was going to defend the IWW, saying his law practice and residence in Aberdeen "will be made most uncomfortable in perfectly legitimate and law abiding but painful ways."[130] This was the same paper that had counseled against vigilante tactics in 1916 because it thought Wobblies "were American citizens." Now the paper felt that Wobblies could not "appreciate decent treatment, and are not entitled to the consideration that the law abiding" people deserve.

Arrests and beatings continued to such an extent that the AWO, now renamed the Agricultural Workers' Industrial Union (AWIU), called a general strike on the state of South Dakota. The *Daily News* gleefully reprinted the union's bulletin denouncing Aberdeen city officials and accusing vigilantes of, among other things, tearing up the draft registration cards of IWW members. "The Home Guard is not a Vigilante society," the *News* editorialized in response. Rather, its members were "the leading citizens of every community in the state."[131] The IWW agreed, telling Thorstein Veblen of the President's Mediation Commission that "the opposition shown towards our members does not come from the farmers who employ these men to sow, cultivate and harvest their grain" but from the "bankers, real estate agents, [and] business men" who made up the region's commercial clubs, the newspapers, and local police.[132] In 1918, the newly created South Dakota State Council of Defense, dominated by commercial club interests, issued an order making it illegal for laborers to demand more than $4.50 per day. The state legislature quickly passed the wage cap and a criminal syndicalism bill into law.[133]

The IWW fared much better in neighboring North Dakota during 1917, largely because of the power of the Non-Partisan League in that state. Governor Frazier issued a letter to state's attorneys and other law enforcement officials ordering that they must not search harvest hands without a warrant or force men to work if they were holding out for higher wages. Nor did North Dakota enact a criminal syndicalism law.[134] The AWIU and the NPL engaged in negotiations toward a mutual agreement as to hiring, wages, and hours of work. The proposed agreement, not a contract in the usual sense, set wages at $4 for a ten-hour day and specified that league farmers would give hiring preference to IWW members and Wobblies would work first for league farmers. Overtime pay was set at 40 cents per hour, and the base rate of pay was tied to the price of wheat. The agreement further specified that "sleeping accommodations were to be the best possible under the conditions surrounding the job," and food was to be "wholesome and plentiful." Workers would receive free board during weather delays three days or less and be paid $1 per day after three days. However, the league abandoned the agreement when it could not reach consensus on the matter. Farmers in western North Dakota favored the plan overwhelmingly, but those in the east opposed it just as strongly. That the plan was considered at all, in the midst of anti-IWW hysteria throughout the region, signified a much more tolerant attitude toward unionization of laborers in North Dakota and the IWW's strong presence in that state.[135]

Widespread vigilante repression and the imprisonment of union leaders limited the ability of the AWIU to recruit members during 1917 and 1918.[136] From a reported membership of 24,000 in 1917, the AWIU dropped to only 6,000 in 1919.[137] The union returned during the 1920–23 harvests reporting a sustained membership of around 15,000.[138] After this, however, the organization shrank, according to its own historian, to 9,219 members in 1924, 8,507 members in 1925, and less than 3,000 by 1928.[139] Just as the organization was becoming more of a fixture in the wheat belt, the twin pressures of labor market changes and internal factionalism sapped its strength. Automobiles began to outpace freight trains as the transportation of choice for harvest hands, altering a pattern of travel that had been an important foundation of laborers' community networks. With the formation of the American Communist party in 1919, the IWW lost many top leaders and rank-and-file activists. Even with all of these problems, the IWW may have survived the 1920s had it not been for the fratricidal schism of 1924, in which two rival groups vied for control of the organization. Thousands of members simply gave up on the IWW in disgust when the leadership split once again on the issue of centralization. In the end there was nothing to centralize and very little power in the hands of workers in the field.[140]

The so-called Battle of Mitchell and armed deportations elsewhere in the wheat belt were skirmishes in a larger conflict over community power and the structure of the labor market. Harvest laborers, farmers, small-town businessmen, railroad companies, and reform-minded government bureaucrats all had a stake in this conflict but were not equal players. The IWW's organizing drive in the wheat belt was a highly decentralized affair, relying on the cooperation of thousands of volunteer organizers and sympathizers to push farm employers to accept the union wage and hour standards. In this way, the IWW hoped to substitute its own class-conscious culture for the employer- and labor agent–controlled structures of the labor market. For their part, farmers and business leaders in small towns wanted to ensure an adequate supply of labor at what they considered reasonable wages. Negative attitudes toward the IWW were tempered by desires for a harmonious community and by the rural economy's need for outside labor.

The emergence of the IWW goaded state and federal governments to rectify some of the worst abuses of the private labor market. Employers raised wages, improved conditions, and lessened the driving intensity of work. State and federal government reformers, troubled by the social unrest caused by transient labor, hoped to substitute their moral expertise for the private institutions of the labor market. State-controlled institutions, such as free employment bureaus, would regularize the idiosyncratic and unregulated labor market and connect the "jobless man with the manless job," to use the common phrase of the time. The IWW was both a threat to this nascent government bureaucracy and the object of its reforming impulse. State control of labor marketing would replace these damaged and dangerous workers with farm laborers who accepted the temporary nature of the work.

Part of this ill-defined reform strategy was the racialization of transient farm labor, that is, to locate laborers whom employers could more easily consider outside the bounds of community. Of course, employment service officials held on to the idea that young, white, rural people and students could be mobilized to replace the hoboes, and therefore sustain the rural community. But industrial employers who relied on seasonal labor began to search for new sources even before the outbreak of World War I. The railroads, big wheat farmers, and especially the emerging sugar beet industry turned to southern migrants, especially African Americans, Mexicans, and Mexican Americans for labor. However, even these workers were not as docile as employers had hoped. In contrast to other areas of industrial agriculture such as California, Florida, and South Texas, the midwestern problem of seasonal labor was resolved more through mechanization than labor market control. By the mid-1930s, there simply were not enough jobs to sustain the massive and harvest migration of earlier times.[141]

The "battles" in the wheat belt in 1916 and 1917 represented the coming together of these local, regional, and national forces. We usually envision rural social conflict in terms of the clash of community and outsiders. This image places harvest hands on the outside of the community when, in fact, harvest hands, vigilantes, farmers, and others were part of a broader regional community. The collusion of employers with local and federal officials in fielding an anti-IWW force of laborers reminds us that laborers' outcast status was not simply cultural or rhetorical. It also was enforced physically through beatings and mass deportations. Defining the boundaries of community through laborers' invisibility and marginalization was an active, ongoing political process. The rise of union organizing among seasonal laborers profoundly affected existing tensions in the rural Midwest. The resulting debates about how communities should treat transient laboring men were very much about what kind of society America would be as it passed from an agricultural to an industrial nation.

NOTES

1. "Shun Mitchell: IWWs Didn't Enjoy Mitchell's Hospitality," *Mitchell (South Dakota) Clarion,* 3 August 1916. See also Haug, "The Industrial Workers of the World in North Dakota," 85–102; Wagman, "The Industrial Workers of the World in Nebraska," 295–337.

2. Stock, *Main Street in Crisis,* 75.

3. *Sioux City (Iowa) Union Advocate* (hereafter *UA*), 15 April 1915, 1.

4. Salerno, *Red November,* 45–67, 146–49.

5. Dubofsky, *We Shall Be All,* 480–82; Foner, *History of the Labor Movement,* 558. The IWW was founded in 1905 as an avowedly revolutionary movement by an alliance of Socialists and unionists who favored organizing on an industry-by-industry basis rather than the craft-based structure of the AFL. The IWW created its AWO in 1915 and renamed it the AWIU in 1917.

6. *Report of the General Secretary-Treasurer to the Second IWW Convention,* 30. In its first years the IWW faced internal struggles over political and economic strategy, some favoring support of a revolutionary political party, others being opposed. This

issue was resolved when a large group of laborer-delegates from Portland and Spokane (known as the "Overalls Brigade") arrived at the 1908 convention and voted to expel Daniel DeLeon and remove the so-called political clause from the preamble to the constitution. DeLeon derisively named this group of delegates the "Bummery." See Brissenden, *The I.W.W.*, 221–33.

7. Edward McDonald, "The Farm Laborer and the City Worker," *Solidarity*, 10 September 1910, 3; Thomas Bogard Autobiography (T-124), pp. 84–85, Washington State Historical Society; *Solidarity* 9 September 1911, 1. See article by Biscay, *Solidarity*, 4 May 1912, 2; *Solidarity*, 30 September 1911, 2.

8. *Solidarity*, 25 October 1913, 2.

9. *Proceedings of the 1912 IWW Convention*, as quoted in Dubofsky, *We Shall Be All*, 261.

10. The internal debate had two strands. The first pitted so-called decentralists against centralists and focused on the relative power of national officers, industrial unions, and locals. The second strand related to organizing structure, in particular whether workers should be grouped in mixed locals (i.e., locals with members working in more than one industry) or strictly along industrial lines. In general, the decentralists were associated with the western mixed locals, especially in Phoenix, Portland, and Seattle, and with philosophical anarchists. Those known as centralists (often associated with Chicago) favored a stronger general executive board with power to call and end strikes and free speech fights. The centralists won the day in 1913, but the tension between the camps ran through all internal debates and eventually contributed to the union's 1924 schism. Brissenden, *The I.W.W.*, 305–19; Foner, *History of the Labor Movement*, 144–46; Gambs, *The Decline of the I.W.W.*, 99–125; *Solidarity*, 3 January 1914, 3.

11. *Solidarity*, 15 October 1913, 2.

12. *Solidarity*, 8 November 1913, 1.

13. Ibid.

14. *Solidarity*, 29 November 1913, 4. On the Sheep Shearers' Union see Jamieson, *Labor Unionism*, 221–32. "The Sheep Shearers' Union, having a local charter in Butte, claims jurisdiction 'over North America.' Union members, while at work during the shearing season, elect delegates by secret ballot to the union convention which takes place every four years. There the delegates in turn nominate and elect officers to the executive board. This body, among its other functions, on or before February 1 of each year sets the union scale for shearing sheep. Any member shearing at less than this scale is liable to suspension" (p. 222).

15. A Socialist party–inspired incident occurred in Mitchell, South Dakota, in 1913; see *Aberdeen Weekly News*, 24 July 1913, 6. See also Koppes, "The I.W.W. and County Jail Reform," 63–86. Kornbluth, *Rebel Voices*, 94; Saunders, "The Road," 131–34, WHMC, St. Louis, Mo.

16. *Solidarity*, 3 January 1914, 3.

17. Ibid.

18. *Solidarity*, 20 June 1914, 1. See also *Solidarity*, 13 June 1914, 4, on organizing at Enid, Oklahoma. See also Sellars, *Oil, Wheat and Wobblies*, 48.

19. *Solidarity*, 27 June 1914, 3.

20. *Solidarity*, 4 July 1914, 1.

21. Ibid.

22. *Solidarity,* 25 July 1914, 1, 4.

23. *ADN,* 15 July 1914, 6.

24. *ADN,* 16 July 1914, 3; *Solidarity,* 8 August 1914, 1 quoting *Aberdeen (South Dakota) Sunday American,* 19 July 1914.

25. *ADN,* 16 July 1914, 4.

26. Carey, "Free Speech Fight in Aberdeen, S.D." (n.d. probably 1914) USCIR: Labor in General, P71-1681, Free Speech Folder, SHSW.

27. The account of the Aberdeen fight comes from Carey, "Free Speech," and the *Aberdeen (South Dakota) Sunday American,* 19 July 1914, as reprinted in *Solidarity,* 8 August 1914, 1. The editors of *Solidarity* headlined the story "No Free Speech Fight Intended," but Carey's account suggests otherwise. On Kitty Solomon, see *Hobo News* 2 (August 1916): 12.

28. *Solidarity,* 10 October 1914, 2. He signed the report, "Yours for turkey with the trimmings."

29. On IWW unemployed organizing during the winters of 1913–15 see Foner, *History of the Labor Movement,* 435–61.

30. *Solidarity,* 17 October 1914, 1.

31. *Solidarity,* 14 November 1914, 1.

32. On Des Moines see *Solidarity,* 16 January 1915, 1; 30 January 1915, 1; 27 February 1915, 4. On Kansas City see *Solidarity,* 5 December 1914, 1.

33. *ADN,* 20 July 1914, 2. See also *SCJ* editorial reprinted in *ADN,* 22 July 1914, 2.

34. *ADN,* 20 July 1914, 2.

35. *ADN,* 23 July 1914, 6.

36. *Aberdeen (South Dakota) Weekly News,* 16 July 1914, reported that 300 hoboes arrived in Mitchell and demanded meals. Officials put them on the next train north.

37. *ADN,* 20 July 1914, 1. For the internal IWW debate over how the union should relate to farmers see Hall, "IWW and Working Farmers," *Solidarity,* 27 March 1915, 4; "Farmers and Workers Should Fraternize Says Writer," *New Solidarity,* 9 August 1919, 3; "Opposes Amalgamation with Non-Partisans," *New Solidarity,* 6 September 1919, 4. See also "Agriculture, the Mother of Industry," (Chicago: Agricultural Workers' Industrial Union No. 110, n.d. [1922]), IWW Collection, Box 156, Walter Reuther Archives.

38. Gruber to Hill, 8 October 1914, GN Railway, VP-Operating: VP and Gen. Manager Subject Files: "Hoboes, Tramps, and Bums (IWW)," MHS.

39. General Superintendent to Gruber, 9 October 1914, GN Railway: VP-Operating: VP and Gen. Manager Subject Files: "Hoboes, Tramps, and Bums (IWW)," MHS. Letter to Honorable J. C. Ross, 9 October 1914, GN: VP-Operating: VP and Gen. Manager Subject Files: "Hoboes, Tramps, and Bums (IWW)," MHS.

40. Morlan, *Political Prairie Fire;* Richardson, "Scientific Organizing and the Farmer," 554–58.

41. Hornbacher, "The Forgotten Heritage," 43–74. Note that the NDSP's newspaper, the *Iconoclast,* had an anti-Catholic tone that may have limited the party's support; Bureau of the Census, *Thirteenth Census of the U.S., 1910, Statistics for North Dakota,* 587.

42. Hornbacher, "The Forgotten Heritage," 57–66. See also Foner, *History of the*

Labor Movement; Allen, "A Review of the Facts Relating to the Free Speech Fight at Minot," *USCIR Unpublished Papers;* "Free Speech. Riot in Minot, North Dakota, July, 1913," USCIR Microfilm (Free Speech, Labor in General), SHSW; "Extract from 'Legalized Bank Robbery' by Grant S. Youmans," USCIR Microfilm (Free Speech, Labor in General), SHSW; Martinson, "'Comes the Revolution,'" 41–109; "Henry R. Martinson" (interview), *North Dakota History* (Spring 1978): 16–22.

43. Hornbacher, "The Forgotten Heritage," 82, 113.

44. *Solidarity,* 17 October 1914, 1; *UA,* 8 October 1914, 8; *SCJ,* 11 October 1914, 7. See Foner, *History of the Labor Movement,* 456–58; Short, "How One Town Learned a Lesson," 106–8. Wobblies had been active in Sioux City at least since 1910. See *Solidarity,* 4 June 1910, 2.

45. *Solidarity,* 2 January 1915, 3.

46. *Solidarity,* 26 December 1914, 4.

47. *UA,* 17 December 1914, 4; *Solidarity,* 2 January 1915, 3.

48. *Solidarity,* 2 January 1915, 4.

49. *SCJ,* 28 December 1914, 8; *Solidarity,* 2 January 1915, 4.

50. *Solidarity,* 30 January 1915, 1.

51. Short, "How One Town Learned a Lesson," 107.

52. Ibid.; *UA,* 14 January 1915, 8.

53. *Solidarity,* 23 January 1915, 1.

54. *Solidarity,* 30 January 1915, 1; Short, "How One Town Learned a Lesson," 107.

55. *UA,* 14 January 1915, 8.

56. *Solidarity,* 2 January 1915, 4.

57. *Solidarity,* 27 February 1915, 4.

58. Ibid.

59. *Solidarity,* 3 April 1915, 1. Thirteen were give thirty-day sentences; one was released. O'Connor was later released.

60. *Solidarity,* 3 April 1915, 1; 10 April 1915, 1.

61. *SCJ,* 1 April 1915, 1.

62. *Solidarity,* 10 April 1915, 1.

63. Ibid.

64. *SCJ,* 4 April 1915, 1; Short, "How One Town Learned a Lesson," 107.

65. *SCJ,* 15 April 1915, 1; *Solidarity,* 24 April 1915, 1; Short, "How One Town Learned a Lesson," 107.

66. *SCJ,* 15 April 1915, 2; *Solidarity,* 24 April 1915, 1; Short, "How One Town Learned a Lesson," 107.

67. *Solidarity,* 24 April 1915, 1; *SCJ,* 17 April 1915, 1, 2.

68. *Solidarity,* 1 May 1915, 1; *SCJ,* 20 April 1915, 1; Short, "How One Town Learned a Lesson," 108.

69. *UA,* 4 March 1915, 4.

70. *UA,* 4 March 1915, 4. See also "Joe Lewis's Stockade," *UA,* 1 April 1915, 1. The stockade was the idea of city councilman Lewis, about whom the *Advocate* editorialized: "Joe has lorded over a bunch of 'free and independent' scab workmen for so many years . . . that he should be eminently qualified to do a bossing job over a half-starved bunch of down and outers." See *Solidarity,* 1 May 1915, 1.

71. *UA,* 15 April 1915, 6.

72. *UA,* 15 April 1915, 1; see also *UA,* 17 December 1914, 4.

73. *UA,* 15 April 1915, 1.

74. Ibid. See the People's party platform of 1892 (Omaha Platform): "From the same prolific womb of governmental injustice we breed the two great classes—tramps and millionaires." Quoted in Hofstadter and Hofstadter, *Great Issues in American History,* 140.

75. Short, "How One Town Learned a Lesson," 107–8.

76. See Short's response to a letter critical of his article on Sioux City: *Survey* 35 (27 November 1915), 225. See Short, *Just One American;* Cumberland, *Wallace Short,* 35–75; Taft, "Mayor Short."

77. *Solidarity,* 6 March 1915, 1.

78. Workman, *History of "400,"* 9. This source reports that the new union was dubbed an "Organization" rather than an "Industrial Union" because "the word 'UNION' was anathema to many workers," 7–8. Only nine IWW delegates and one representative of the IBWA were present for the opening session; see "Minutes of Conference of Harvest Workers Held in Kansas City, Missouri, April 15th, 1915," IWW Collection, Box 44, Folder 1, Walter Reuther Archives. See also Haywood's announcement of the April conference in *Solidarity,* 28 November 1914, 3 (and reprinted in *Solidarity,* 13 February 1915, 2).

79. *Solidarity,* 27 March 1915, 1, 4. Local 64 also advised an effort to educate small-town residents and home guard workers.

80. *Solidarity,* 27 March 1915, 4.

81. Foner, *History of the Labor Movement,* 475–78; Doree, "Gathering the Grain," 740–43; *Solidarity,* 18 March 1916, 4.

82. For example, see Spink Co. Case #694, July 1917, Spink Co. Courthouse, Redfield, SD, especially the trial transcripts. See also "Ridding Mellette" *ADN,* 1 August 1917.

83. Foner, *History of the Labor Movement,* 480–82; "Hi-Jacks, Boot-Leggers, Hold-ups, Gamblers, Etc., in the Harvest Fields Warning to You," IWW Pamphlet, n.d. [c. 1915–16], IWW Collection, Box 163, Walter Reuther Archives.

84. Thomas Bogard, "Autobiography," 158–60, 189–91, 301, WSHS. See also McGuckin, *Memoirs of a Wobbly,* 73–74; Joseph Murphy in Bird et al., *Solidarity Forever,* 46.

85. *ADN,* 10 September 1915, 1; 11 September 1915, 1; 15 September 1915, 5; 16 September 1915, 3; "Harvest Hands Must Protect Themselves," *Solidarity,* 9 October 1915, 1. See also *Solidarity,* 5 November 1915, 4, on bootlegging and gambling in North Dakota.

86. The more carefully considered IWW texts usually defined sabotage in the first way, especially those published after the passage of criminal syndicalism laws: "The IWW has never advocated crime, violence, or any methods of terrorism, either lawful or unlawful," Rowan, *The I.W.W. in the Lumber Industry,* 29. See *Solidarity,* 21 October 1916, 4: "The greatest violence we believe in is folding our arms. If all the workers did that the wheels of industry would stop." A 1924 letter from the secretary-treasurer of the AWIU to fellow worker Bob Hall goes to great lengths to distance the IWW from violence. In addition to a 1923 AWIU resolution requiring all new members to oppose "violence and destruction of property," the letter cites a 1917 IWW executive board resolution declaring that the IWW "does not now, and never

has believed in or advocated either destruction or violence as a means of accomplishing industrial reform" and finally points to the 1912 pamphlet "On the Firing Line," which actually does not renounce violence but states that employers historically set the tone for industrial struggle, and if they choose to use violence, the IWW will meet them openly but not secretively. (See Hanley to Hall, 11 March 1924, Box 44, Folder 7, IWW Collection, Walter Reuther Archives. On the sabotage debate see Foner, *History of the Labor Movement,* 398–400, 406–8, 551.

87. The IWW was also accused of setting forest fires in Montana and Idaho during World War I, but reports from Forest Service officials praise IWW members for their hard work in fighting these fires. See "Exhibit C," *Papers of the President's Mediation Commission.* In a 1922 union bulletin, the AWIU suggested that fire insurance companies were spreading fear of Wobbly-set fires in hopes of selling policies to farmers; see "AWIU No. 110 of the IWW, Bulletin No. 25, 26 July 1922, Chicago, Ill," IWW Seattle Branch, Box 4, Folder 13, University of Washington Libraries, Manuscripts and Archives Division.

88. *Solidarity,* 4 September 1915, 1. Some farmers reportedly found railroad spikes inside their bundles, apparently for the purpose of destroying threshing machines; see *ADN,* 27 August 1915, 4.

89. *Solidarity,* 4 September 1915, 4. See also Hanson, "Threshing the Wheat," 344–47.

90. *Solidarity,* 11 September 1915, 1. Elsewhere, however, police were sympathetic with harvesters' demands and did not intervene in wage negotiations with farmers. "Even the Cop Scratched His Head," *Solidarity,* 4 September 1915, 1.

91. *Solidarity,* 4 September 1915, 1.

92. *Solidarity,* "Berthod Police," 18 September 1915, 4.

93. *Solidarity,* 23 October 1915, 4.

94. *Solidarity,* 16 October 1915, 2.

95. *Solidarity,* 4 March 1916, 2.

96. *ADN,* 27 July 1916, 5.

97. Ibid., 2.

98. Ibid., 3.

99. *SCJ,* 26 July 1916, 14. This article was reprinted in the *ADN,* 28 July 1916, 5.

100. *SCJ,* 25 July 1916, 5, 26 July 1916, 14.

101. Among the more typical stories were "Hobo with Razor Goes to Bastille," *Mitchell (South Dakota) Daily Republican,* 21 June 1916, 1; and "Say Tramp Is Carrying Knife—Ethan Folks Worried about Hobo Running Amuck," *Mitchell (South Dakota) Daily Republican,* 18 July 1916, 1. On the heat wave see Mitchell *Gazette,* 1 August 1916, 3.

102. *Mitchell (South Dakota) Daily Republican,* 25 July 1916, 4.

103. For examples of police attempts to contain migrants to a particular section of town see, "IWW Hands in City Today," *Mitchell (South Dakota) Daily Republican,* 18 July 1916, 5; and reporting on Sioux Falls, SD, "Handling the IWW Situation Easily," *Mitchell (South Dakota) Gazette,* 27 July 1916, 1.

104. *Mitchell (South Dakota) Daily Republican,* 25 July 1916, 4.

105. *ADN,* 27 July 1916, 1; *Redfield (South Dakota) Journal Observer,* 3 August 1916, 2; *Redfield (South Dakota) Press,* 3 August 1916, 3. Five men were charged with carry-

ing concealed weapons; see *State of South Dakota, Spink County v. John Bassinger,* case 665; *State of South Dakota, Spink County v. William Astor,* case 666; *State of South Dakota, Spink County v. Albert Gray,* case 667; *State of South Dakota, Spink County v. George McFarland,* case 668; *State of South Dakota, Spink County v. Fred J. Kelly,* case 669. Two others also were charged with assault with a deadly weapon; see *State of South Dakota, Spink County v. Charles Lewis and George Hughes,* case 671. All received sentences of thirty days in jail, but the *Redfield Press* reported that they were released soon after the incident. However, the *Press* (3 August 1916, 4) also reported that "a number of negroes" remained in jail because of the fight. It is not clear whether they were among those formally charged.

106. *SCJ,* 29 July 1916, 1; *Redfield (South Dakota) Press,* 3 August 1916, 4.

107. *Redfield (South Dakota) Journal-Observer,* 3 August 1916, 2; *Redfield (South Dakota) Press,* 3 August 1916, 4. On the KKK in the upper Midwest see Duffus, "The Ku Klux Klan," 363–72; Stock, *Main Street in Crisis,* 66–67; Harwood, "The Ku Klux Klan in Grand Forks," 301–35: Cumberland, *Wallace Short,* 76–83.

108. *Mitchell (South Dakota) Clarion,* 3 August 1916, 1; *Solidarity,* 19 August 1916, 1.

109. *Solidarity,* 19 August 1916, 1.

110. *Mitchell (South Dakota) Clarion,* 3 August 1916, 1.

111. Quoted in *Mitchell (South Dakota) Clarion,* 3 August 1916, 2.

112. *ADN,* 28 July 1916, 4.

113. *ADN,* 1 August 1916, 2.

114. Ibid.

115. *Mitchell (South Dakota) Gazette,* 29 July 1916, 2.

116. *Mitchell (South Dakota) Gazette,* 3 August 1916, 3.

117. *Mitchell (South Dakota) Gazette,* 1 August 1916, 2.

118. *Mitchell (South Dakota) Gazette,* 3 August 1916, 2. Thomas Bogard recalls that The Jungles in Mitchell was started by a former laborer and IWW member and that all the patrons were Wobblies. See Bogard, "Autobiography," 159, WSHS.

119. *SCJ,* 28 July 1916, 1; *ADN,* 28 July 1916, 1; *Ortonville (Minnesota) Journal,* 3 August 1916, 1. On conflicts in Minot see *Solidarity,* 2 September 1916, 4.

120. Foner, *History of the Labor Movement,* 479. *Solidarity,* 9 September 1916, 3; 21 October 1916, 1; Sellars, *Oil, Wheat, and Wobblies.*

121. Foner, *History of the Labor Movement,* 475–79; Workman, *History of "400";* Edwards, "The Class War in the Harvest Country," *Solidarity,* 19 August 1916, 1; "New AWO Methods," *Solidarity,* 9 September 1916, 3; see also Sellars, *Oil, Wheat and Wobblies;* Reese, "The AWO—An Example of a Successful Union," *Solidarity,* 18 March 1916, 1.

122. Haynes, "Revolt of the 'Timber Beasts'"; Betten, "Riot, Revolution, Repression," 82–94; See also "Remarks for 1917," Yearly Reports Binder, Frank Gillmor Papers, MHS.

123. Chrislock, *Watchdog of Loyalty,* 36–37, 97–98; Hearings, Labor Troubles in Northern Minnesota, 30 January 1917, John Lind Papers (P933), Box 8, MHS. The Minnesota Commission of Public Safety (MCPS) also tried to undermine the Non-Partisan League and the IWW in North Dakota; see correspondence between Thomas G. Winters and J. D. Bacon, 30 June, 1 July, and 6 July 1917, Public Safety Commission, Agents Reports to T. G. Winter, MHS. Minnesota became the first state to con-

vict anyone under a criminal syndicalism law when lumberjack Jesse Dunning was convicted in September 1917; see Dowell, *A History of Criminal Syndicalism Legislation*, 139.

124. *Solidarity*, 9 September 1916, 3.

125. On Frank Little's lynching see *Solidarity*, 4 August 1917, 1; on Sioux City Civilian Unit see *Solidarity*, 14 July 1917, 8.

126. *Industrial Worker*, 21 July 1917, 8.

127. *ADN*, 30 July, 17, 4.

128. *Solidarity*, 11 August 1917, 5; 4 August 1917, 8. See also affidavits of W. E. Teston, A. B. Holtsman, John Gilmartin, Harvey Shearer, Michael Sapper, and Ed Hurley in *Papers of the President's Mediation Commission*.

129. *ADN*, 27 July 1917, 8.

130. *ADN*, 28 July 1917, 2.

131. *ADN*, 4 August 1917, 2. Note that figures given in the report suggest that the majority of Wobblies in the area already had registered for the draft.

132. Maurice G. Bresnan to Thorstein Veblen, 8 April 1918, *Papers of the President's Mediation Commission*.

133. Dowell, *History of Criminal Syndicalism Legislation*, 53, 58, 61. See also *State of South Dakota, Spink County v. C. Hamilton*, Case 77, Spink County Courthouse, Redfield, South Dakota. The court found Hamilton guilty of demanding wages of $5 per day. He was fined $25 and sentenced to twelve and one-half days in jail

134. Dowell, *History of Criminal Syndicalism Legislation*, 92–94, 148. The lower house passed a criminal syndicalism bill in 1918, but the NPL-controlled upper house amended it to include monopoly, profiteering, price fixing, financial manipulation, and antilabor combination. Dowell quotes the *Fargo Courier-News*, an NPL paper, as saying the NPL "is willing to pass laws preventing syndicalism and sabotage by labor; all that it asks is that syndicalism and sabotage by big business be made equally a crime." The bill died in conference committee, according to Dowell.

135. *Fargo (North Dakota) Courier-News*, 15 July 1917, 3; AWIU Bulletin #53, William Langer Papers, University of North Dakota.

136. More than 300 IWW leaders were arrested in the federal and state raids of 1917; see Gambs, *Decline of the IWW*, 26–32; Dubofsky, *We Shall Be All*, 398–422.

137. Rand School, *American Labor Yearbook, 1919–1920*, 195–96; Thompson and Murfin, *The IWW*, reports even lower membership figures of 4,000 in 1919 (p. 130).

138. "The Farm Hand," 526; Rand School, *American Labor Yearbook, 1923–1924*, 93; Thompson and Murfin, *The IWW*, 149. The 1923 membership of the IWW as a whole was 58,000.

139. Thompson and Murfin, *The IWW*, 149.

140. Gambs, *The Decline of the IWW*, 89, 99–125; Sellars, *Oil, Wheat and Wobblies*, 143–84; Draper, *Roots of American Communism*, 318.

141. Wright, "American Agriculture and the Labor Market," 207–9.

5 "We Thought of Ourselves as Men after Awhile": Mutuality, Violence, and the Apprenticeship of the Road

ANTON JOHANNSEN climbed into a boxcar half full of shelled corn as it pulled out of his hometown of Clinton, Iowa, and headed for Chicago. At eighteen years of age, he was beginning seven years of life as a hobo. He was already experienced with work, getting his first job at twelve in a brick-yard and two years later working in a sash and door factory. As a teenager in the mid-1880s he had witnessed a Knights of Labor strike in Clinton and immediately understood that employers were "our enemies, and were trying to get all they could out of us and give us as little in return as we would accept." In light of this class resentment, he "felt justified in killing as much time as I could without being discharged." When his boss caught him and his friends playing cards at work, however, he was fired. Rather than face the anger of his father, he slipped out of town on a freight train.[1]

On the road, his first friend was an older tramp mechanic "with a philosophic turn of mind." The mechanic spoke approvingly of Marxism and unions and disparagingly of religion. Together they "beat, begged and worked their way" across Iowa. The older man's politics and friendship made an impression on Johannsen but didn't make him a radical right away. He hired out to jobs that he was unqualified for and, though quickly fired, he gained a little more experience every time. By this method he had a kind of apprenticeship in work and human nature. He came to know a wide variety of people, from mechanics, to shopkeepers, to hoboes, to criminals. Working his way south through Louisiana, Texas, and into Mexico, he relied on acquaintances as much as his own wits to find jobs, free meals, and places to sleep. In one small Texas town he connived his way into social relations with a respectable family, but lacking money to maintain his front, he hit the road again. In Corpus Christi, he passed himself off as a stranded actor and performed blackface minstrelsy to great local acclaim. Eventually he returned to Clinton and married. Finding his hometown too small after his worldly travels, Johannsen moved his family to Chicago, where he later became a leader of the city's woodworkers' union and a well-known anarchist. As he told Hutchins Hapgood, a middle-class progressive who wrote Johannsen's biography, this early education on the road gave him the insight into workers' thinking that helped him succeed as a union leader. "I knew men," he told Hapgood, "and felt instinctively that it was best to appeal mainly to the manhood in a man."[2]

Several decades after Johannsen hopped his first boxcar, in July 1915, seventeen year-old Earl Coole arrived in Ashton, South Dakota looking for farm work. There were already a number of other men in the small town waiting for harvest work to begin, so when a farmer, Ethan Young, came to town looking for a hand who would hire out by the month, Coole opted for steady work over higher-paying but less secure jobs. He worked on Young's farm for a month, but the two seem to have had little social interaction, for Young knew only that Coole lived in Fort Pierre, South Dakota and that his father lived in Dennison, Iowa. On August 21, with the harvest winding down and with paychecks in his pocket, Coole set off for Aberdeen, the nearest large town. As he walked north along the tracks of the Chicago, Milwaukee and St. Paul railroad he met two other harvest hands, W. G. Campbell and B. C. "Reb" Wilds, boyhood friends from Arkansas. Since early summer the two had followed the wheat harvest north from Oklahoma through Kansas to South Dakota, stopping in Ashton because Wilds had worked in the area during the previous year's harvest. Like Coole, Campbell and Wilds had made their stake and were on their way to Aberdeen for entertainment.

The three laborers stood by a crossroads, perhaps discussing what they would do with their earnings, drinking some "whiskey" that Campbell had purchased the previous day. The "whiskey" probably was grain alcohol, but it must have tasted good to Coole because he bought a small bottle for himself from his new friends. After some more small talk and a few more rounds, the men parted company. Campbell and Wilds walked off quickly toward Ashton while Coole, heading in the wrong direction, "sort of staggered as he walked along and then sat down on the track and put his head in his hands," according to a passing farmer. About an hour later Coole lay passed out with his legs hanging over the rail as a speeding northbound locomotive drew upon him. Engineer Delbert Haldeman spotted the body, threw on the train's emergency brake, and blasted its whistle. But Coole did not move as the locomotive and four cars ran him over, severing one leg below the hip and leaving the other dangling "by a few tissues." Running back to the body, Haldeman and his crew found Coole barely alive: "The death rattle was in his throat. He gasped and rolled his eyes."[3]

The contrast between the untimely end of Earl Coole's young life and Anton Johannsen's successful passage from hobo to union leader calls attention to the chaotic nature of the hoboing experience: Some men survived and settled, others were literally torn apart. This chapter is an effort to make sense of the contrast between those who burned out and those who settled out. In his book *Violent Land,* David Courtwright suggests that the essential distinction between the Cooles and Johannsens of the world was innate intelligence. This assertion is as untestable as it is dubious. However, it is also a marker of the powerful tendency to view the lives of poor people in terms of degradation. For instance, Peter Way characterizes as romantics the labor historians who find evidence of resistance to exploitation in the institutions of working-class culture. Working people in general, Way argues, "were largely powerless in the face of broad material forces that sought to shift them from place to place and strip them of resources."[4] In other words, they were more like Earl Coole than Anton Johannsen.

The issue of hobo workers' power in the face of social forces is interwoven with questions of manliness and violence, individuality and community. Where some historians see an ethos of self-destructive hypermasculinity, others see a conscious political strategy, a "virile syndicalism" based on collective action and intended to counter bourgeois masculinity.[5] Where Peter Speek and Carleton Parker saw perversion and the inevitable degradation of workers into tramps, many young men viewed seasonal work and life on the road as a rite of passage and an opportunity to see the world. As the poet Carl Sandburg wrote of his youthful experiences as a hobo, "I was meeting fellow travelers and fellow Americans. What they were doing to my heart and mind, my personality, I couldn't say then nor later and be certain. I was getting a deeper self-respect than I had had in Galesburg, so much I knew. I was getting to be a better storyteller." Or as Vincent Dunne summarized his youthful work and travels, "We thought of ourselves as men after awhile."[6]

While many young men searched for a sense of independence from family, home town, and employers, none could survive the road alone. In fact, their efforts to stand alone often led to extreme privation. The supposed independence of the road turns out to have been structured by a distended network of advice, assistance, and care: A man with money would buy a meal for a hungry man, homemakers and hoboes exchanged chores for food, and jobs could be found through friends, distant relatives, and acquaintances. These acts were in turn predicated on a vague but real ethic of mutuality, what I call transient mutuality. When laborers with money or food shared it with those without, they did so with the expectation that the favor would be returned, not necessarily by the same person but by a future acquaintance. Likewise, homemakers who fed men at their back doors often had sons, brothers, and husbands on the road. To be sure, acts of "mutuality" sometimes masked less than altruistic motives. A fast friendship might turn into a setup for a robbery; drinking buddies sometimes stole from their passed-out friends or left their dangerously drunken acquaintances unconscious on railroad tracks. Migrants' reliance on transient mutuality was a sign of their social marginalization. But it was also a marker of community among migrants and between migrants and nonmigrants who chose to help them. Individuality and community hung in an uneasy balance. Laborers needed the support of their transient communities to survive as physical, and therefore social, beings. Their lives as freewheeling travelers, that is, as individuals, depended on the collective.[7]

This chapter draws on the memoirs of former laborers, especially IWW members, to explore the meaning of the contrast between Earl Coole and Anton Johannsen. It is not my contention that all laboring men shared the political outlooks of the Wobblies; rather, the rich documentary basis surrounding the union allows us to understand the subculture of laboring men, a subculture with deep connections to working-class culture in general. The lessons learned from the road were rarely as direct as those offered by radical songs, newspapers, and speeches. Instead, radical propaganda offered one important model from which former laborers retold their life stories, what we might call the radical coming-of-age story. As Joan Scott argues, memoirs of this kind often are not a window onto experience but an obfuscation. By reading these stories critically, however, we can describe the uneven terrain of hobo experience, here conforming to a brightly lit heroic narrative of solidarity and there departing into a shadowy world of hunger, crime, violence, illicit sex, and shame. Building on a broader Midwestern populist intellectual network, laborers attempted to recast the privation and alienation of their experience into a more meaningful story. In contrast to the inevitable downward drift predicted by social investigators, socialist and populist journalism and literature offered laboring men a variety of more pleasant imagined futures.

Among the millions of laborers who did not meet Earl Coole's fate, most settled into communities and grew old. Later in life, a few decided to write their own memoirs, and historians gathered a larger number of life narratives for various oral history projects. The stories told by men who survived take on quite a different tone from those collected by Progressive Era social investigators: They reflect hard experiences overcome, solidarities celebrated, or a passing phase in a long life. To be sure, men looking back on their youth are prone to romanticize, and memoirists often use their life stories in service of latter-day agendas. Just as investigators used case studies and life histories to repackage working-class experience into a coherent reform narrative, laboring men often retold their own stories with a eye to relating a specific message. However, the life on the road that emerges from these working-class narratives—both retrospective and contemporaneous—is less the inverse of the investigators' version of a downward life course than an alternative perspective on the same basic information. To borrow a phrase from Michael Denning, these are life stories with working-class accents. Of course, the ring of this accent has been decisively shaped by the caprice of history and the agendas of historians and radicals themselves.[8] Clearly, we do not have life narratives from a representative sample (in the statistical sense) of men who experienced life on the road. But even from so obviously biased a sample as the memoirs of ex-Wobblies, we have much to learn about the broader experience of seasonal labor.

These memoirists commonly framed their experiences as a radical coming-of-age story. Indeed, IWW literature offered an important interpretive venue for laborers' life experiences, and few items achieved greater popularity than "The Little Red Song Book," a pocket-sized volume of radical verse. One song in particular, "The Mysteries of a Hobo's Life," by T-Bone Slim, is an illustrative coming-of-age model:

> I took a job on an extra gang,
> Way up in the mountain,
> I paid my fee and shark shipped me
> And ties I soon was counting.
>
> The boss he put me driving spikes
> And the sweat was enough to blind me,

He didn't seem to like my pace,
So I left the job behind me.

I grabbed a hold of an old freight train
And around the country traveled,
The mysteries of a hobo's life
To me were soon unraveled.

I traveled east and I traveled west
And the "shacks" could never find me,
Next morning I was miles away
From the job I left behind me.

I ran across a bunch of "stiffs"
Who were known as Industrial Workers,
They taught me how to be a man—
And how to fight the shirkers.

I kicked right in and joined the bunch
And now in the ranks you'll find me.
Hurrah for the cause—To hell with the boss!
And the job I left behind me.[9]

The song tells of experiences that any seasonal laborer would have recognized: an abusive and hard-driving boss, stealing rides on freight trains to find work, and struggling to avoid railroad police. The "mysteries" of life on the road are left largely to the imagination, but the resolution of the problems identified in the first two verses is not. When the hobo joins the IWW, he learns "how to be a man" less through independence than through belonging to the cause.

Not surprisingly, memoirs of former Wobblies offer a remarkably similar story of hard work and manly belonging. Among the more literary coming-of-age narratives is the autobiography of the IWW leader Ralph Chaplin (1887–1961). Chaplin was born on a Kansas farm, but he grew up in Chicago. Driven by their desire for adventure, Chaplin and his working-class friend "Blackie" Donovan landed jobs on an East St. Louis construction crew through a Chicago employment agency one summer around 1905. From there, they moved on to the wheat harvest in northern Texas. As inexperienced young workers, the pair had trouble finding steady jobs and spent many nights sleeping in the open. "We learned of the magnitude and beauty of the American continent," Chaplin wrote, "and we learned how the underdog was forced to live." Their "farmer bosses" sometimes refused to pay and "were inclined to treat us as human outcasts beyond the law."[10]

Despite such hardships, Chaplin looked back fondly on his time as a harvest laborer. When he returned home "rich in suntan and experience" but completely broke, he was proud of his callused hands. Chaplin's father was distressed to hear that his son had begged for food. Suspecting that he had not really worked at all, the elder Chaplin demanded to see his son's hands. "I held them out to him," Chaplin wrote; "They were brown from the sun and callused. I was proud of those calluses. Dad studied them carefully on both sides. I saw that he was impressed. Dad held his hands out to me. I had never noticed that they were so horny and hard."[11] The passage to manhood came in socially productive work, at once uniting the son with the father and distancing them from the beggar who did not share their callused hands.

Other autobiographies and oral testimonies suggest that conflicted relations with parents often drove young men toward sojourns as migrant workers. Henry McGuckin (1893–1974), who, like Chaplin, later became an IWW activist, left his Paterson, New Jersey home at age ten or eleven after a fight with his father. In contrast to Chaplin, McGuckin recounted his initiation into wage labor less as one dramatic event than as a litany of lessons in kindness amid exploitation. He had good jobs and bad. The good ones were always too short; the bad ones he soon quit. Shortly after leaving home, McGuckin met an older hobo who befriended him and taught him how to live on the road. McGuckin wrote that the man never took advantage of him or made any inappropriate advances. "In spite of all you hear about older men taking up with kids on the road," McGuckin wrote, "this hobo—and he was that, pure and simple—never made a wrong move or a dirty crack while I was with him." After a few months together, the two parted. McGuckin took a job on a farm near Bath, New York; the hobo went south alone, saying the region was too rough for a youngster.[12] Years later, when McGuckin encountered the IWW, he found other fatherly role models. There was the soapbox speaker Tommy Whitehead, whose arguments first drew him to the Wobblies and who issued McGuckin his first "red card." There was Jack Graves, a well-educated radical known as the "Big Professor," from whom McGuckin learned about economics around jungle campfires. McGuckin summed up his early life by saying, "I guess I'm proud of this: that I worked for a better world for people to live in and did my part within the structure of an organization I was sure had the answers, and for that day and time, it did."[13]

Like McGuckin, Thomas Bogard remembered a series of father figures in his early life, and their eagerness to help him reflects the social currency of fatherliness, or mentorship, among laboring men on the road. Bogard grew up in a poor rural family in southern Illinois; both his mother and father worked for wages in other peoples' homes. When he was fifteen he went to work for a neighbor, an older farmer who had been in the Knights of Labor and "who taught me things about the class struggle as we sat around the fireplace on those long winter nights and many times while resting ourselves out in the woods while cutting wood and splitting rails." Discussions of the hard rock miners' strikes in Colorado made Bogard "long for the rockies of the West and . . . to become a Union man," and in May 1905, with a mixture of sadness and excitement, he left home.[14] On his way west he met up with several older men who taught him about the road. Among the things Bogard learned was that "all good workmen keep clean on the road," that you should "always keep a tow[e]l and some soap with you and keep your face clean when you are on the road and a clothes brush and a comb to comb your hair," and finally, "never leave a town or a city unless you got tobac[c]o and matches."[15] Bogard quickly found that the old Knight's political lessons would earn him respect on the road. Several of the older men who helped him were also former Knights of Labor, and their companionship led him to a couple of members of the Western Federation of Miners. These miners asked Bogard to travel with them to their homestead in the mountains, where he could become a miner and join the union. It was at that homestead that Bogard found a new family of radicals, who gave him the nickname "Powderly" after the leader of the Knights of Labor.[16]

In comparison to McGuckin and Bogard, Walter Harju's (1900–1981) travels were much more parochial. Although he later became a Communist party organizer, Harju was raised by his mother's family, who were very strict Norwegian Lutherans in rural Brown County, South Dakota. His father, a Finnish-born miner, died in 1911 in Hibbing, Minnesota; the two did not know each other. Like other young men from poor families, Harju went to work out of necessity and gained important skills and political outlooks from itinerant laborers. As a teenager he worked on farms around Brown County and learned carpentry from his uncle. He tried to join the army during World War I but was rejected for medical reasons, and instead he worked the wheat harvest for several years. He joined the IWW so he could ride freight trains unmolested, and he found his fellow workers ready to help him when he was shot by a railroad employee. However, when telling his life story, Harju highlighted a lesson he learned from a middle-aged Native American "whose philosophy and friendship I will never forget." As Harju recounted in a 1977 interview, they traveled through the Dakotas in boxcars and his partner told him about the values of his people's culture. "We award eagle feathers to all who learn from life's lessons," his partner explained, "for useful work; for devotion to the commonweal of our tribe; for honesty and truth; for devotion to the common good and well-being; for valor; for the love of our neighbors and our fellow human beings; for the love of children—of your own as well as your neighbors'; for devotion to peace among all peoples of the world; for charity toward the weak and ailing; for kindness and compassion toward all our sisters and brothers regardless of race or color of skin."[17]

Harju did not elaborate on this experience in his lengthy interview; he simply read the story into the tape recorder before the interviewer asked any questions. It is significant that a working-class radical of Norwegian and Finnish background would frame his political commitment in this way. Neither Marxism, nor the defense of immigrant culture, nor any other theory framed his commitment to radical politics. Rather, Harju retrospectively justifies his life through a Native American voice heard in a hobo jungle.[18] To be sure, "Eagle Feathers," like many other remembered life stories, has a sentimental bent, and he uses a conspicuously stock character, the wise Indian, as its messenger. However, it is entirely possible that the story is based on a real event, even if it has been elaborated for effect. More significantly, the story does not validate any of the so-called traditionally masculine traits of laborers' rough culture. The Native American Harju credits for shaping his own political outlook insisted on decidedly compassionate values.

The importance of these partners extended well beyond moral teachings: Life on the road would have been very difficult without their material support for one another. This was especially the case for young men who had yet to learn how to survive on the road. The actions of the Wobblies whom Walter Harju remembered as "very compassionate" and "some of the most beautiful people in the world" reflected both politicized community and a broader ethic of mutual aid. We see this dynamic in its reverse in the autobiographical narrative of Robert S. Saunders (1893–1971), a St. Louis man who took to the road eight times between 1911 and 1916. In contrast to memoirists who seemed to slip effortlessly into their first boxcar, Saunders's early efforts were foiled by inexperience, fear, and homesickness. Saunders and a friend left on their first trip in late November 1911, with vague plans to go to the West Coast and afterwards "China, perhaps, or the islands of the South Seas." They made it to Kansas City, but going broke and failing as beggars in their first week away from home took away the romance. Saunders and his partner decided that the "prospect of actually being a hobo, in the very next day or so, was not nearly as attractive as viewing the possibility from a greater distance had been."[19] On subsequent trips, Saunders was more successful. He visited Chicago and got a factory job making electric motors, and in a few weeks his brother arrived from St. Louis and joined him in the factory. After two months of factory work, he and a friend decided to try their hand at the wheat harvest. They made it to the wheat belt, but being "inexperienced and soft," they never found work. They were aided along the way by fellow hoboes bound for the harvest and were regaled with stories of road life told by an older one-armed hobo. Later that summer, Saunders traveled to Indianapolis, where he found work but was again hampered by inexperience. With little spare cash and payday a week away, he could not afford a room and nearly exhausted himself "working ten hours a day, and then walking half of each night," catching short naps in parks and on streetcars. After a week of this, a chance meeting with a friend from St. Louis led Saunders to a shared bed, and after payday he got his own room.[20]

After these brief forays into hobo life, Saunders was much more successful at hopping freight trains, begging for meals, and finding jobs. These things he had learned from fellow hoboes as they rode together in boxcars, shared meals, drinks, and campfires. From 1913 to 1916 he made three long trips, each time returning to his family in St. Louis. His previous experiences helped him survive these trips, not by making him more independent but by teaching him the necessity of relying on the advice and assistance of others. His travels were aided by chance meetings with acquaintances, brief partnerships with other hoboes, and many a meal from housewives in exchange for household chores. A bachelor farmer allowed Saunders and his partner to sleep in his barn. In the morning he invited the two to join him for breakfast and lectured the men on socialism. "He found us to be an appreciative audience," Saunders wrote.[21] Later in his trip he made quick friendships with hoboes from different backgrounds (Americans, Irishmen, a Scotsman, a Mexican), friendships that allowed him to stave off homesickness. He also got advice on where to find jobs, how to avoid hostile train crews, and at which houses to beg. He became a member of the IWW, did some organizing, read books, spent time in jail, and gained a cosmopolitan education in economics and sociology.

Although Saunders was a member of the IWW, his life story reflects experiences in common with those beyond the radical milieu as well. He maintained connection with his family home in St. Louis. He traveled to find work and to see the world. When in need he fell back on the assistance of friends, acquaintances, and total strangers. Similarly, men such as Andrew Devich, Charles Brown, Nels Anderson, and even Josiah Flynt relied on partners and fast friendships: companions who eased the loneliness of strange cities and remote work camps and helped locate work, food, and transportation.[22] Men huddled for warmth in freezing boxcars, slept together in bunkhouses, and set up "bachelor shacks" to share expenses during periods of unemployment. When it came time to celebrate at their remote work camps, they often danced together, with some taking the "female" role. Partnerships of varied intensity between men were an integral part of the laborers' world.[23]

Read with twenty-first-century eyes, these partnerships seem potentially sexual, especially given the gay subculture among the hoboes. Were memoirists who avoided discussing homosexuality hiding something about which they felt guilty? Did they want to protect the reputation of the IWW? Should we read as homosexual Henry McGuckin's youthful friendship with a coworker that "grew out of our common needs and the misery of cold nights when our bodies lying close on a pile of straw was the only blanket we had"? What of his later friendships with men named "Lone Wolf" and "Saffo"?[24] In another case, historian Philip Taft, who was a hobo and a Wobbly in his youth, stumbled over how to explain his relationships with older men in the IWW. In describing the union's membership, he noted, "You had all sorts of people in the IWW. You had some very good, fine men, generous, and then of course, you had a lot of stewbums, really, in there. I mean, really just border alcoholics. And you also had more than the normal number of active male homosexuals in the IWW." After suggesting that some of the latter might try to "bother" other young men, Taft clarified that "the older men would protect you in a sort of way, not—you really don't need protection in these matters, but there were some of them that were very kind."[25] Although Taft's comments elide homosexuals with the alcoholics and stewbums, they also suggest a certain interpretive confusion surrounding intense male relationships. Given the widely known stereotype of the "jocker" and the "prushin," Taft may have felt his audience would not understand that protection from older men did not always signify a sexual relationship.

Questions about individuals' sexual practices, however, are less important than questions about the meaning of various types of relationships. Regardless of Taft's opinion on homosexuality, he did share something with the hoboes who were open to having sex with other men. For laborers living on the edge of destitution, partnership often tipped the balance between getting by and washing out. Those who could draw on the solidarity of kin, friends, or lovers often found life much easier. Although the early twentieth century witnessed the emergence of new sexual and social norms in which affinity and sexual desire became linked in a heterosexual ideology, earlier norms of same-sex sociality hung on much longer among laborers who traversed the rural-urban frontier. Even when physical contact and intense feelings of attachment carried an erotic potential, they were not necessarily sexual.[26] Moreover, laborers' razor-thin margin of survival meant that every interaction carried an economic potential as well. Just as single women looked to their better-paid male companions to pay for food, clothing, or rent, male partners could logically hope to get a free meal, a job, or other favors in return for various types of companionship. In the context of the commercialization of relationships between men and women in the bars, dance halls, and brothels of the entertainment industry, we might also think of intimate relationships between men—whether dancing, sleeping, or mutual sexual gratification—as one way to express desire and have fun for free.[27] The youthful partnerships described in laborers' radical coming-of-age stories were both a nod to the socialist ethic of solidarity and a reflection of labor market structures. In their effort to keep body and spirit together, laborers fell back on a *transient* mutuality, one that balanced affinity and exchange with mixed results.

Just as transient mutuality was a mechanism that made the independence of living on the road possible, it reflected the hard economic facts of working-class life. Although acts of kindness, mutuality, and love were common enough, violence, prostitution, and starvation were just as common. Reflecting on his early years, Wobbly leader Ralph Chaplin wrote that the pressures of unemployment, poverty, and powerlessness usually did not support worker solidarity. "The normal relationship between harvest workers was one of suspicion and distrust. We shared the policy of dog-eat-dog with the human pack who preyed upon us," he concluded starkly.[28] In the world of laborers' manly apprenticeships, violence and privation brought their complex feelings toward independence and dependency into stark relief.

Indeed, the harvest months were open season on laboring men, a window of opportunity for legitimate and illegitimate businesses alike to turn a profit. While small-town businesses serviced the legal trade, gamblers, prostitutes, and bootleggers operated with a degree of freedom "as long as they left the natives alone, and limited their activities to plundering the harvest hands," wrote Robert Saunders.[29] On the freight trains, harvest hands were held up by professional hijackers and hostile train crews alike; some were brutally beaten by train crews simply because they were easy to victimize. Charles Brown, who was both a hobo and a railroad brakeman (and not a Wobbly), explained in his memoir that the railroad companies "hire the floating element of railroad men (known as boomers) to help handle and move their trains during the big wheat rush." These boomer brakemen often had been fired for drinking on the job or otherwise blacklisted by companies. They saw the harvest season as a chance to earn "'bo money from the harvest hands," Brown recounted, "and as they was out after all the jack that they could get, they sure was hostile, and it was dig up or hit the grit," that is, pay a bribe or risk being thrown from a speeding train.[30] Railroad company records show that crews regularly "collected fares" from trespassing hoboes and that company officials were aware of the practice. In fact, the Great Northern and other railroad companies defended the right of their employees to beat trespassers. True, they noted, when protecting company property trainmen sometimes "overstep the line of defense and perform acts which are unwarranted in the law." But they should not be disciplined or fired because "under very aggravated circumstances it cannot be expected that they will always use good judgment," a company lawyer concluded.[31]

Robbery, assault, and murder were part of the experience of migrant workers, every bit as common as political discussions and worker solidarity. Injury and even death from fighting or robbery were common during the wheat harvest, when tens of thousands of laborers converged on the Great Plains in a short time. The coroner's records of wheat belt towns include cases in which men were shot while walking along railroad tracks, run over by trains (like Earl Coole), killed in bar fights, and shot by farmers while allegedly stealing chickens.[32]

Although the IWW aimed to reform the way laborers sold their labor, they did not eliminate violence from the harvest. Instead, they redirected the balance of violence. Wobblies participated in aggressive confrontations with employers, railroad brakemen, holdup men, nonunion workers, and local authorities for a number of reasons: to defend friends, to further the goals of the organization, and especially as public displays of manhood. Although violence to some extent had always been part of migrants' experiences and interactions with townspeople, the presence of the IWW tended to provide coherence and direction to an otherwise diffuse anger. In numerous street-corner and workplace conflicts, Wobblies demonstrated their political message that marginalized, disfranchised workers should collectively fight for respect, fair wages, and better working conditions. The source of the IWW's success might be attributed to its ability to draw on the rough, exuberant, and even violent elements of migrants' cultural milieu to establish a measure of organization, regularity, and decorum among migrant workers.

Ralph Chaplin summed up the noble public face of the IWW harvest campaigns saying, "There were brave and devoted friendships among us. We would stand together, fight for one another, steal for one another, and share our last crust with one another."[33] Behind the image of a well-organized and orderly revolutionary movement, a quieter strategy aimed to clear the wheat belt of the "parasites" who preyed on harvest hands. As Henry McGuckin recounted, groups of "the most tested and time-proven Wobs" were organized into "Flying Squadrons," autonomous units of two or three men who carried out a covert strategy that was unheard of by the membership at large. "Their purpose," McGuckin wrote, "was to clean up the harvest fields of holdup men, whether they were parts of train crews, railroad detectives, law officers, or just plain holdup men. During the clean-up, freight trains might pull into their divisions points with a brakeman missing, never to be found."[34] A similar strategy was described by Joseph Murphy: "We took them hijacks, many of them; we took a razor, a Gem razor blade, and cut 'IWW' on their face, 'I' on the forehead and 'W' on each cheek."[35] Likewise, F. G. Peterson reported in *Solidarity* that Wobblies carved a large "W" on the back of an antiunion worker after he and his partners drew knives on the unionists.[36]

Acts of direct resistance to criminals, hostile train crews, and employers gave pause to those who would exploit harvest hands, and the meaning of these acts reverberated widely. For instance, when an IWW Flying Squadron confronted a group of hijackers who were preparing to rob homeward-bound harvest hands near Poplar, Montana, in October 1914, they were joined by railroad employees.[37] Similarly, just as stories of "hostile bulls" circulated among the men on the road, instilling fear and caution, reports of successful resistance suggested new boundaries for the social interaction between migrants and so-called respectable citizens. A former hobo, Jack Miller, recalled confronting the head brakeman on a train in Council Bluffs, Iowa, in the summer of 1916. His refusal to pay a bribe drew a blow from the brakeman that Miller easily dodged. Then, with the rest of the train crew and his companions looking on, Miller soundly beat the brakeman by wrestling him into a swampy area near the tracks and holding his head under water until he gave up. "I found out later that he was the champion bully of this division" and that his defeat delighted the rest of the train crew.[38]

Confrontations with train crews gave weight to IWW promises of solidarity and partnership on the road. In the words of Richard Brazier's song "When You Wear That Button," "No need to hike, boys, along these old pikes, boys / Every 'Wobbly' will be your pard."[39] Likewise, public confrontations with bosses signaled the potential to change long-standing power relations. One such incident took place on Main Street in Mitchell, South Dakota, during the 1916 harvest when IWW members quarreled with a former employer. When the employer refused to pay the back wages the laborers believed they were due, the argument became violent. Outnumbered, the employer succumbed to the Wobblies' blows, and his former employees escorted him to the police department, where they again demanded their back pay. Surprisingly, the police did not arrest the Wobblies, and the employer agreed to pay his assailants what he owed them. Laborers observing the incident could hardly fail to read its cultural significance. Normally, harvest hands were the victims of beatings by brakemen, sheriffs, and vigilantes. For one moment, the world was turned upside-down. The workers beat the boss and dragged him to the police. As Brazier's song intoned,

> The boss will be leery, the "stiffs" will be cheery
> when we hit John Farmer hard.
> They'll all be affrighted, when we stand united
> and carry that Red, Red Card.

Such inversions of the established social order were no doubt part of the growing unease among authorities that led to the organized suppression of the IWW in 1917.[40]

These episodes also remind us that as the Wobblies rose above the "dog-eat-dog" subculture, as Chaplin called it, they were not above using violence to further their ends. According to Henry McGuckin, the recourse to violence also could turn inward. "There were times when to take an opposing view from that of the top leadership would not only put you out of activity, but might just as easily end you up along a railroad right-of-way with your brains bashed in," he wrote in his memoir.[41] During the period of government repression in 1917 and 1918, with agents provocateurs turning fellow workers against each other, McGuckin recalled, "old-timers began to look at each other with suspicion. Men turned up missing and were never heard from again." He was almost "bumped off" but was saved by the last-minute intervention of the long-time Wobbly organizer Jack Law. "We had some self-styled saviors of the working class who had murder in their hearts," he concluded.[42]

McGuckin's close brush with assassination suggests the frightening possibilities of an organization that justifies violence against its enemies. But a broader problem for understanding the IWW concerns the organization's relations with criminals. Just as railroad employees and local officials engaged in criminal depredations against harvest workers, there were connections between the subculture of seasonal laborers, the IWW, and the criminal underworld. Each of these subcultures organized along similar lines: small groups of young men traveling by boxcar. They shared the same class background, even if their goals were quite different. And they shared a disdain for "duly constituted authorities": the police, property law, and the courts. The loose structure of the IWW also allowed easy infiltration by criminals seeking cover and government agents seeking to disrupt the union.

The autobiography of Robert Saunders offers a telling glimpse at the opportunities for slippage between labor and criminal organizations. In the fall of 1915, Saunders worked the North Dakota wheat harvest and acted as an IWW field delegate. During rainy weather he met a man named Kelly who claimed to be an IWW member. Kelly was also a member of a criminal gang that was robbing harvest hands as they returned from work. The gang's leader, Big Ace, never took money from members of the IWW. Kelly claimed credit for this policy, but it may have simply reflected the gang's recognition that the Wobblies were likely to put up an organized resistance. After an all-night poker game in which a portion of the winnings went to the defense fund for the soon-to-be-executed Wobbly bard Joe Hill and the losers were treated to breakfast, Saunders's initial suspicion of Kelly and Big Ace gave way to a mutual "let alone" policy. Saunders knew that Big Ace's gang was robbing freight trains, but he did nothing to stop them.[43]

Later that fall, Saunders and his partner "Shorty" met up with a fellow Wobbly named "Blackie" when the three were in the Spokane jail during the free speech fight there. Saunders had met Blackie before but had not known he was an IWW member. When they were released at the conclusion of the free speech fight, Saunders chaired a joint Socialist party–IWW celebration meeting, and afterwards the three hungry and broke men traveled by freight train to Seattle. Arriving on Thanksgiving Day, they begged enough for a meal and then visited the IWW Hall, where they ran into Kelly and Big Ace, the hijackers from North Dakota. Blackie soon convinced Shorty and Saunders to participate in a burglary he had planned. "Just a suit of clothes for each of us. And a pair of overalls, and a jumper to wear over the suit to keep it clean. And a new pair of shoes, and a hat, and some underwear, and a Mackinaw, and any money that might be in the till," Saunders wrote of their aims. But when they arrived at the store, they noticed it was equipped with an alarm and decided to call off the robbery. This was a major turning point in Saunders's young life. "It was with a feeling of relief that I found that we were not going through with the job. I realized then the direction in which I had been drifting. Condoning the robberies of Kelly and Big Ace. And now almost taking part in one myself. . . . For the first time in my life I took a long, hard, look at myself. I was an adult. I was twenty-two." He explained his thoughts to his partners, and found that Shorty agreed. They were "determined not to be drawn into anything of the sort again."

Although Blackie ridiculed his erstwhile partners in crime, saying they "were going soft, or going crazy," Saunders made good on his pledge to stay out of trouble.[44] But his experiences suggest the need to move beyond "rough culture" as an analytical frame. Although gambling, drinking, and fighting were ever-present for young men who sought out work and adventure in the West and easily identified with masculinity, we should also consider their experiences that were rough but not usually considered part of manliness. Transient laborers suffered hunger, cold, heat, and sickness, as well as dismemberment and death. At times they were lonely or ashamed of what they perceived as their own failure in life. Reflecting on his first reading of Henry McGuckin's autobiographical manuscript, the IWW leader Fred Thompson wrote that support for the union among nonmember laborers sprang "from a consciousness of kind born, not of books, but of the very unpleasant sense of singularity when on a summer day one walks through a small town with a winter overcoat over one arm, knowing he will need it to keep warm that night, even though it marks him as a pesky go-about meanwhile." Thompson noted that these nonmember supporters knew that if the IWW lost their fight, "they and their kind would have to mope and move furtively, ashamed, expecting harassment wherever they went."[45]

Although we encounter these experiences through words alone, for laborers they were both corporeal and cultural. Consider, for instance, the central role of the gastrointestinal system in laborers' worldview. Hunger was enough of an issue for them that they coined the term "stomach-robber" to refer to a low-wage employer. As Robert Saunders noted, "Hungry men have food on their minds," and whenever hoboes gathered each had a story that began with a "brief and sketchy description of the circumstances under which the meal was obtained, then a long, complete, detailed, and drooling description of each item of the food. And the stories always ended—'and three cups of coffee.'" Or consider the description of the afterlife offered in the song "The Big Rock Candy Mountain": no police, good weather, no need to change your socks, and a land overflowing with food, liquor, and cigarettes. For hoboes, these references were not abstract. After participating in a free speech fight in Aberdeen, Washington, Henry McGuckin passed out in a doctor's office and was hospitalized five days for malnutrition. The cure was simply to stay in bed and eat all that he wanted. Similarly, Saunders drifted toward committing a burglary no doubt in part because he was hungry and bitter. In Spokane he had chaired a public meeting while nearly "fainting from hunger." He and his partners left town because, as he recalled, "I had gained some publicity, and was ashamed to beg for fear that I might be recognized." At other times Saunders, like many laborers, suffered from dysentery. Spoiled food from inexpensive restaurants and cookhouses and bad water supplies usually were the culprits. But whatever the cause, dysentery left Saunders and other sufferers physically weakened and forced to defecate in boxcars, railyards, and other unsanitary and embarrassing locations.[46]

Len De Caux recalled similar moments of physical deprivation. In one incident, he entered a diner in a small North Dakota town after hiking all day in search of work. He had not eaten in two days and had only two cents to his name. In the diner, he showed his pennies and asked for bread and water. "The waitress gave me an already filled glass of lukewarm water. I didn't look at it—just poured the water down my parched throat. Halfway my glance caught something black in the glass. It was a dead fly. I didn't, couldn't stop."[47] A few years later he arrived in Chicago similarly "dirty and hungry." Outside a cheap diner he saw a "dishwasher wanted" sign, so he entered and took the job. It was unbearable: "the grease, the filth, the stench, the sweat, the piling pressure" made him want to "go berserk." He managed to keep working until it was time for his free meal, and having eaten his fill he took off his apron and walked out, the manager shaking his fist and cursing him as he rushed away.[48]

❖ ❖ ❖

Progressive Era reformers and some historians consistently connect these physical experiences of class to individual degradation, but the laborers who had the experiences needed to find a way to reinterpret them more positively or to situate them within a broader understanding of where the world was heading. Consider the following passage from Len De Caux's memoir, in which he recalls a night in a Chicago lodging house where the thin partitions and chicken-wire ceilings made it difficult to sleep amid the cacophony of bodily necessities:

> Instead of sheep, I counted the shufflings, mutterings, cussings, as each cubicle was occupied. In this tune-up, I noted the remarkable acoustics of the big hall's thinly tintinnabulating partitions.
>
> The symphony began. It started pianissimo with the winds—belches, groans, farts, incipient snores. It rose in a crescendo of tubercular coughing, bibulous slurping, snorting and snoring, a vomit, and many-stringed cot-creaking. After a climax of nightmare yells, partitions-pounding, and cries of protest, a brief intermission called by the night clerk. Then on again, till dawn's early light brought the quiet of windless exhaustion.

Although De Caux's colorful vocabulary reveals more about his middle-class family background than his years as a laborer and union organizer, it nonetheless runs counter to the tendency of most middle-class observers to compare even the most benign aspects of migrant life with animals, disease, and disaster. Instead, De Caux compares the misery of the nighttime lodging house to a symphony orchestra and at the same time brilliantly conveys the comedic, the ridiculous, the disgusting, and the enervating aspects of migrant life.[49]

Investigators identified bad conditions with degradation because they ignored or underestimated the importance of the working-class cultural milieu. In part, they failed to see the importance of family networks that laborers relied on in tough times. But they also underrated the power of a broadly populist intellectual subculture as a basis for alternative interpretations of working-class existence. Moreover, investigators rarely took hobo intellectual life seriously because they could not agree with its radical tone. Josiah Flynt noted the keen interest of tramps in all kinds of reading material, especially dime novels and books on political and economic topics. They would use the latter at their "hang out conferences," where they competed to offer the most compelling social analysis. According to Flynt, they liked "any book . . . which 'shows up' what the tramps consider the unreasonable inequalities in our social conditions." Flynt saw these debates as self-serving escapism on the part of men who wanted to blame society for their condition. However, laborers' memories of their coming to intellectual maturity through the IWW and other radical movements suggests a more authentic engagement with ideas. Thomas Bogard linked his radicalism to his early reading of Terence Powderly's *Thirty Years of Labor* and the popular socialist weekly *Appeal to Reason,* along with stories about the Knights of Labor told by his first employer. Although Vincent Dunne left school at fourteen to work as a lumberjack and harvest hand, later he was befriended and tutored by a fellow radical worker with a large private library. Laborers of Finnish background recalled the extensive Finnish socialist and religious press. And laborers of varied backgrounds read—and often wrote letters to—the *International Socialist Review* and the IWW's newspapers *Solidarity* and *Industrial Worker.*[50]

Given their frequent unemployment, laborers had plenty of time on their hands, and many of them used that time to read and talk. The Chicago hobo bookstore owner Daniel Horsely guessed that at least half of the migrant workers were avid readers. Generally, they favored "liberal, free thought and radical" magazines, scientific works, and realistic fiction, in addition to newspapers and whatever they could acquire with their limited means. Magazines such as the *International Socialist Review* were intended to meet these needs and interests as well as promote socialism. Published by Chicago's Charles H. Kerr Company until federal officials denied them access to the mails during World War I, the *Review* featured well-illustrated, brief articles on politics, world geography, and literature. Likewise, the Haldeman-Julius Publishing Company offered pocket-sized books for five cents each through the Little Blue Book series. Among the nearly one thousand titles in print by 1929 were works of European literature and drama (Balzac, Tolstoy, Wilde, Ibsen, Shakespeare); popular histories, political tracts, and works of science and religion; treatises on marriage, fascism, and sexuality; and how-to books on gardening, home ownership, psychoanalysis, and hypnosis. The Haldeman-Julius books were an inspiration to such budding worker-intellectuals as Jack Conroy and Harry Haywood. Conroy eventually started his own magazine of literature, *The Anvil,* which published unknown midwestern authors including Richard Wright and Nelson Algren. Haywood became a Communist party organizer. He began his education reading Kerr and Haldeman-Julius books that prepared him to read Darwin, "armed with a dictionary." Other workers took part in radical or trade union educational programs that drew on the abundant and inexpensive output of these populist publishers. The hobo colleges and open forums of Chicago, the IWW-affiliated Work People's College in Duluth, and other loosely organized institutions provided a rough, class-conscious education for laborers.[51]

Like many other men, Robert Saunders considered his connection to the Wobblies in a positive light, despite his brush with crime. Unable to go to school steadily as a child because his family moved so often, Saunders used his time on the road to acquire the beginnings of an education and a lifelong thirst for reading. He found his books in public libraries, at rescue missions, in IWW halls, and in prison libraries. "To a green horn, like me," Saunders wrote, "the conversations in the jungles was interesting, colorful, and informative. Among the 'boes I met more men who thought in abstract terms than in any other group that I have been thrown with in all of my life."[52] Another laborer, Jack Miller, recalled, "If it had not been for my contact with the IWW and what I gained from them, I would have probably become a criminal. . . . Like many migratory workers, I had left the mill of religion behind me. I couldn't even be threatened with hell. I had no respect for institutions, because I saw how they worked. I had no way to evolve a sense of values that would make me a social being." Similarly, Philip Taft recalled that the presence of an IWW hall in a town "meant that you could talk to someone, and that you didn't have to go into the Skid Row bar. A hall meant that you could read." For one Mexican worker, Primo Tapia, the IWW was an ideological home away from home during his ten-year sojourn working in the U.S. mining, sugar beet, railroad, and wheat industries. Anthropologist Paul Friedrich argues that his contact with the Wobblies equipped him with the skills necessary to become a leader of his community upon his return to Mexico in 1920.[53]

Amid this intellectual atmosphere the IWW fashioned its particular response to laborers' conditions. Whereas the dominant culture described laboring men, their rough bachelor culture, the spaces they inhabited, and their very bodies as pathological, broken, and beyond the margins of community, Wobblies refashioned laborers' bodies, actions, and places into manly sites of rebellion that defined their own community. They often portrayed this newly fashioned man in the most masculinist terms, muscular and alone, perhaps with intentional homoerotic appeal (see figures 16 and 17). But they might also depict their struggle with less decisive masculinism. For instance, a mural in

Figure 16. Radicals often depicted laborers as single, muscular men. From the *International Socialist Review* 16 (August 1915). Courtesy of the Newberry Library, Chicago.

Figure 17. This IWW organizing pamphlet, c. 1922, speaks to the harvest hands out to make a winter stake. Courtesy of the Walter Reuther Library, Wayne State University, Detroit.

the Duluth IWW hall rendered the weight of the industrial cityscape balancing on the shoulders of a human figure of ambiguous gender crouching beside a wooded river bank. Is this a world divided between a romanticized feminine nature and its masculine opposite, industry? Should Wobbly men see themselves as restoring the natural world by casting off the contamination of capitalism? Or perhaps the mural signals the indeterminate nature of the struggle, for it is not clear whether the human figure is casting off the weight of modernity, supporting it, or being crushed by it (see figure 18).[54]

The Wobbly discourse on work and manliness also reveals a complicated and contradictory picture that outlines both manly behavior and its negative. For the Wobblies, manliness was opposed not only to effeminacy but also to lack of class consciousness. For instance, Ernest Riebe's cartoons about the exploits of "Mr. Block" made light of workers who rejected class organi-

Figure 18. Gust Hanula's mural in the Duluth, Minnesota, IWW Hall. Courtesy of the Walter Reuther Library, Wayne State University, Detroit.

zation. Mr. Block was the consummate fool, ever believing the platitudes of capitalist society even in the face of experience. Walker C. Smith, editor of the *Industrial Worker*, noted that Mr. Block was "representative of slaves who think in terms of their masters." Owning nothing, Mr. Block "speaks from the standpoint of the millionaire; he is patriotic without patrimony; he is a law-abiding outlaw; he boasts of 'our tremendous wheat exports,' yet has no bread on his table; he licks the hand that smites him and kisses the boot that kicks him; he is the personification of all that a worker should not be." Despite these harsh words, readers were supposed "to see their reflection" in Mr. Block because, according to Smith, "it is from the Blocks that we must recruit our forces to overthrow wage slavery."[55]

In the cartoon "Mr. Block: He Has Some Uplifting Done," we see Mr. Block as the object of charity workers' efforts (see figure 19). The cartoon opens with Block despondent, thinking of suicide and, perhaps, agreeing with the IWW. An upper-class woman sees him in this state and invites him to her "Uplift Club," where he is entered into the charity case files and given a package to take home, which he thinks contains food for his family. Mr. Block's faith in America is restored, only to be dashed again when upon opening the

MR. BLOCK

HE HAS SOME UPLIFTING DONE

Figure 19. "Mr. Block: He Has Some Uplifting Done." From Ernest Riebe, *Mr. Block: Twenty-four IWW Cartoons* (1913; Chicago: Charles H. Kerr, 1984). Used by permission of the Charles H. Kerr Publishing Company.

package before his wife and son he finds only a sign with healthy-minded statements. The enclosed letter reads, "The latest authorities on mental science say that suicide is caused by the wrong kind of living. We suggest you follow our health hint[s]," which include singing and smiling after breakfast, resting after dinner, and walking after supper. Mr. Block's son laments that he will have to pawn his scout uniform to buy food, and Mrs. Block shows her displeasure by breaking the sign over her husband's head.[56]

Riebe pokes fun at workers with middle-class pretensions by attacking their manliness. Block cannot support his family, and he is a fool who does not know his own interests. Other Mr. Block cartoons focused on workers' individualism as the cause for their woes, and almost every one ends with Block being hit over the head or painfully realizing the error of his ways. According to Smith, the point was "to weaken the foundation [of capitalism] by joking some knowledge into those Blocks which have been split open a trifle in the College of Hard Knocks." Given the physical deprivation of laborers' experiences, we can guess that Mr. Block's "hard knocks" would have resonated with readers as more than a figure of speech. Invited to see their reflection in the negative example of the blockhead, readers were expected to understand the lesson: Solidarity is more manly than individualism. However, as is often the case in Riebe's cartoons, it is Mrs. Block who must drive home the ideological lesson, suggesting the ambivalent role of women in the manly culture of the IWW.

In their cartoons, letters, speeches, and memoirs, radicals sought to counter the widespread perception of laborers as pathological outcasts. In other words, they tried to redraw the image of the floating laborer and redefine the social practices associated with laborers in a positive light. This process was especially visible when radical laborers wrote about the value of a job. Whereas investigators focused on laborers' slow pace at work or tendency to roam from job to job, laborers celebrated the hobo tendency to quit and roam as a measure of independence from the boss. For instance, T-Bone Slim wryly noted that there was no need to worry about being fired from any particular job because "there are 2,000,000 bosses waiting with power to hire me as soon as I am at liberty." At that rate, Slim joked, a working man would never run out of bosses. Indeed he calculated that if he were fired "twice per day I'll be 2,739 years old when the last pair of bosses request my resignation."[57] Alternatively, workers could hope for a future with less work. James Cole, a laborer from Indiana, wrote to the *International Socialist Review* that his boss had purchased a "steam dipper" for digging trenches. "Using this machine three men and one boy perform the work of 50 teams and 100 men and do it better." Along with his subscription request Cole sent a photograph of the device, which the magazine reprinted, and noted that "in the good days a-coming the world's work will be done by machinery used and owned by the working class for the BENEFIT of the worker. No one will have to work more than two or three hours a day and all the good things of life will be ours to enjoy" (see figure 20)."[58] How distant this was from the investigator Whiting Williams's belief that the workers' utopia consisted of "a job for everyman, everyday." This dream of a world with less work—as opposed to steady work, or even the traditional socialist vision of ennobled work—was a popular one for men and women who worked hard for little reward.

Of course, not all laboring men shared these radical visions. However, their experiences demonstrated to them that most jobs and most bosses were the same and that no particular job was worth holding at all costs. For instance, a Belgian laborer told Nels Anderson that he refused to work on railroad extra gangs because "they don't treat a man like a man. They treat him like a slave." Yet despite this Wobbly-esque analysis, he declined the offer of a radical newspaper, telling Anderson that nothing would change. Anderson concluded that "he does not seem like a radical."[59] There were good jobs and bad

Figure 20. "The New Ditch Diggers." From the *International Socialist Review* 15 (December 1914). Courtesy of the Newberry Library, Chicago.

jobs, but they were jobs all the same. In times of economic depression, laborers clung to whatever job they could find. To keep a job or to avoid vagrancy arrest, laborers learned to cheerfully agree to the demands of bosses and police and then do as they pleased after the authorities had gone. As Len De Caux learned from the Italian laborers at his first job on a railroad construction crew, "Bosses demanded you both obey . . . and like it."[60] Workers nurtured their revenge in plans to use "short shovels," that is, to reduce their own efficiency. Most workers knew that it was all too easy to work oneself out of a job, so they adhered to T-Bone Slim's aphorism, "half a loaf is better than no loafing at all."[61] Wobblies spoke boldly of making this kind of behavior more overtly political, and when possible they acted on their sentiments. During periods of labor surplus, however, laborers' "manly bearing toward the boss" went underground because most recognized that openly confronting an abusive boss was job suicide. When the labor market was tight, laborers could more easily say "to hell with the boss," and when they did they usually just walked off the job, alone or in groups, leaving their boss short-handed.

Delving into the thinking of people who left few records is a risky business. Much of what we know about laborers in North America's seasonal industries comes from middle-class social investigators. As I have argued in other sections of this book, we must approach these sources not only as reflections of lived experience but also as representations of a contested social order. Memoirists were also part of this contest. Because they lived the life stories that social investigators told, their narratives are both engagements in old fights and part of the historians' storytelling repertoire. They reveal a shadow world within the radical coming-of-age story where crime and violence were tolerated and sometimes promoted. But they also help us understand what Alice Solenberger called "the philosophy" of seasonal laborers, and they explain why a man might quit a job when he made his stake, not out of laziness but out of a sense of obligation to the unemployed and a desire to escape the tedium of work.

Memoirists also help us understand the physicality of solidarity and deprivation. The historical record rarely gives us a laborer's whole life but regularly gives us bodies and minds broken by trains, guns, and loneliness. It is all too easy to leave these injuries in the realm of statistical or anecdotal abstraction, one more case illustrating the exploitation of a marginal social group. Reading laborers' memoirs side by side with social investigators' case studies, I am struck by the intense interaction of experiences of class in the body and in the mind. Whether their hard knocks came from dizzying hunger or the "very unpleasant sense of singularity" travelers experienced in a hostile small town, the abstract boundaries we think of as social class were lived by individuals as assaults on their whole personhood. The education that seasonal laborers received on the road was a varied and contradictory one, but it was deeply connected to laborers' sense of manhood and community. The culture in which these men came of age was held together by a tenuous ethic of mutuality. It was tenuous because poverty and marginality demanded that it be so. But without transient mutuality, individuality itself was much more difficult to maintain. Some took from this experience the lesson that society valued the ability to make victims of other people. Many others fashioned more sustainable lives out of the broken experiences of the road.

NOTES

1. Hapgood, *Spirit of Labor,* 34. See also Hapgood, *A Victorian in the Modern World.*

2. Hapgood, *Spirit of Labor,* 103. Sandburg, "The Dynamiter," *Collected Poems,* 21; Reitman, "Life among the Outcasts," 339, Charles Kerr Company Archives, Newberry Library, Chicago.

3. Verdict of Jury, Testimony of Ethan Young, W. G. Campbell, B. C. Wilds, W. D. Haldeman, Louis Young, and R. D. Twaddle: Coroner's Inquest upon the Body of Earl Coole, Case #43, Mellette, Spink County, South Dakota. Because Campbell and Wilds had two jugs, it is possible that one of the jugs contained pure alcohol and the other the diluted solution. Robert Saunders wrote that many alcoholics drank laboratory alcohol diluted with water, a mixture known as "white mule" or "white line." See Saunders, "The Road," 137, WHMC, St. Louis. Investigators in North Dakota found inexpensive alcohol available in the form of "lemon extract," which they reported as 85–95 percent alcohol; see "Report of George Kreil," 8 August 1919 (F. L. Watkins to William Langer), William Langer Papers, University of North Dakota.

4. Way, "Labour's Love Lost," 21–22.

5. Shor, "'Virile Syndicalism,'" 65–77; Shor, "Masculine Power and Virile Syndicalism," 83–99; Fairbanks, "Fifty-Thousand Lumberjacks and the Rebel Girl," paper presented at 1996 North American Labor History Conference.

6. Sandburg, *Always the Young Strangers,* 391; Interview of Vincent Raymond Dunne by Lila Johnson Goff, 17 April 1969, 11, MHS; see also Saunders, "The Road," 124, 147, WHMC, St. Louis.

7. Conversations with historian Tapio Bergholm from the University of Helsinki, Finland have helped me clarify this idea.

8. Denning, *Mechanic Accents,* 1–5, 65–84; Scott, "Evidence of Experience," 773–75. Many of the oral histories that I draw on were collected by the Twentieth-Century Radicalism in Minnesota Project; see Ross, *Radicalism in Minnesota.* Similarly, this study would have been much more difficult without the publication of autobiographies, reprinted editions of earlier radical works, and the historical recovery work

of Franklin and Penelope Rosemont at the Charles H. Kerr Company. See also Maynes, *Taking the Hard Road.*

9. *IWW Songs,* 54. A "shack" is a railroad detective. T-Bone Slim was the moniker for Matt Valentine Huhta, a Finnish-American hobo intellectual. See Rosemont, *Juice Is Stranger Than Friction,* 7–14.

10. Chaplin, *Wobbly,* 87, 89. Compare the "Life Story of Joseph Burke," Peter Speek "Case 3," and William Duffus "Case 1" in *USCIR Unpublished Papers.* Chaplin was the author of a much more famous IWW song, "Solidarity Forever," which has since become a mainstream labor anthem.

11. Chaplin, *Wobbly,* 91–92.

12. McGuckin, *Memoirs of a Wobbly,* 10–13. See also Life Story of Raymond Harvey, *USCIR Unpublished Papers;* Brown, *Brownie the Boomer,* 7–13.

13. McGuckin, *Memoirs of a Wobbly,* 35–40, 87.

14. Bogard Autobiography, 1–2, WSHS.

15. Ibid., 1–3.

16. Ibid., 4–10.

17. Interview with Walter Harju, 1977, MHS.

18. Compare the coming-to-radical-awareness narrative of the immigrant laborer in Nelson, Barrett, and Ruck, *Steve Nelson,* 15–16. Other examples of seasonal or migrant work as a kind of rite of passage include Jack Maloney (harvester and teamster, involved in 1934 Teamsters' strike), Patrick McMillen (railroad, coal dock worker, sailor, professional wrestler), and the interview with Frank Ellis, MHS; Powers Hapgood, "Journal," [1920], Powers Hapgood Papers, Lilly Library, Indiana University; Douglas, *Go East, Young Man* (in which the Supreme Court justice recounts his time wheat harvesting in Washington state and comments favorably on his IWW fellow workers); Ashleigh, *Rambling Kid,* especially part three; Reitman, "Following the Monkey," undated manuscript in Ben L. Reitman Papers, Manuscripts Collection, University of Illinois at Chicago; Hak, "The Harvest Excursion Adventure," 247–65.

19. Saunders, "The Road," 13.

20. Ibid., 32–34.

21. Ibid., 47.

22. Devich, "My Memoirs," IHRC; Brown, *Brownie the Boomer;* Anderson, *American Hobo;* Flynt, *My Life.*

23. Smith, "The Minnesota Lumberjack," 3; Woodward, *Checkered Years,* 184; Johnson, "Bulls, Bears, and Dancing Boys," 4–37.

24. McGuckin, *Memoirs of a Wobbly,* 16, 55–56, 59.

25. Neufeld, "Portrait of the Labor Historian," 62–63.

26. In his study of nineteenth-century sexuality, D. Michael Quinn identifies a widespread "homocultural orientation" that valued intense same-sex relationship, recognized the homoerotic potential of these relationships, but placed strict taboos on homosexuality. Quinn, *Same-Sex Dynamics,* 1–2, 156–59, 401–3.

27. Meyerowitz, *Women Adrift,* 110–13, Cressy, *The Taxi-Dance Hall,* 121–23; Saunders, "The Road," 71–72, WHMC, St. Louis; Montgomery, *Fall of the House of Labor,* 89–90; Peck, *Reinventing Free Labor,* 139–40.

28. Chaplin, *Wobbly,* 88–89.

29. Saunders, "The Road," 123.

30. Brown, *Brownie the Boomer,* 22–23.

31. Chief of Special Agents Records, NP Records, MHS; E. C. Lindley to R. A. Jackson, 19 August 1914; E. C. Lindley to C. J. Murphy, 11 August 1914; General Superintendent to J. M. Gruber, 26 August 1914; Great Northern Railway Company Records, VP-Operating: VP and General Manager Subject Files: Hoboes, Tramps and Bums (IWW), Box 5. In these particular cases local residents in North Dakota brought suit against railroad employees for assaulting transients. Regular hi-jacks who were not railroad employees also threw men off moving trains, a process known as "greasing the wheels." See Bird et al., *Solidarity Forever,* 46.

32. Spink County, South Dakota, Coroner's Inquest over the Body of Bert Hunt, 11 July 1907; Brown County, South Dakota, Inquest Record, vol. 1, pp. 32, 37, 98.

33. Chaplin, *Wobbly,* 89.

34. McGuckin, *Memoirs of a Wobbly,* 73–74.

35. Bird et al., *Solidarity Forever,* 46.

36. "Solidarity Wins All the Time," *Solidarity,* 4 September 1915, 3. See also *Sioux City Journal* 21 July 1916, 9; 22 July 1916, 1; Bogard Autobiography, 158, 189–92, WSHS.

37. *Solidarity,* 24 October 1914, 1; McMullin to Leach, 3 October 1914, and Bergin to Leach, 4 October 1914, GN Railway Co., Vice President—Operating: VP and Gen. Mgr. Subject Files: "Hoboes, Tramps and Bums." The latter two sources corroborate the IWW press committee report on the incident, but from the perspective of the Great Northern employees.

38. Bird et al., *Solidarity Forever,* 38–39.

39. Brazier, "When You Wear That Button," *IWW Songs,* 41.

40. *Mitchell, South Dakota, Daily Republican,* 25 July 1916, 4; Brazier, "When You Wear That Button," in *IWW Songs,* 41.

41. McGuckin, *Memoirs of a Wobbly,* 87.

42. Ibid., 83–84, 87.

43. Saunders, "The Road," 123–29, WHMC. See also "Hi-Jacks, Boot-Leggers, Holdups, Gamblers, Etc., in the Harvest Fields. Warning to You," IWW pamphlet, n.d. (probably 1916), IWW Collection, Box 163, Walter Reuther Archives. Gambs, *Decline of the IWW,* 92, states that several former Wobblies had become bootleggers and labor racketeers, but his sources on this may be former Wobblies who became Communist party members and therefore had an interest in discrediting the IWW. See also Frankel, "Report on Labor Disturbances in Northern Minnesota, December 1919 to January 1920," MHS, which claims that Wobblies were working as bootleggers and gamblers and that prostitutes were signing their clients up with the IWW. The 1921 AWIU Convention had to remind members and officers that union bylaws provided for the expulsion of officials found intoxicated or gambling and members found bootlegging liquor. See AWIU Convention Minutes, 1921, 9, Box 44, IWW Collection, Walter Reuther Library.

44. Saunders, "The Road," 134, WHMC.

45. Fred Thompson to Henry McGuckin, Jr., June 10, 1974, Charles H. Kerr Company Records, Box 7, Newberry Library, Chicago.

46. Rammel, *Nowhere in America,* 104–7; Saunders, "The Road," 54–55, 66–67, 79–80, 134, WHMC; McGuckin, *Memoirs of a Wobbly,* 38–39.

47. De Caux, *Labor Radical,* 60.

48. Ibid., 89.

49. Ibid., 56. See also the description of Kansas City's Helping Hand Mission in Brown, "*Broke*," 76–78: "The odor of the hundred unwashed bodies was nauseating. There was the usual consumptive and asthmatic coughing, and the expectoration upon the floor; there were no cuspidors, and the air was stifling." Compared with Walter Wyckoff's description of his night in the Chicago police station (see chapter 2), DeCaux's and Brown's accounts are both more detailed and less condescending toward homeless men. See Wyckoff, *The Workers, the West,* 38–39.

50. Flynt, *Notes of an Itinerant Policeman,* 216–17; Bogard Autobiography, 1–2, WSHS; Interview with Vincent Dunne by Lila Johnson Goff, 4, 14–15, MHS; Walker, *American City,* 193, reports that the Dunne brothers were expelled from Catholic school when the priest caught the oldest brother reading aloud to other boys from a Victor Hugo novel; Interview with Raymond Wright by Carl Ross, 1992, p. 35, Radicalism in Minnesota Project, MHS.

51. Daniel Horsley, "What the Hobo Reads," Anderson Document 150, 1–6, Burgess Papers; Ruff, "*We Called Each Other Comrade,*" 160–75, 201–6; Mordell, *The World of Haldeman-Julius,* 5–7; Haywood, *Black Bolshevik,* 96–101; Wixson, *Worker-Writer in America,* 186–208; Thompson and Murfin, *The I.W.W.,* 101, 151; Fagin, *Public Forums in Chicago,* 31–47.

52. Saunders, "The Road, 54, WHMC.

53. Bird et al., *Solidarity Forever,* 40; Neufeld, "Portrait of the Labor Historian," 67–68. Friedrich, *Agrarian Revolt,* 67–70.

54. "Harvest Time Is Honey Time," IWW Collection, Walter Reuther Archives, Wayne State University. On the gendered iconography of the IWW see Faue, *Community of Suffering and Struggle,* 69–99; Fairbanks, "Fifty-Thousand Lumberjacks and the Rebel Girl," paper presented at 1996 North American Labor History Conference. IWW Mural, "From original painting by IWW artist, painting in hall at Duluth. Painted by Gust Hannula," IWW Collection, Walter Reuther Archives.

55. Smith, "Introductory," in Riebe, *Mr. Block,* 10.

56. Riebe, *Mr. Block,* n.p.

57. Rosemont, *Juice Is Stranger Than Friction,* 45.

58. "The New Ditch Diggers," *ISR* 15 (December 1914): 381; Webb, *The Migratory-Casual Worker,* 99–100.

59. Anderson Document 11, Burgess Papers.

60. De Caux, *Labor Radical,* 45.

61. Rosemont, *Juice Is Stranger Than Friction,* 153. See also Mathewson, *Restriction of Output among Unorganized Workers.*

❖

CONCLUSION

ON A SUMMER DAY IN 1921, U.S. Department of Agriculture economist Don Lescohier was shocked to meet a self-educated hobo. "I talked with this man Doyle for more than four hours," Lescohier wrote in his notes, "and found him one of the brainiest and most thoroughly read in his line of any man I have ever met." Originally from Ireland, Doyle came to the United States around 1895. Since the turn of the century he had followed the yearly wheat harvest from Texas to Canada. "He has been all around the earth several times," Lescohier noted, "visited every important port and interior city in South America, every important city in Europe and on this continent." Lescohier was frankly astonished at Doyle's wide-ranging knowledge of economics, history, and politics. "I drew him, or rather he drew me, into an economic discussion. This hobo, this bum, this chap *who had never been inside of a school* . . . knew the classical economists well and quoted readily from Ricardo and Adam Smith" as well as Marx and a host of contemporary economists. Lescohier quibbled with Doyle's Marxian analysis but found that the laborer's knowledge of current politics "made [him] ashamed of [his] own ignorance."[1]

A Bolshevik and a Wobbly, Doyle was earning his stake in 1921 so he could enroll in a course with the socialist economist Scott Nearing at the Rand School of Economics in New York. Like many other self-taught, working-class radicals who looked forward to a coming social revolution, Doyle was preparing for what he considered the inevitable "supremacy of the proletariat." The university-trained Lescohier could not agree with the politics of men such as Doyle and other Wobblies, but he recognized in them something special. "The 'Red' is on a higher social level than the unorganized hobo," Lescohier later wrote in *Harper's Monthly Magazine.* "He respects himself, he makes claims for himself, he fights for social justice. However erroneous his theories, he plays a man's part."[2]

For middle-class investigators, the existence of self-educated workers such as Doyle threw the world of labor into a different light. Lescohier's shock that a man who had not been inside a schoolhouse might know more about the world than a college professor illuminates both the class divide and the role of gender in articulating and bridging class worlds. Central to the investigator's manhood were his sense of mastery over the social world in terms of scholarly learning and his advocacy for social justice through reform organizations. Middle-class investigators and audiences assumed these were beyond the capacity of workers, and especially transient laborers. For Lescohier, meeting Doyle undermined all of this. Middle-class men had often realized that working men were more "masculine" in the sense that they were less refined. But an educated worker might also be "manly," that is, knowledgeable about the world, self-respecting, and working for social justice. Certainly, the fate of capitalism was challenged more by the intellectual hobo than by the working-class tough or the degraded floating laborer.

Laboring men pushed against the roles society laid out for them, driving ideas about reform through their own actions and in the ways middle-class reformers interpreted their lives. Until the twentieth century, seasonal laborers appeared in mainstream discourse as "tramps," men who traveled about the country with no particular plan and no attachment to work. Increasingly, the tramp problem was linked to structural unemployment as social scientists moved closer to the analysis of labor radicals who argued that industrial capitalism necessitated a certain amount of unemployment. Nevertheless, the footloose ways of the seasonal laborer remained a focus of investigation, and social scientists generally agreed that there was something wrong with these men. The tramp problem quickly merged into the problems of unemployment, labor turnover, and floating labor. Together with concern about monopoly control of the economy and the chaotic nature of industrialism, these "labor problems" were part of a powerful complex of social fears that called for greater scientific understanding and control of social relations.[3]

The existence of floating laborers also highlighted the shifting linkages between rural and urban life. Between 1870 and 1930, historian Hal Barron argues, northern rural communities experienced the "Second Great Transformation" as rural life was increasingly integrated in the emerging urban, corporate, and state-centered society. During this period, rural people sought to preserve their local communities and use modern society to their own ends. The so-called parity years between 1900 and 1920, when prices of farm products were roughly equal to those of manufactured goods, stimulated agricultural expansion and farm family consumerism. Automobiles and radios eased the isolation of farm life and helped strengthen local community ties by making visiting easier and connecting families to a wider rural community. As the cost of maintaining a farm business increased, farm laboring became a less viable pathway to farm ownership, and marginal farms failed in increasing numbers. But this process took some time, and those living through changes often hoped to retain their connection to rural life. Families abandoning farming often migrated only as far as the nearest city, where family members could piece together a living through various urban and rural seasonal jobs. Many young men from these families could travel widely in search of jobs in railroad construction, logging, and agriculture, where they worked side by side with men from cities. Along with their sisters, they were expected to send money home to "raise the household" as Vincent Dunne put it, that is, to support their parents and younger siblings.[4]

The disruption of the World War I years marked the beginning of a reorientation of these labor markets. Farm wages did not bounce back as fast as urban wages from their collapse during the postwar depression and remained much lower than industrial wages throughout the rest of the twentieth century. It is not clear whether this was because low commodity prices undermined farmers' ability to pay or because of the suppression of rural and urban worker organizations that had demanded higher wages. Both trends probably influenced rural wages in the 1920s and 1930s. As opportunities for rural industrial employment declined because of mechanization, exhaustion of natural resources, and the waning of the railroad construction boom, workers had fewer opportunities to shift between rural and urban areas. The exception to this trend was the emerging sugar beet industry. This capital-intensive industry, supported by government tariffs and research, began around 1900 and spread to Minnesota, North Dakota, and eastern Colorado from 1910 through the 1920s. Although beet farmers, especially those in Michigan, initially drew on the urban poor, women, and children to tend their crops, by the 1920s beet labor was synonymous with Mexican immigrants and Mexican-American migrants. The large sugar-refining corporations contracted and provisioned these workers, often in family groups. Although some of these workers filtered into the farm work sector familiar to earlier immigrants to the region, historians suggest that they were more likely to use beet work as an avenue toward better-paying urban industrial jobs.[5]

While rural industrial job opportunities in the region were in decline, large urban employers, having successfully shut out union regulation of work, moved to stabilize the labor market. High labor turnover cut into profits by increasing training costs, but it also undermined workers' "spirit of loyalty to the management," as one personnel executive argued.[6] During the flush 1920s, many firms offered incentives ranging from cash bonuses to stock ownership and leisure activities to workers who stayed on the job. As a result, urban working-class communities developed greater stability and identification with the goals of consumer culture, as Lizabeth Cohen argues.[7] In this context there was less need to send members of the household into seasonal work. By the late 1920s, however, even this urban employment was declining in the upper Midwest. In contrast, the number of farm wage laborers continued to grow in Minnesota and North Dakota, probably as a result of urban unemployment. Given the choice between subsistence wages on the farm and no wages in the city, laborers appeared to choose the former. By the 1940s, however, drought and depression continued the trend toward a decline in the farm laboring population.[8]

When government investigators and progressive reformers spoke of the "problem of floating labor" they referred to more than the bad conditions laboring men experienced on work sites and in urban lodginghouse districts. Low wages, corrupt employment agents, and the destructive behavior of laborers themselves were the most visible problems. They also worried that laborers were perpetual outsiders, inevitably moving down the social scale from worker to hobo to tramp to bum, according to many investigators. Observers of many political orientations considered laborers "birds of passage," migrating from place to place as if by natural instinct, or worse, simply floating willy-nilly without a plan. But most floating laborers did not "float" at all. Their movements across the land were structured by the geography of job opportunity, by seasonal change, and by their connections to families and communities. Employers and their agents had an interest in maintaining the pattern of "floating" labor migration. The supposed anomie and the real invisibility of transient working men obscured the structures of the labor market, maintained the steady flow of fees for employment agents, and suppressed wages. Similarly, the sense that laborers were outside the boundaries of community with resident workers was reinforced by beating, deportation, and pervasive descriptions of laborers as degraded.

If laborers' status as perpetual outsiders was consistently reiterated by employers and resident workers, we should remember that seasonal laborers often chose their line of work. Admittedly, their choices were constrained by economic necessity, age, and other factors. Some took to the road to escape abusive parents, crimes committed, or families abandoned. But we should not discount that something about seasonal labor appealed to the "manhood in a man," as Anton Johannsen would say. For instance, when a hobo going by the name of Bill Quirke wrote to the *Hobo News* of his experience working in an ill-ventilated brush factory, he compared the "home guards" to "a dip candle that gutters along in smut and smoke until it eventually smothers in its own grease."[9] He preferred hoboing.

Laborers' efforts to cope with short-term work, low income, and marginalization from community power took organized and unorganized forms. They worked slowly, they quit swiftly, they relied on networks of mutuality between strangers on the road, and they acted together to force employers to pay a decent wage. Like their reasons for taking seasonal work, these forms of resistance were structured by economics and by notions of manly action. Laborers quit to protest injustices on the job ranging from the unfair firing of friends, to excessively close supervision, to bad food. They often characterized these varied injustices as violations of their manhood. Even the explicitly class-based protest of the IWW hinged on appeals to "be a man." Likewise, the rough culture laborers lived within or passed through constantly egged men on to prove their manhood through excessive drinking, fighting, gambling, and whoring. These were the destructive elements of the manly ethic, but they were not the only elements. Laboring men also valued temporary friendships and reveled in the opportunity to instruct neophytes in the ways of the road. I have called this "transient mutuality": an ethic of sharing among people who shared little or no affiliation other than being together and being in need. Of course, some men used their fast friends poorly. But most helped because they had been in need themselves and expected to be again. That laborers needed transient mutuality was both a mark of their marginalization and a means of transcending it. It facilitated their wide-ranging travels and demonstrated their need for social relations, solidarities, and dependence on other people to survive.

The encounter between investigator and laborer reflected the divide between class worlds and the fascination of the (mostly) male investigators with laboring men's masculinity. Laborers' rough ways seemed more vital despite the troubling, violent, and self-destructive elements. It is perhaps too easy to condemn these investigators who, after all, sought understanding in an era of conflict. To be sure, some deserve criticism. Investigators such as Walter

Wyckoff and Whiting Williams hoped to bridge the cultural misunderstandings between workers and managers, but their brief stints among the toilers left their opinions of social relations little changed. Williams, in particular, used his experience to further his career as a management consultant. Others, such as Edwin Brown and Peter Speek, had a better sense of the reality of laborers' lives and were part of sincere and profound reform efforts. My intent has not been to vilify all reform movements without distinction. Certainly, the USCIR was an unusually progressive force in American society. It is also worth noting that large government investigations such as the USCIR often put forward more than one message, especially at the level of internal reports. Although the USCIR structured its investigation in opposition to the IWW, for instance, the message that the IWW was the chosen union of many laborers came through clearly in life histories and affidavits. Similarly, although the President's Mediation Commission made common cause with military intelligence, employers, and the justice department to undermine IWW power in the West, one of its researchers, Thorstein Veblen, advocated cooperation with the IWW to ensure an adequate supply of farm labor.[10]

Seasonal laborers of the early twentieth century were a lightning rod for tensions over class, citizenship, and manhood because their existence disrupted widely accepted narratives about the character of American society. Most Americans wanted to believe that a man could rise from hired hand to independent farmer or could earn enough to support himself and a family. Yet as Peter Speek's life histories illustrated, hard work and determination were almost useless because bad conditions and the chaos of the labor market ensured that laborers inevitably moved downward on the social scale. Despite the ideological function of the focus on bad conditions, investigators reported on very real hardships. Laboring men did indeed experience hunger, cold, beatings, robbery, alcoholism, and other maladies. But did these experiences necessarily and wholly define laborers? Were laborers so oppressed as to lose their humanity? For some, the answer was certainly yes. They turned their anger and hurt to crime, murder, or self-destruction. But most found ways to "get by" amid the indignities, and many others were able to refocus their experiences in less destructive directions through community organizations, religion, and radicalism.

The history of the marginal hobo sheds a good deal of light on the dramas of the Progressive Era. As "floaters," "tramps," or "migratories," laborers working in seasonal industries were both real people and signifiers of abstract social problems. They could at once embody the decline of rural life, the need for state regulation of the economy, and the widening gulf between workers and the middle class. The downward mobility and radicalization of "white" farmhands were especially troubling for the mythology of middle America. Seasonal laborers were simply an extreme manifestation of what a growing number of Americans believed was a dysfunctional economy, and historians have inherited the results of these anxieties. Fear of the IWW floater often lurked behind sociological debates on high turnover and chronic unemployment among factory operatives, influencing research protocols and findings. Former laborers wrote their memoirs in response to this reform literature, hoping to balance out the prevalent images of hoboes and Wobblies as social derelicts beyond salvation. The task of the historian, however, is not simply to weigh the balance but also to read the social conflicts written into our assumptions about work, community, and citizenship.

Eighty years after Whiting Williams first put on overalls, a new fascination with hobo life percolates through American popular culture. Spurred on by a desire to "live off the grid," a new generation of middle-class adventurers has taken up freight train riding as a hobby. In part this trend takes off from a decades-long cultivation of folksy hobo culture among people who have experienced more or less brief stints on the road. There is a National Hobo Association with a Web site and a monthly newsletter, the *Hobo Times.* Several guidebooks offer suggestions on how to catch a freight train, what clothes to wear, and other details of the modern hobo life. These guidebooks also describe the dangers associated with the hobby, but just enough to offer a sensational thrill. Much as Allan Pinkerton celebrated tramping as a personally liberating experience in the 1870s, one manual notes that today's hoboes ride freights "because [they] have a ball and at the same time *beat the system in every way.* Riding the rails is the last pure red-blooded adventure in North America." What's more, the author assures his safely middle-class hobo audience, riding the rails is not just for bums: "All sorts of professional types do it for sport."[11]

Not surprisingly, middle-class would-be hoboes do not care to compare themselves to migrants along the U.S.-Mexico border who routinely hop rides on northbound freight trains. For labor organizers and community activists, however, few issues are more relevant today than the conditions of immigrant and contingent workers. Like their predecessors, today's unions struggle to square their traditional organizing tactics with new workplace realities and often find the traditions lacking. In today's contingent labor market, workers are less likely to have a strong association with one employer or industry. Like the "floaters" of the early twentieth century, contemporary workers slip in and out of the labor market as opportunities appear and necessities dictate.

The roots of labor's confusion and disorganization in the face of a changing workforce lie in modern conceptions of work and class that emerged in the post–World War II era. For the first time in American history powerful industrial unions and government commitment to full-employment policies instituted a measure of labor market regulation and helped to ensure that industrial workers could reasonably hope to have a steady job, for better or worse. Our image of "the working class" became associated with this particular historical and geographic juncture: urban, heavy industry, male breadwinners. This particular working class never represented the majority of working people, but it is a powerful legacy just the same. Even in that era of relative prosperity industrial labor markets were segmented by race, gender, and region. Technological change undermined the stability of many jobs in mining, railroad, and textile work. With the failure of industrial unionism in the South and its continuing weakness in less urbanized areas of the North and West, manufacturers spied an opportunity to find less expensive labor. The geographic reorientation of American industry southward and into the countryside began as early as the 1950s and was the quiet precursor to the flight of jobs abroad. Since the 1970s, inflation, global competition, and an employer-led antiunion drive have combined to undermine the heavy industries and their unions. For instance, meatpacking has shifted from an urban-centered, strongly unionized sector to a largely nonunion, rural industry.[12] In this context, labor markets reminiscent of the early twentieth century have reappeared.

At the base of many of these changes is a new management philosophy known as "just-in-time production" that seeks to maximize profits by limiting expenses on inventory, supply chain, and employees. Relying on the emerging global interconnection among suppliers, producers, and distributors, manufacturing employers strip down to what they consider "core" workers and processes. A smaller number of core workers are usually permanent and receive higher pay and full benefits, while noncore workers or processes can be spun off to subsidiary companies or wholly independent contractors. The automobile industry has been an important example of these trends. In the 1970s, the Big Three automakers produced most of the parts that went into their cars, and two-thirds of autoworkers were unionized. By 1990, 40 percent of autoworkers were "low wage," labor activists complained, up from 17 percent in 1975. In addition, by 1997 upwards of 70 percent of the components that went into Chrysler, Ford, and GM cars were made by contractors, many of whose workers were nonunion.[13]

Well-publicized strikes have drawn attention to contingent work, subcontracting, and stagnant wages. In the summer of 1997, the Teamsters Union went on strike against United Parcel Service, one of the largest private package delivery firms in the world. UPS had been making record profits and expanding its use of part-time workers. The union made full-time jobs the major issue of the strike, attracting a great deal of positive publicity. A public opinion polling executive noted that the UPS strike was "a consciousness-raising event. . . . an event like this suddenly and unexpectedly focuses attention on something that is on people's minds and makes their concerns more of a political issue." In settling the strike, UPS agreed to create 10,000 full-time jobs as well as limit the use of outside contractors.[14] Industrial outsourcing also has been at issue in several major strikes by the United Auto Workers, such as the unsuccessful six-year struggle at Caterpillar, and strikes against GM and various auto parts manufacturers. The reorganization of work scheduling has been another frontier of employer power and union resistance with long and bitter struggles by A. E. Staley and Bridgestone-Firestone workers in Decatur, Illinois. In both cases union defeat ushered in mandatory ten- and twelve-hour days and increased worker turnover.[15]

As work becomes less regulated by union and government intervention, employers are transforming the ideological balance between *security* and *opportunity* with unsure results for working people and the labor movement. Management rhetoric, of course, emphasizes the dynamic qualities of the new economy and the wonderful opportunities for economic improvement open to those who would work hard. The dynamism of the labor market may be alluring to younger workers; however, workers who expected to provide for their families on one income find the "opportunity" to piece together a household budget on multiple incomes less than satisfying. No doubt these labor market changes have fueled the political backlash among some white workers against efforts to gain equal workplace rights for women and African Americans.[16]

Also complicating assessments of the relative benefits and pitfalls of the contingent workforce is the presence of a range of workers under one category. "Contingent workers" include professionals and manual laborers, full-time workers and occasional workers out to make a little extra cash. The debate is often framed by the extremes. Among the fastest-growing sectors of market-mediated employment are the highly skilled computer, engineering, and educational professions in which workers have greater autonomy on the job and sometimes earn comfortable incomes. Although companies can exploit employees' nominal status as "contractors" to avoid providing benefits to otherwise long-term workers, highly skilled contract workers are often considered privileged because they can tailor work to the needs of family and social life.[17] At the other extreme of the symbolic social spectrum, so-called welfare mothers participate in "workfare" and "work experience" programs that place them as temporary employees. As in the case of New York City's Work Experience Program, these workers displace unionized city employees, are paid subminimum training wages, and are prohibited from unionizing. Because these workers have faced long-term dependence on government support, their transition into the labor market is celebrated as "liberating." For participants in these programs work is presented as an opportunity to escape dependence on government subsidies, even as changes in welfare law now mandate employment and restrict access to higher education.[18]

Between the well-paid professionals and the forced-to-work welfare recipients, contingent workers experience a great range of freedom and compulsion. These workers suffer the worst effects of the contingent labor market: inadequate pay, no benefits, and excessive payroll deductions. The Bureau of Labor Statistics estimated that in 1995 some 4.4 million workers with full-time jobs entered the temporary labor market to compensate for the low wages paid by their primary employers. These estimates do not include undocumented immigrant workers.[19] Many, if not most, temporary employment agencies cater to these low-wage workers rather than the higher-paid professionals, and unknown numbers of unregulated employment contractors operate from shopping mall parking lots and street corners. One rapidly-growing company is a good example of how today's employment agencies echo and surpass those of the hobo era. Labor Ready, Inc., frankly promotes itself as a service to companies that want to avoid hiring permanent workers. With its "work today–paid today" slogan the company also poses as a friend to underemployed workers who need cash in a hurry. With nearly eight hundred hiring halls in the United States, Puerto Rico, and the United Kingdom, Labor Ready claims to employ more than half a million workers per year and to bring in more than $900 million in revenue. Most of their clients are light manufacturing, construction, and warehouse employers. As with the employment agencies of the early twentieth century, Labor Ready's clientele includes stable workers looking for extra pay, those employed in seasonal industries, and homeless people, some facing drug and alcohol problems. In a notice to potential investors, Labor Ready emphasizes that its business is highly seasonal with peak periods in the spring, summer, and early fall. Resistant to unionization and able to increase its profits in a recession, Labor Ready is just one example of a company that is remaking labor relations in contemporary America. Other low-wage employers like Wal-Mart have developed elaborate personnel policies to keep unions out of the workplace.[20]

Alice Solenberger's "Irishman" and Don Lescohier's "Doyle" would have found these developments all too familiar. Although the language has changed, the message is remarkably similar: citizenship and submission to the labor market go hand in hand. But working people have always taken opportunities to use wage work to their own ends, and when possible they have tried to escape work altogether. Progressive Era reformers and governments were baffled by this kind of behavior. It was simply not appropriate for a modern industrial society. Shifting between employers and industries, following the seasonal swings of the labor market, and sometimes dropping out of sight altogether, today's contingent workers are similarly mystifying to the sociological thinking of government bureaucrats. Only slowly are unions overcoming their belief that these workers are "unorganizable," and they are usually following the lead of community-based organizations. If history is a guide, effective organizing strategies will emerge in fits and starts, but they will certainly be unorthodox. Unions and activists who hope to organize contingent workers will have to look beyond single workplaces and industries and beyond the legalities of collective bargaining. In addition to these traditional aims, they must channel workers' everyday struggles to make a living into a movement for social and economic citizenship.

NOTES

1. Emphasis in original. Notes on interview with Doyle, 1921. Don D. Lescohier Papers, Box 1, Folder 1. State Historical Society of Wisconsin. This was one of the few items that Lescohier saved from his long career as a researcher. See also Lescohier, "With the I.W.W. in the Wheat Lands," 374–75.
2. Lescohier, "With the IWW," 380.
3. Sklar, *The Corporate Reconstruction of American Capitalism,* 4–14; Furner, "Social Scientists and the State," 145–81; Fraser, "The 'Labor Question,'" 55–84.
4. Interview with Vincent Dunne, 4, MHS; Barron, *Mixed Harvest,* 243–45; Jellison, *Entitled to Power;* Neth, *Preserving the Family Farm;* Saloutos and Hicks, *Agricultural Discontent,* 286–320, 372–434.
5. Valdés, *Barrios Norteños,* 48–64; Mapes, "Defining the Boundaries"; Vargas, *Proletarians of the North,* 24–34.
6. Alexander, "Hiring and Firing," 143; see also Lescohier, "The Supply of Labor after the War," 83–89; Minnesota Industrial Commission, *Fourth Biennial Report,* 158.
7. Cohen, *Making a New Deal,* 99–212.
8. Minnesota Industrial Commission, *Fourth Biennial Report,* 165; Minnesota Industrial Commission, *Fifth Biennial Report,* 254–55.
9. Quirke, "Amongst the Home Guards," *Hobo News* 9 (July 1921): 5. Quirke died in an accident in 1921; his obituary noted that he had a tattoo reading "NO GOD, NO COUNTRY, NO MASTER." See "Loving Memory," *Hobo News* 9 (December 1921): 9.

10. Veblen, "Memorandum: Farm Labor and the IWW," Reel 3, *Papers of the President's Mediation Commission, 1917–1919.*

11. Littlejohn, *Hopping Freight Trains,* 1, 261–63. See also Leen, *Freighthopper's Manual;* Christopher Ketcham, "Hoboes from Hell," *Stuff Magazine,* July 2002, 94–98 (my thanks to Sara Austin for directing me to this article). Among the Web sites available in November 2002, see <http://www.hobo.com> and <http://www.ftra.org>.

12. Rose, "Class Formation and the Quintessential Worker," 141–47; Davis, *Prisoners of the American Dream,* 52–101; Fink, *Cutting into the Meatpacking Line,* 39–71; Horowitz, *"Negro and White, Unite and Fight,"* 259–86; Sugrue, *The Origins of the Urban Crisis,* 153–77; Honey, *Southern Labor and Black Civil Rights,* 215–44.

13. Jim West, "UAW Strike against Johnson Controls," 3–4.

14. Uchitelle, "Gap between Full-time and Part-time Workers"; Dishwasher Pete, "I'd Rather Be a Dishwasher," *TempSlave #11,* 35–36; West, "Big Win at UPS!" 1, 14.

15. West, "Union to Drop 441 Unfair Labor Practice Charges," 7; West, "UAW Strike against Johnson Controls;" Franklin, *Three Strikes.*

16. Faludi, *Stiffed,* 51–101; Davis, *Prisoners of the American Dream,* 171–80.

17. Polivka, "Profile of Contingent Workers," 10–21. According to this study, between 10 and 26 percent of college teachers were contingent in the mid-1990s. See also Clinton, "Flexible Labor," 3–27; Wilson, "For Some Adjunct Faculty Member," A9–A10; Barker, "Toiling for Piece-Rates," in Barker and Christensen, *Contingent Work,* 195–220. The Communications Workers of America is currently supporting union campaigns among high-tech workers at IBM, Microsoft, Boeing, and other companies. See <http://www.allianceibm.org> and <http://www.washtech.org>, accessed on 23 November 2002.

18. Ream, "New York Workfare Workers Vote Union," 1, 12.

19. Outside of the high-tech contingent workforce, woman and African Americans hold a disproportionate share of contingent jobs. See Polivka, "Profile of Contingent Workers," 10–21; "A Different Look at Part-time Employment," *Issues in Labor Statistics,* Summary 96-9 (April 1996): 1–2.

20. "Work and Pay Same Day," *Champaign-Urbana (Illinois) News-Gazette,* 4 April 1999, C1–3; Annual Report of Labor Ready, Inc., 1995 (Form 10K), filed with the U.S. Securities and Exchange Commission, 31 December 1995; Quarterly Report of Labor Ready, Inc., (Form 10Q), filed with the U.S. Securities and Exchange Commission, 12 November 2002. Labor Ready's chief competitive edge is a software system that handles all the tax paperwork for hiring companies and workers. For a fee, workers can use an ATM-type device in the hiring hall to cash their pay stubs daily; see the company's Web site, <http://www.laborready.com>, accessed on 20 February 1999 and 23 November 2002. See also Christopher D. Cook, "Street Corner, Incorporated," *Mother Jones* (March–April 2002): 65–69; "Labor Law Not Working," *Chicago Tribune,* 2 July 2002; Ehrenreich, *Nickel and Dimed.*

BIBLIOGRAPHY

Manuscript and Archival Sources

Bancroft Library, University of California, Berkeley
Paul S. Taylor Papers
Bentley Historical Library, University of Michigan, Ann Arbor
Floyd V. Ames Papers
Burton Historical Collection, Detroit Public Library, Detroit, Michigan
Papers of the International Seamen's Union of America
Center for Western Studies, Augustana College, Sioux Falls, South Dakota
V. H. Masters Collection
Sioux Falls Oral History Project
Department of Special Collections, Chester Fritz Library, University of North Dakota, Grand Forks
William Langer Papers
Immigration History Research Center, University of Minnesota, Minneapolis
Andrew Devich Papers
John Wiite Papers
Iron Range Research Center, Chisolm, Minnesota
Gonska, Hilda Elizabeth Warra. "Cradle of Iron" (n.d., probably 1973)
Interview with Cecilia and Arthur Sabattini
Interview with Arvid and Fred Ukura
Life in a Mining Location Oral History Project (interviews with Walter Alt, Sigurd Anderson, William Barke, and John Begich)
Silica Location Oral History Project (interviews with Richard Graff and Robert Lundin)
Minnesota Historical Society, St. Paul
Personal Papers
Hyman Berman, "Education for Work and Labor Solidarity: The Immigrant Miners and Radicalism on the Mesabi Range," unpublished manuscript, 1963

Hiram D. Frankel, "Report on Labor Disturbances in Northern Minnesota, December 1919 to January 1920"
Frank Gillmor Papers
Powers Hapgood Papers
Arthur LeSueur Papers
John Lind Papers
Fred S. Rutledge Papers
Robert E. Smith Papers
Government and Corporate Records
City of Minneapolis. Annual Reports of the Board of Charities and Corrections, Municipal Lodging House, 1911–1916
City of Minneapolis, Board of Charities and Corrections
Minnesota Commission of Public Safety Papers
Minnesota Department of Labor and Industry
Records of the Great Northern Railway
Records of the Northern Pacific Railway
United States General Land Office Records
Interviews
Interview with Vincent Raymond Dunne by Lila Johnson Goff, April 17, 1969
Interview with Frank Ellis
Interview with Walter Harju
Interview with Jack Maloney
Interview with Sam Swanson by Jack Spiese, October 27, 1967
Radicalism in Minnesota Oral History Project (interviews with Karl Rølvaag, Jack Maloney, Patrick McMillen, Raymond Wright, and Harry DeBoer)
The Newberry Library, Chicago, Illinois
Charles H. Kerr Publishing Company
Newberry Library Archives, Records of the Center for Family and Community History, Chicago Area Labor History Group Papers
North Dakota Institute for Regional Studies, Fargo
Amenia and Sharon Land Company Papers
Belle Prairie Farm Scrapbook
James H. Carter Collection
Interview with John Hanson
Interview with Olaus Hanson
Interview with Thorfin Jestin
George Tracy Collection
Redfield Town Hall, Redfield, South Dakota
Minutes of Town Meetings, 1914–1920
Roosevelt University Oral History Project, Roosevelt University, Chicago, Illinois
Interview of Christ Yankoff by Frank Ninkovich
Sioux City Public Museum, Sioux City, Iowa
Wallace Short Papers
Social Welfare History Archives, University of Minnesota, Minneapolis
Minnesota Social Service Association Papers
Spink County Courthouse, Redfield, South Dakota
Coroner's Inquests, 1903–1915

Petitions for Mother's Pensions, 1911–1918
Records of the State Circuit Court, Ninth District, 1908–1920
State Historical Society of Wisconsin, Madison
Don D. Lescohier Papers
William Lieserson Papers
United Packinghouse Workers of America Oral History Project
U.S. Commission on Industrial Relations
Wisconsin Agriculturalist Oral History Project
Wisconsin Industrial Commission Papers
United States National Archives
Records of the Adjutant General's Office, Regular Army of Enlistment, RG 94, Washington, D.C.
Records of the Bureau of Employment Security, Files of the U.S. Employment Service, Early History Files, RG 183, Washington, D.C.
Records of the Bureau of Employment Security, Omaha, Nebraska, Branch, RG 183, Kansas City, Missouri
Records of the U.S. Department of Labor, Secretary's General Subject Files, RG 174, Washington, D.C.
Records of the U.S. Fish and Wildlife Service, RG 22, Washington, D.C.
University of Chicago Library, Department of Special Collections, Chicago, Illinois
Ernest W. Burgess Papers, Student and Collaborators, Nels Anderson
University of Illinois at Chicago, Manuscripts Collection
Ben L. Reitman Papers
University of Washington Libraries, Manuscripts and Archives Division, Seattle
Industrial Workers of the World Seattle Branch
Walter Reuther Library, Archives of Labor and Urban Affairs, Wayne State University, Detroit, Michigan
Charles Ashleigh Papers
Leonard Howard De Caux Papers
Industrial Workers of the World Collection
Industrial Workers of the World Minneapolis Branch Collection
Washington State Historical Society Research Center, Tacoma
Thomas Bogard Collection
Western Historical Manuscript Collection, Columbia, Missouri
Clarence W. Alvord Collection
Curtis F. Marbut Papers
Peter Tamony Papers
Western Historical Manuscript Collection, St. Louis, Missouri
Robert S. Saunders Papers

Microfilm Collections

The President's Mediation Commission, 1917–1919. Frederick, Md.: University Publications of America, 1985.
The Social Reform Papers of John James McCook. Hartford, Conn.: Antiquarian and Landmarks Society, 1977.

U.S. Commission on Industrial Relations, 1912–1915: Unpublished Records of the Division of Research and Investigation. Frederick, Md.: University Publications of America, 1985.

Computerized Data Sets

Integrated Public Use Microdata Samples, 1995 release. <http://www.hist.umn.edu/~ipums/>

Published Sources and Theses

Abbott, Grace. "Chicago Employment Agencies and the Immigrant Worker," *American Journal of Sociology* 14 (November 1908): 289–305.

Adams, Graham, Jr. *Age of Industrial Violence, 1910–15: The Activities and Findings of the U.S. Commission on Industrial Relations.* New York: Columbia University Press, 1966.

Adams, Jane. *The Transformation of Rural Life: Southern Illinois, 1890–1990.* Chapel Hill: University of North Carolina Press, 1994.

Adelman, Jeremy. *Frontier Development: Land, Labour, and Capital on the Wheatlands of Argentina and Canada, 1890–1914.* Oxford, England: Clarendon Press, 1994.

Adrian, Lynne Marie. "Organizing the Rootless: American Hobo Subculture, 1893–1932." Ph.D. diss., University of Iowa, 1984.

"Agriculture, the Mother of Industry." Chicago: Agricultural Workers' Industrial Union No. 110 [1922?].

Ahearn, Daniel J., Jr. *The Wages of Farm and Factory Laborers, 1914–1944.* New York: Columbia University Press, 1945.

Alanen, Arnold R. "Years of Change on the Iron Range." In *Minnesota in a Century of Change: The State and Its People Since 1900.* Ed. Clifford E. Clark. St. Paul: Minnesota Historical Society Press, 1989. 157–61.

Alexander, Magnus. "Hiring and Firing: Its Economic Waste and How to Avoid It." *Annals of the American Academy of Political and Social Science* 65 (1916): 128–44.

Allen, Henry J. "The New Harvest Hand." *American Review of Reviews* 76 (September 1927): 279–84.

Almaguer, Tomás. *Racial Fault Lines: The Historical Origins of White Supremacy in California.* Berkeley: University of California Press, 1994.

Anderson, Margo J. *The American Census: A Social History.* New Haven, Conn.: Yale University Press, 1988.

Anderson, Nels. *The American Hobo: An Autobiography.* Leiden: E. J. Brill, 1975.

———. *The Hobo: The Sociology of the Homeless Man.* 1923. Reprint, Chicago: University of Chicago Press, 1961.

———. *Men on the Move.* Chicago: University of Chicago Press, 1940.

——— [Dean Stiff]. *The Milk and Honey Route: A Handbook for Hobos.* New York: Vanguard Press, 1930.

Applen, Allen G. "Migratory Harvest Labor in the Midwestern Wheat Belt, 1870–1940." Ph.D. diss., Kansas State University, 1974.

Ashleigh, Charles. *Rambling Kid.* London: Faber and Faber, 1930.

Ayers, Edward L. *The Promise of the New South: Life after Reconstruction.* New York: Oxford University Press, 1992.
Baltensperger, Bradley H. "Farm Consolidation in the Northern and Central States of the Great Plains." *Great Plains Quarterly* 7 (Fall 1987): 256–65.
Barker, Kathleen, and Kathleen Christensen, eds. *Contingent Work: American Employment Relations in Transition.* Ithaca, N.Y.: ILR Press/Cornell University Press, 1998.
Baron, Ava, ed. *Work Engendered: Toward a New History of American Labor.* Ithaca, N.Y.: Cornell University Press, 1991.
Barrett, James R. "Americanization from the Bottom Up: Immigration and the Remaking of the Working Class in the United States, 1880–1930." *Journal of American History* 79 (December 1992): 996–1020.
———. "Why Paddy Drank: The Social Importance of Whiskey in Pre-Famine Ireland." *Journal of Popular Culture* 11 (1977).
———. *William Z. Foster and the Tragedy of American Radicalism.* Urbana: University of Illinois Press, 1999.
———. *Work and Community in the Jungle: Chicago's Packinghouse Workers, 1894–1922.* Urbana: University of Illinois Press, 1987.
Barron, Hal S. *Mixed Harvest: The Second Great Transformation in the Rural North, 1870–1930.* Chapel Hill: University of North Carolina Press, 1997.
Beaulieu, David. "A Place among Nations: Experiences of Indian People." In *Minnesota in a Century of Change: The State and Its People Since 1900.* Ed. Clifford E. Clark. St. Paul: Minnesota Historical Society Press, 1989.
Bederman, Gail. *Manliness and Civilization: A Cultural History of Gender and Race in the United States, 1880–1917.* Chicago: University of Chicago Press, 1995.
Bell, Colin, and Howard Newby. *Community Studies: An Introduction to the Sociology of the Local Community.* New York: Praeger Publishers, 1972.
Bell, Earl H. *Culture of a Contemporary Rural Community: Sublette, Kansas.* Vol. 2. Washington: Government Printing Office, 1942.
Benson, Ben (Hobo). *Hoboes of America.* New York: Hobo News, 1942.
Berdahl, Andrew J. *The Berdahl Family.* Sioux Falls, S.Dak.: n.p., 1942.
Berlanstein, Lenard R., ed. *Rethinking Labor History: Essays on Discourse and Class Analysis.* Urbana: University of Illinois Press, 1993.
Betten, Neil. "Riot, Revolution, Repression in the Iron Range Strike of 1916." *Minnesota History* 41 (Summer 1968): 82–94.
———. "Strike on the Mesabi: 1907." *Minnesota History* 40 (Fall 1967): 340–47.
Bird, Stewart, Dan Georgakas, and Deborah Shaffer. *Solidarity Forever: An Oral History of the IWW.* Chicago: Lake View Press, 1985.
Björkman, Frances Maule. "The New Anti-Vagrancy Campaign." *The American Review of Reviews* 37 (February 1908): 206–11.
Blaisdell, Lowell L. *The Desert Revolution: Baja California, 1911.* Madison: University of Wisconsin Press, 1962.
Blewett, Mary. "Masculinity and Mobility: The Dilemma of Lancashire Weavers and Spinners in Late-Nineteenth-Century Fall River, Massachusetts." In *Meanings for Manhood: Constructions of Masculinity in Victorian America.* Ed. Mark C. Carnes and Clyde Griffen. Chicago: University of Chicago Press, 1990. 164–78.

———. *Men, Women and Work: Class, Gender, and Protest in the New England Shoe Industry, 1780–1910.* Urbana: University of Illinois Press, 1988.

Bodnar, John, Roger Simon, and Michael P. Weber. *Lives of Their Own: Blacks, Italians, and Poles in Pittsburgh, 1900–1960.* Urbana: University of Illinois Press, 1982.

Boose, Arthur. "The Lumber Jack." *International Socialist Review* 16 (January 1916): 414–16.

Borchert, John R. *America's Northern Heartland: An Economic and Historical Geography of the Upper Midwest.* Minneapolis: University of Minnesota Press, 1987.

Bourdieu, Pierre. "Structures, Habitus, Power: Basis for a Theory of Symbolic Power." In *Culture/Power/History: A Reader in Contemporary Social Theory.* Ed. Nicholas B. Dirks, Geoff Eley, and Sherry B. Ortner. Princeton, N.J.: Princeton University Press, 1994. 155–99.

Bradwin, Edmund W. *The Bunkhouse Man: A Study of Work and Pay in the Camps of Canada, 1903–1914.* 1928. Reprint, Toronto: University of Toronto Press, 1972.

Brantlinger, Patrick. *Crusoe's Foot-prints: Cultural Studies in Britain and America.* New York: Routledge, 1990.

Brissenden, Paul F. *The I.W.W.: A Study of American Syndicalism.* New York: Columbia University, 1920.

Brody, David. *Workers in Industrial America: Essays on the Twentieth-Century Struggle.* New York: Oxford University Press, 1980.

Brown, Charles P. *Brownie the Boomer: The Life of Charles P. Brown, an American Railroader.* Ed. H. Roger Grant. DeKalb: Northern Illinois University Press, 1991.

Brown, Edwin. *"Broke": The Man without the Dime.* Chicago: Browne and Howell Co., 1913.

Bruns, Roger A. *The Damndest Radical: The Life of Ben Reitman, Chicago's Celebrated Social Reformer, Hobo King, and Whorehouse Physician.* Urbana: University of Illinois Press, 1987.

———. *Knights of the Road: A Hobo History.* New York: Methuen, 1980.

Burris, Martin. *True Sketches of the Life and Travels of Martin Burris on the Western Plains, the Rocky Mountains and the Pacific Coast, U.S.A.* Salina, Kansas: Padgett's Printing House, 1910.

Bussel, Robert. *From Harvard to the Ranks of Labor: Powers Hapgood and the American Working Class.* University Park: Pennsylvania State University Press, 1999.

Canning, Kathleen. "Feminist History after the Linguistic Turn: Historicizing Discourse and Experience." *Signs* 19 (Winter 1994): 368–404.

———. "Gender and the Politics of Class Formation: Rethinking German Labor History." *American Historical Review* 97 (June 1992): 736–68.

Chaplin, Ralph. *Wobbly, the Rough-and-Tumble Story of an American Radical.* Chicago: University of Chicago Press, 1948.

Chauncey, George. "Christian Brotherhood or Sexual Perversion? Homosexual Identities and the Construction of Sexual Boundaries in the World War One Era." *Journal of Social History* 19 (Winter 1985): 189–211.

———. *Gay New York: Gender, Urban Culture, and the Making of the Gay Male World, 1890–1940.* New York: Basic Books, 1994.

Chicago Vice Commission. *The Social Evil in Chicago: A Study of Existing Conditions with Recommendations by the Vice Commission of Chicago.* Chicago: Gunthorp-Warren Printing Co., 1911.

Chrislock, Carl H. *Watchdog of Loyalty: The Minnesota Commission of Public Safety during World War I.* St. Paul: Minnesota Historical Society Press, 1991.

Chudacoff, Howard P. *Mobile Americans: Residential and Social Mobility in Omaha, 1880–1920.* New York: Oxford University Press, 1972.

Ciolli, Dominic T. "The 'Wop' in the Track Gang." *The Immigrants in America Review* 2 (July 1916): 61–64.

Clark, Clifford E., ed. *Minnesota in a Century of Change: The State and Its People Since 1900.* St. Paul: Minnesota Historical Society Press, 1989.

Clifford, James. *The Predicament of Culture: Twentieth-Century Ethnography, Literature, and Art.* Cambridge, Mass.: Harvard University Press, 1988.

Clifford, James, and George Marcus, eds. *Writing Culture: The Poetics and Politics of Ethnography.* Berkeley: University of California Press, 1986.

Clinton, Angela. "Flexible Labor: Restructuring the American Workforce." *Monthly Labor Review* 120 (August 1997): 3–27.

Closson, Carlos, Jr. "The Unemployed in American Cities." *Quarterly Journal of Economics* 8 (January 1894): 168–217.

Cockburn, Cynthia. "Forum: Formations of Masculinity, Introduction." *Gender and History* 2 (Summer 1989): 159–63.

Cohen, Lizabeth. *Making a New Deal: Industrial Workers in Chicago, 1919–1939.* New York: Cambridge University Press, 1990.

Commons, John R., ed. *Trade Unionism and Labor Problems.* 2nd Series. Boston: Ginn and Co., 1921.

Conroy, Jack. *The Disinherited.* 1933. Reprinted, Columbia: University of Missouri Press, 1991.

———. *A World to Win.* 1935. Reprinted, Urbana: University of Illinois Press, 2000.

Cooper, Frederick. "Colonizing Time: Work Rhythms and Labor Conflict in Colonial Mombasa." In *Colonialism and Culture.* Ed. Nicholas B. Dirks. Ann Arbor: University of Michigan Press, 1992. 209–45.

———. *On the African Waterfront: Urban Disorder and the Transformation of Work in Colonial Mombasa.* New Haven, Conn.: Yale University Press, 1987.

Cooper, Patricia A. *Once a Cigar Maker: Men, Women, and Work Culture in American Cigar Factories, 1900–1919.* Urbana: University of Illinois Press, 1987.

Coulter, John Lee. "Industrial History of the Valley of the Red River of the North." In *Collections of the State Historical Society of North Dakota.* Vol. 3. Bismark, N.Dak.: State Printers and Binders, 1910. 569–612.

Courtwright, David T. *Violent Land: Single Men and Social Disorder from the Frontier to the Inner City.* Cambridge, Mass.: Harvard University Press, 1996.

Cox, LaWanda F. "The American Agricultural Wage Earner, 1865–1900." *Agricultural History* 22 (April 1948): 95–114.

Crapanzano, Vincent. "Life-Histories." *American Anthropologist* 86 (December 1984): 953–60.

Creel, George. "Harvesting the Harvest Hands." *Harper's Weekly* 59 (26 September 1914): 292–94.

Cressey, Paul. *The Taxi-Dance Hall: A Sociological Study of Commercialized Recreation and City Life.* Chicago: University of Chicago Press, 1932.

Cronon, William. *Nature's Metropolis: Chicago and the Great West.* New York: W. W. Norton, 1991.

Cumberland, William H. *Wallace Short: Iowa Rebel.* Ames: Iowa State University Press, 1983.

Danbom, David. *The Resisted Revolution: Urban America and the Industrialization of Agriculture, 1900–1930.* Ames: Iowa State University Press, 1979.

Daniel, Cletus. *Bitter Harvest: A History of California Farmworkers, 1870–1941.* Ithaca, N.Y.: Cornell University Press, 1981.

Daniel, Pete. *Breaking the Land: The Enclosure of Cotton, Tobacco, and Rice Cultures.* Urbana: University of Illinois Press, 1984.

Danysk, Cecilia. *Hired Hands: Labour and the Development of Prairie Agriculture, 1880–1930.* Toronto: McClelland and Stewart, 1995.

Davis, Michael. "Forced to Tramp: The Perspective of the Labor Press, 1870–1900." In *Walking to Work: Tramps in America, 1790–1935.* Ed. Eric Monkkonen. Lincoln: University of Nebraska Press, 1984. 142–70.

De Caux, Len. *Labor Radical: From the Wobblies to CIO, a Personal History.* Boston: Beacon Press, 1970.

D'Emilio, John, and Estelle B. Freedman. *Intimate Matters: A History of Sexuality in America.* 2nd Ed. Chicago: University of Chicago Press, 1997.

Denning, Michael. *Mechanic Accents: Dime Novels and Working-Class Culture in America.* New York: Verso, 1987.

DePastino, Todd Allan. "From Hobohemia to Skid Row: Homelessness and American Culture, 1870–1950." Ph.D. thesis, Yale University, 1997.

Deutsch, Sarah. *No Separate Refuge: Culture, Class, and Gender on an Anglo-Hispanic Frontier in the American Southwest, 1880–1940.* New York: Oxford University Press, 1987.

DiGirolamo, Vincent. "The Women of Wheatland: Female Consciousness and the 1913 Wheatland Hop Strike." *Labor History* 34 (1993): 236–55.

Doree, E. F. "Gathering the Grain." *International Socialist Review* 15 (June 1915): 740–43.

Douglas, William O. *Go East, Young Man: The Early Years.* New York: Dell Publishing Co., 1974.

Dowell, Eldridge F. *A History of Criminal Syndicalism Legislation in the United States.* 1939. Reprinted, New York: Da Capo Press, 1969.

Drache, Hiram. *The Day of the Bonanza: A History of Bonanza Farming in the Red River Valley of the North.* Fargo: North Dakota Institute for Regional Studies, 1964.

Draper, Theodore. The *Roots of American Communism.* New York: Viking Press, 1957.

Draper, W. R. "Solving the Labor Problem of the Wheat Belts." *American Review of Reviews* 26 (July 1902): 70–72.

Dublin, Thomas. *Transforming Women's Work: New England Lives in the Industrial Revolution.* Ithaca, N.Y.: Cornell University Press, 1994.

Dubofsky, Melvyn. *We Shall Be All: A History of the Industrial Workers of the World.* 1969. Reprinted, Urbana: University of Illinois Press, 1988.

Duffus, Robert L. "The Ku Klux Klan in the Middle West." *World's Work* 46 (August 1923): 363–72.

Eaton, Geoffrey Dell. *Backfurrow.* New York: G. P. Putnam's Sons, 1925.

Edge, William. *The Main Stem.* New York: Vanguard Press, 1927.

Edwards, P. K. *Strikes in the United States, 1881–1974.* Oxford, England: Basil Blackwell, 1981.

Edwards, Richard. *Contested Terrain: The Transformation of the Workplace in the Twentieth Century.* New York: Basic Books, 1979.
Ehrenreich, Barbara. *Nickel and Dimed: On (Not) Getting By in America.* New York: Metropolitan Books, 2001.
Emmons, David M. *The Butte Irish: Class and Ethnicity in an American Mining Town, 1875–1925.* Urbana: University of Illinois Press, 1989.
Engberg, George B. "Collective Bargaining in the Lumber Industry of the Upper Great Lakes States." *Agricultural History* 24 (October 1950): 205–11.
Engerman, Stanley, and Claudia Goldin. "Seasonality in Nineteenth-Century Labor Markets." In *American Economic Development in Historical Perspective.* Ed. Thomas Weiss and Donald Schaefer. Stanford, Calif.: Stanford University Press, 1994. 99–126.
Erickson, Halford. *Tenth Biennial Report of the Bureau of Labor and Industrial Statistics, State of Wisconsin, 1900–1901.* Madison: State Printer, 1902.
Fagin, Sophia. *Public Forums in Chicago.* Chicago: Work Projects Administration, 1940.
Faludi, Susan. *Stiffed: The Betrayal of the American Man.* New York: William Morrow and Co., 1999.
"The Farm Hand" (Editorial). *The Locomotive Engineers Journal* 57 (July 1923): 526.
Faue, Elizabeth. *Community of Suffering and Struggle: Women, Men and the Labor Movement in Minneapolis, 1915–1945.* Chapel Hill: University of North Carolina Press, 1991.
———. "Gender and the Reconstruction of Labor History." *Labor History* 34 (Spring–Summer 1993): 169–77.
Fellows, Will, ed. *Farm Boys: Lives of Gay Men from the Rural Midwest.* Madison: University of Wisconsin Press, 1996.
Fields, Barbara. "Ideology and Race in American History." In *Region, Race and Reconstruction: Essays in Honor of C. Vann Woodward.* Ed. J. Morgan Kousser and James M. McPherson. New York: 1982.
Fink, Deborah. *Agrarian Women: Wives and Mothers in Rural Nebraska, 1880–1940.* Chapel Hill: University of North Carolina Press, 1992.
———. *Cutting Into the Meatpacking Line: Workers and Change in the Rural Midwest.* Chapel Hill: University of North Carolina Press, 1998.
Fink, Leon. *In Search of the Working Class: Essays in American Labor History and Political Culture.* Urbana: University of Illinois Press, 1994.
———. "Looking Backward: Reflections on Workers' Culture and Certain Conceptual Dilemmas within Labor History." In *Perspectives on American Labor History: The Problems of Synthesis.* Ed. Carroll Moody and Alice Kessler-Harris. DeKalb: Northern Illinois University Press, 1990. 5–29.
———. *Workingmen's Democracy: The Knights of Labor and American Politics.* Urbana: University of Illinois Press, 1983.
Flynt, Josiah [Willard]. *My Life.* New York: The Outing Publishing Co., 1908.
———. *Notes of an Itinerant Policeman.* Boston: L. C. Page and Co., 1900.
———. *Tramping with Tramps: Studies and Sketches of Vagabond Life.* 1899. Reprinted, New York: The Century Co., 1907.
Foley, Neil. *The White Scourge: Mexicans, Blacks, and Poor Whites in Texas Cotton Culture.* Berkeley: University of California Press, 1997.

Foner, Philip S. *History of the Labor Movement in the U.S., Volume 4: The Industrial Workers of the World, 1905–1917.* New York: International Publishers, 1965.

Foster, William Z. *Pages from a Worker's Life.* 1939. Reprinted, New York: International Publishers, 1970.

Fox-Genovese, Elizabeth, and Eugene D. Genovese. "The Political Crisis of Social History: A Marxian Perspective." *Social History* 10 (Winter 1976): 205–20.

Frank, Gelya. "Finding the Common Denominator: A Phenomenological Critique of Life History Method." *Ethos* 7 (Spring 1979): 68–94.

Fraser, Steve. "The 'Labor Question.'" In *The Rise and Fall of the New Deal Order, 1930–1980.* Ed. Steve Fraser and Gary Gerstle. Princeton, N.J.: Princeton University Press, 1989. 55–84.

Friedmann, Harriet. "World Market, State, and Family Farm: Social Bases of Household Production in the Era of Wage Labor." *Comparative Studies in Society and History* 20 (October 1978): 545–86.

Friedrich, Paul. *Agrarian Revolt in a Mexican Village.* Chicago: University of Chicago Press, 1977.

Frizell, E. E. "About Farm Labor." In *Wheat in Kansas.* Topeka: Kansas State Board of Agriculture, 1921.

Fry, C. L. "Migratory Workers of Our Industries." *World's Work* 40 (October 1920): 600–611.

Furner, Mary O. "Knowing Capitalism: Public Investigation and the Labor Question in the Long Progressive Era." In *The State and Economic Knowledge: The American and British Experiences.* Ed. Mary O. Furner and Barry Supple. New York and Cambridge, England: Woodrow Wilson International Center for Scholars and Cambridge University Press, 1990. 274–84.

———. "Social Scientists and the State: Constructing the Knowledge Base for Public Policy, 1880–1920." In *Intellectuals and Public Life: Between Radicalism and Reform.* Ed. Leon Fink, Stephen T. Leonard, and Donald M. Reid. Ithaca, N.Y.: Cornell University Press, 1996. 145–81.

Gambs, John S. *The Decline of the I.W.W.* 1932. Reprinted, New York: Russell & Russell, 1966.

Gardner, James B., and George Rollie Adams, eds. *Ordinary People and Everyday Life: Perspectives on the New Social History.* Nashville, Tenn.: American Association for State and Local History, 1983.

Garland, Hamlin. *Boy Life on the Prairie.* 1899. Reprinted, Boston: Allyn and Bacon, 1926.

Gillespie, L. D. "Hunger in the Midst of Plenty." *International Socialist Review* 17 (November 1916): 282–85.

Gjerde, Jon. *The Minds of the West: Ethnocultural Evolution in the Rural Middle West, 1830–1917.* Chapel Hill: University of North Carolina Press, 1997.

Gordon, Robert, Richard Edwards, and Michael Reich. *Segmented Work, Divided Workers: The Historical Transformations of Labor in the United States.* New York: Cambridge University Press, 1982.

Gorn, Elliot J. "'Gouge and Bite, Pull Hair and Scratch': The Social Significance of Fighting in the Southern Backcountry." *American Historical Review* 90 (February 1985): 18–43.

———. *The Manly Art: Bare-Knuckle Prize Fighting in America.* Ithaca, N.Y.: Cornell University Press, 1986.

Graziosi, Andrea. "Common Laborers, Unskilled Workers: 1890–1915." *Labor History* 22 (1981): 512–44.

Green, Archie. *Wobblies, Pile-Butts and Other Heroes: Laborlore Explorations.* Urbana: University of Illinois Press, 1993.

Green, James R. *Grass-Roots Socialism: Radical Movements in the Southwest, 1895–1943.* Baton Rouge: Louisiana State University Press, 1978.

Griffen, Clyde. "Reconstructing Masculinity from the Evangelical Revival to the Waning of Progressivism: A Speculative Synthesis." In *Meanings for Manhood: Constructions of Masculinity in Victorian America.* Ed. Mark C. Carnes and Clyde Griffen. Chicago: University of Chicago Press, 1990.

Grossardt, Ted. "Harvest(ing) Hoboes: The Production of Labor Organization through the Wheat Harvest." *Agricultural History* 70 (Spring 1996): 283–302.

Grossman, James. *Land of Hope: Chicago, Black Southerners and the Great Migration.* Chicago: University of Chicago Press, 1989.

Groth, Paul. *Living Downtown: The History of Residential Hotels in the United States.* Berkeley: University of California Press, 1994.

Guha, Ranajit. "The Prose of Counter-Insurgency." *Subaltern Studies* II (1983): 1–42.

Gullickson, Gay L. "Commentary: New Labor History from the Perspective of a Women's Historian." In *Rethinking Labor History: Essays on Discourse and Class Analysis.* Ed. Lenard R. Berlanstein. Urbana: University of Illinois Press, 1993. 200–214.

Gutman, Herbert. *Work, Culture and Society in Industrializing America: Essays in American Working-Class and Social History.* New York: Vintage Books, 1977.

Hader, John J. "Honk, Honk Hobo." *The Survey* 60 (August 1928): 453–55.

Hagg, Harold T. "The Lumberjacks' Sky Pilot." *Minnesota History* 31 (June 1950): 65–78.

Hahamovitch, Cindy. *The Fruits of Their Labor: Atlantic Coast Farmworkers and the Making of Migrant Poverty, 1870–1945.* Chapel Hill: University of North Carolina Press, 1997.

Hahn, Steven, and Jonathan Prude, eds. *The Countryside in the Age of Capitalist Transformation: Essays in the Social History of Rural America.* Chapel Hill: University of North Carolina Press, 1985.

Hak, Gordon. "The Harvest Excursion Adventure: Excursionists from Rural North Huron–South Bruce, 1919–1928." *Ontario History* 78 (December 1985): 247–65.

Hall, Covington. *Labor Struggles in the Deep South and Other Writings.* Ed. David R. Roediger. Chicago: Charles H. Kerr, 1999.

Hall, John R., ed. *Reworking Class.* Ithaca, N.Y.: Cornell University Press, 1997.

Halonen, Arne. "The Role of Finish-Americans in the Political Labor Movement." Master's thesis, University of Minnesota, 1945.

Hanagan, Michael. "Commentary: For Reconstruction in Labor History." In *Rethinking Labor History: Essays on Discourse and Class Analysis.* Ed. Lenard R. Berlanstein. Urbana: University of Illinois Press, 1993. 182–99.

Hanson, Nils H. "Among the Harvesters." *International Socialist Review* 16 (July 1915): 75–78.

———. "Threshing Wheat." *International Socialist Review* 16 (November 1915): 344–47.
Hapgood, Hutchins. *The Spirit of Labor.* New York: Duffield and Co., 1907.
———. *A Victorian in the Modern World.* Seattle: University of Washington Press, 1972.
Harrison, Shelby M., et al. *Public Employment Offices: Their Purpose, Structure and Methods.* New York: Russell Sage Foundation, 1924.
Hartsough, Mildred Lucile. "The Development of the Twin Cities (Minneapolis and St. Paul) as a Metropolitan Market." Ph.D. diss., University of Minnesota, 1924.
Harwood, William. "The Ku Klux Klan in Grand Forks, North Dakota." *South Dakota History* 1 (Fall 1971): 301–35.
Hatton, Timothy J., and Jeffrey G. Williamson. *The Age of Mass Migration: Causes and Economic Impact* New York: Oxford University Press, 1998.
———. "What Explains Wage Gaps between Farm and City? Exploring the Todaro Model with American Evidence, 1890–1941." *Economic Development and Cultural Change* 40 (January 1992): 267–94.
Haug, Charles James. "The Industrial Workers of the World in North Dakota, 1913–1917." *North Dakota Quarterly* (Winter 1971): 85–102.
Haynes, John E. "Revolt of the 'Timber Beasts': IWW Lumber Strike in Minnesota." *Minnesota History* 42 (Spring 1971): 163–74.
Haywood, Harry. *Black Bolshevik: Autobiography of an Afro-American Communist.* Chicago: Liberator Press, 1978.
Haywood, William D. *Bill Haywood's Book: The Autobiography of William D. Haywood.* 1929. Reprinted, New York: International Publishers, 1983.
Heard, Wilby. "'Our' Cililo Canal." *International Socialist Review* 14 (February 1914): 483–86.
Heron, Craig, ed. *The Workers' Revolt in Canada, 1917–1925.* Toronto: University of Toronto Press, 1998.
Higbie, Frank Tobias. "Indispensable Outcasts: Seasonal Laborers and Community in the Upper Midwest, 1880–1930." Ph.D. thesis, University of Illinois, Urbana-Champaign, 2000.
Hiles, Theron L. *The Ice Crop: How to Harvest, Store, Ship and Use Ice, A Complete Practical Treatise.* New York: Orange Judd Company, 1893.
Hoare, Quintin, and Geoffrey Nowell-Smith, eds. and trans. *Selections from the Prison Notebooks of Antonio Gramsci.* New York: International Publishers, 1971.
Hobsbawm, Eric. *Primitive Rebels: Studies in Archaic Forms of Social Movements in the 19th and 20th Centuries.* New York: W. W. Norton, 1959.
Hofstadter, Richard, and Beatrice K. Hofstadter, eds. *Great Issues in American History.* Vol. 3: *From Reconstruction to the Present Day, 1864–1981.* New York: Vintage Books, 1982.
Honey, Michael K. *Southern Labor and Black Civil Rights: Organizing Memphis Workers.* Urbana: University of Illinois Press, 1993.
Hornbacher, Perry Joel. "The Forgotten Heritage: The North Dakota Socialist Party, 1902–1918." Master's thesis, North Dakota State University of Agriculture and Applied Science, 1982.
Horowitz, Roger. *"Negro and White Unite and Fight": A Social History of Industrial Unionism in Meatpacking, 1930–1990.* Urbana: University of Illinois Press, 1997.

Hunt, Lynn, ed. *The New Cultural History.* Berkeley: University of California Press, 1989.

Iowa Writers' Program. *Woodbury County History, Iowa.* Sioux City: Work Projects Administration/Woodbury County Superintendent of Schools, 1942.

Irwin, Will. "The Floating Laborer: The Case of John Smith." *Saturday Evening Post* (9 May 1914): 3–5, 41–51.

———. "The Floating Laborer: The Need for Teamwork." *Saturday Evening Post* (4 July 1914): 14–15, 45–46.

———. "The Floating Laborer: Some Humble Biographies." *Saturday Evening Post* (6 June 1914): 8–9, 61–63.

Isern, Thomas D. *Bull Threshers and Bindlestiffs: Harvesting and Threshing on the North American Plains.* Lawrence: University Press of Kansas, 1990.

IWW Songs to Fan the Flames of Discontent. 1923. Reprinted, Chicago: Charles H. Kerr, 1989.

Jameson, Elizabeth. *All That Glitters: Class, Conflict, and Community in Cripple Creek.* Urbana: University of Illinois Press, 1998.

Jamieson, Stuart. *Labor Unionism in American Agriculture, U.S. Department of Labor, Bureau of Labor Statistics, Bulletin No. 836.* Washington, D.C.: GPO, 1945.

Janiewski, Dolores. "Southern Honor, Southern Dishonor: Managerial Ideology and the Construction of Gender, Race, and Class Relations in Southern Industry." In *Work Engendered: Toward a New History of American Labor.* Ed. Ava Baron. Ithaca, N.Y.: Cornell University Press, 1991. 70–91.

Jellison, Katherine. *Entitled to Power: Farm Women and Technology, 1913–1963.* Chapel Hill: University of North Carolina Press, 1993.

Johnson, Fred R. "The Lodging House Problem in Minneapolis." Undergraduate thesis, University of Minnesota, 1910.

Johnson, Susan Lee. "Bulls, Bears, and Dancing Boys: Race, Gender, and Leisure in the California Gold Rush." *Radical History Review* 60 (Fall 1994): 4–37.

Jones, Gareth Stedman. *Languages of Class: Studies in English Working-Class History, 1832–1982.* Cambridge, England: Cambridge University Press, 1983.

Kansas City Board of Public Welfare. *Seventh Annual Report of the Board of Public Welfare of Kansas City, Missouri, April 20, 1915 to April 16, 1916.* Kansas City, Mo.: n.p., 1916.

Kansas State Board of Agriculture. *Twentieth Biennial Report of the Kansas State Board of Agriculture.* Topeka: Kansas State Board of Agriculture, 1917.

———. *Wheat in Kansas.* Topeka: Kansas State Board of Agriculture, 1921.

Katz, Jonathan, ed. *Gay American History: Lesbians and Gay Men in the USA.* New York: Thomas Crowell Co., 1976.

Katznelson, Ira, and Aristide Zolberg, eds. *Working-Class Formation: Nineteenth Century Patterns in Western Europe and the United States.* Princeton, N.J.: Princeton University Press, 1986.

Kazin, Michael. *Barons of Labor: The San Francisco Building Trades and Union Power in the Progressive Era.* Urbana: University of Illinois Press, 1986.

Keesing, Felix M. *The Menomini Indians of Wisconsin: A Study of Three Centuries of Cultural Contact and Change.* Philadelphia: American Philosophical Society, 1939.

Kelley, Robin D. G. "'We Are Not What We Seem': Rethinking Black Working-Class Opposition in the Jim Crow South." *Journal of American History* 80 (June 1993): 75–112.

Kelly, Edmond. *The Elimination of the Tramp.* New York: G. P. Putnam's Sons, 1908.
Kelly, Jeff, ed. *Best of "Temp Slave."* Madison: Garrett County Press, 1997.
Kessler-Harris, Alice. "Treating the Male as 'Other': Redefining the Parameters of Labor History." *Labor History* 34 (Spring–Summer 1993): 190–204.
Keyssar, Alexander. *Out of Work: The First Century of Unemployment in Massachusetts.* New York: Cambridge University Press, 1986.
Kimmel, Michael. *Manhood in America: A Cultural History.* New York: The Free Press, 1997.
Kirby, Jack Temple. *Rural Worlds Lost: The American South, 1920–1960.* Baton Rouge: Louisiana State University Press, 1987.
Koppes, Clayton R. "The I.W.W. and County Jail Reform in Kansas, 1915–1920." *Kansas Historical Quarterly* 41 (1975): 63–86.
Kornbluh, Joyce, ed. *Rebel Voices: An IWW Anthology.* 1964. Reprinted, Chicago: Charles H. Kerr, 1998.
Kusmer, Kenneth L. *Down and Out, on the Road: The Homeless in American History.* New York: Oxford University Press, 2002.
Lacey, Michael J., and Mary O. Furner, eds. *The State and Social Investigation in Britain and the United States.* Washington, D.C.: Woodrow Wilson Center Press, 1993.
Lankton, Larry. *Cradle to Grave: Life, Work, and Death at the Lake Superior Copper Mines.* New York: Oxford University Press, 1991.
Laubach, Frank. "Why There Are Vagrants: A Study Based on an Examination of One Hundred Men." Ph.D. thesis, Columbia University, 1916.
Lauck, W. Jett, and Edgar Sydenstricker. *Conditions of Labor in American Industries: A Summarization of the Results of Recent Investigations.* New York: Funk and Wagnalls Company, 1917.
Leen, Daniel. *The Freighthopper's Manual for North America.* Santa Barbara, Calif.: Capra Press, 1979.
Leiserson, William. "Labor Camps in Wisconsin." Madison: Industrial Commission of Wisconsin, 1913.
———. "The Problem of Unemployment Today." *Political Science Quarterly* 31 (March 1916): 1–24.
Lescohier, Don D. "Conditions Affecting the Demand for Harvest Labor in the Wheat Belt." *USDA Bulletin No. 1230.* Washington, D.C.: GPO, 1924.
———. "The Farm Hand in the Middle West." *The Locomotive Engineers Journal* 57 (July 1923): 539–40, 606.
———. "Hands and Tools of the Wheat Harvest." *Survey* 50 (1 July 1923): 376–82, 409–12.
———. "Harvest Labor Problems in the Wheat Belt." *USDA Bulletin No. 1020.* Washington, D.C.: GPO, 1922.
———. "Harvesters and Hoboes in the Wheat Fields." *Survey* 50 (1 August 1923): 482–87, 503–4.
———. *The Labor Market.* New York: Macmillan, 1919.
———. "Sources of Supply and Conditions of Employment of Harvest Labor in the Wheat Belt." *USDA Bulletin No. 1211.* Washington, D.C.: GPO, 1924.
———. "The Supply of Labor after the War." *American Labor Legislation Review* (1919): 83–92.

———. "With the I.W.W. in the Wheat Lands." *Harper's Monthly Magazine* 147 (July 1923): 371–80.

———. "Work-Accidents and the Farm Hand." *Survey* 27 (October 1911): 946–51.

Levine, Louis. "The Development of Syndicalism in America." *Political Science Quarterly* 28 (September 1913): 451–79.

Lewis, Earl. "Expectations, Economic Opportunities, and Life in the Industrial Age: Black Migration to Norfolk, Virginia, 1910–1945." In *The Great Migration in Historical Perspective: New Dimensions of Race, Class, and Gender.* Ed. Joe William Trotter Jr. Bloomington: Indiana University Press, 1991. 22–45.

Littlejohn, Duffy. *Hopping Freight Trains in America.* Los Osos, Calif.: Sand River Press, 1993.

Lohse, Albert. "From a Construction Worker." *International Socialist Review* 16 (March 1916): 550–51.

London, Jack. "South of the Slot." *International Socialist Review* 15 (July 1914): 7–17.

———. "South of the Slot." In *The Strength of the Strong.* New York: Macmillan, 1914. 34–70.

"Loving Memory." *Hobo News* 9 (December 1921): 9.

"The Lure of the City." Kansas City, Mo.: Helping Hands Institute, 1909.

MacDonald, A. B. "The Moving Army of Harvest Hands." *County Gentleman* 89 (9 August 1924): 15.

Macdonald, J. A. "A New Chapter in Industrial Revolution." *International Socialist Review* 16 (November 1915): 347–49.

Mapes, Kathleen A. "Defining the Boundaries: Family Farmers, Migrant Labor, Industrial Agriculture and the State in the Rural Midwest, 1898–1938." Ph.D. diss., University of Illinois, 2000.

Marcosson, Issac F. "Harvesting the Wheat." *World's Work* 9 (November 1904): 5459–77.

Martinson, Henry R. "'Comes the Revolution . . .': A Personal Memoir." *North Dakota History* 36 (Winter 1969): 41–109.

———. "Interview with Henry Martinson." *North Dakota History* (Spring 1978): 16–22.

Massachusetts Board to Investigate the Subject of the Unemployed. *Report of the Massachusetts Board to Investigate the Subject of the Unemployed, Part II: Wayfarers and Tramps (House Document No. 50).* Boston: State Printers, 1895.

Mathewson, Stanley B., et al. *Restriction of Output among Unorganized Workers.* New York: Viking Press, 1931.

Maynes, Mary Jo. *Taking the Hard Road: Life Course in French and German Workers' Autobiographies in the Era of Industrialization.* Chapel Hill: University of North Carolina Press, 1995.

McCartin, Joseph A. *Labor's Great War: The Struggle for Industrial Democracy and the Origins of Modern American Labor Relations, 1912–1921.* Chapel Hill: University of North Carolina Press, 1997.

McCook, John J. "A Tramp Census and Its Revelations." *The Forum* 15 (August 1893): 753–66.

McGuckin, Henry. *Memoirs of a Wobbly.* Chicago: Charles H. Kerr, 1987.

McMath, Robert. *American Populism: A Social History, 1877–1898.* New York: Hill and Wang, 1993.

McWilliams, Carey. *Factories in the Field: The Story of Migratory Farm Labor in California.* Boston: Little, Brown, 1939.

———. *Ill Fares the Land.* Boston: Little, Brown, 1942.

Meriwether, Lee. *The Tramp at Home.* New York: Harper and Brothers, 1889.

Meyerowitz, Joanne J. *Women Adrift: Independent Wage Earners in Chicago, 1880–1930.* Chicago: University of Chicago Press, 1988.

"The Militant Harvest Workers." *International Socialist Review* 17 (October 1916): 229–30.

Mills, Frederick C. *Economic Tendencies in the United States: Aspects of Pre-War and Post-War Changes.* New York: National Bureau of Economic Research, 1932.

Minneapolis Civic and Commerce Association. *Minneapolis: The Market of the Northwest, Brief Compiled for Presentation to the Federal Farm Loan Board,* 2nd Ed. n.p. [1916?].

Minneapolis Civic and Commerce Association, Committee on Housing. *The Housing Problem in Minneapolis.* Minneapolis: n.p., 1914.

Minnesota Bureau of Labor. *Seventh Biennial Report of the Bureau of Labor of the State of Minnesota, 1899–1900.* St. Paul: Pioneer Press Co., 1901.

Minnesota Bureau of Labor, Industries and Commerce. *Twelfth Biennial Report of the Bureau of Labor, Industries and Commerce of the State of Minnesota, 1909–1910,* n.p. [1911].

———. *Thirteenth Biennial Report of the Bureau of Labor, Industries and Commerce of the State of Minnesota, 1911–1912,* n.p. [1913].

Minnesota Department of Labor and Industry. *Fourteenth Biennial Report of the Department of Labor and Industry of the State of Minnesota, 1913–1914.* Minneapolis: Syndicate Printing Co. [1915].

———. *Fifteenth Biennial Report of the Department of Labor and Industries, 1915–1916.* Minneapolis: Syndicate Printing Co., 1916.

———. *Sixteenth Biennial Report of the Department of Labor and Industries, 1917–1918.* Minneapolis: Syndicate Printing Co. [1919?].

———. *Seventeenth Biennial Report of the Department of Labor and Industries, 1919–1920.* Minneapolis: Syndicate Printing Co., n.d.

Minnesota Industrial Commission. *First Biennial Report of the Industrial Commission of Minnesota, 1921–1922.* Minneapolis: Syndicate Printing Co., n.d.

———. *Second Biennial Report of the Industrial Commission of Minnesota, 1923–1924.* Minneapolis: Syndicate Printing Co., n.d.

———. *Third Biennial Report of the Industrial Commission of Minnesota, 1925–1926.* Minneapolis: Syndicate Printing Co., n.d.

———. *Fourth Biennial Report of the Industrial Commission of Minnesota, 1927–1928.* Minneapolis: Syndicate Printing Co., n.d.

———. *Fifth Biennial Report of the Industrial Commission of Minnesota, 1929–1930 (Twenty-Second Biennial Report, Department of Labor and Industry).* St. Paul, Minn., n.p., n.d.

Mitchell, Don. *The Lie of the Land: Migrant Workers and the California Landscape.* Minneapolis: University of Minnesota Press, 1996.

Moe, Edward O., and Carl C. Taylor. *Culture of a Contemporary Rural Community: Irwin, Iowa.* Vol. 5. Washington, D.C.: GPO, 1942.

Monkkonen, Eric, ed. *Walking to Work: Tramps in America, 1790–1935.* Lincoln: University of Nebraska Press, 1984.

Montejano, David. *Anglos and Mexicans in the Making of Texas, 1836–1986.* Austin: University of Texas Press, 1987.

Montgomery, David. *Citizen Worker: The Experience of Workers in the United States with Democracy and the Free Market during the Nineteenth Century.* New York: Cambridge University Press, 1993.

———. *The Fall of the House of Labor: The Workplace, the State, and American Labor Activism, 1865–1925.* New York: Cambridge University Press, 1987.

———. *Workers' Control in America: Studies in the History of Work, Technology, and Labor Struggles.* Cambridge, England: Cambridge University Press, 1979.

Moody, Carroll, and Alice Kessler-Harris, eds. *Perspectives on American Labor History: The Problems of Synthesis.* DeKalb: Northern Illinois University Press, 1990.

Mordell, Albert, comp. *The World of Haldeman-Julius.* New York: Twayne Publishers, 1960.

Morlan, Robert. *Political Prairie Fire: The Nonpartisan League, 1915–1922.* Minneapolis: University of Minnesota, 1955.

The National Cyclopaedia of American Biography. New York: J. T. White, 1906.

Nef, Walter T. "Job Control in the Harvest Fields." *International Socialist Review* 17 (September 1917): 141–43.

Nelson, Steve, James R. Barrett, and Rob Ruck. *Steve Nelson, American Radical.* Pittsburgh: University of Pittsburgh Press, 1981.

Nesbit, Robert C. *Wisconsin, A History.* Madison: University of Wisconsin Press, 1989.

Neth, Mary. *Preserving the Family Farm: Women, Community and the Foundations of Agribusiness in the Midwest, 1900–1940.* Baltimore: Johns Hopkins University Press, 1995.

Neufeld, Maurice, ed. "Portrait of the Labor Historian as a Boy and Young Man: Excerpts from the Interview of Philip Taft by Margot Honig." *Labor History* (Winter 1978): 39–71.

"The New Ditch Diggers." *International Socialist Review* 15 (December 1914): 381.

Ngai, Mae. "Braceros, 'Wetbacks,' and the National Boundaries of Class, 1942–1964." Paper presented to Newberry Library Labor History Seminar, November 30, 2001.

Nylander, Towne. "The Migratory Population of the United States." *The American Journal of Sociology* 30 (September 1924): 129–53.

Oberdeck, Kathryn J. "Popular Narrative and Working-Class Identity: Alexander Irvine's Early Twentieth-Century Literary Adventures." In *Labor Histories: Class Politics, and Working-Class Experience.* Ed. Eric Arnesen and Julie Greene. Urbana: University of Illinois Press, 1998.

O'Connor, Jessie Lloyd, and Harvey O'Connor. *Harvey and Jessie: A Couple of Radicals.* Philadelphia: Temple University Press, 1988.

Ownby, Ted. *Subduing Satan: Religion, Recreation, and Manhood in the Rural South, 1865–1920.* Chapel Hill: University of North Carolina Press, 1990.

Palmer, Bryan. *Descent into Discourse: The Reification of Language and the Writing of Social History.* Philadelphia: Temple University Press, 1990.

Pangborn, Major. "Discussion on Vagrancy." *Proceedings of the National Conference of Charities and Corrections.* Indianapolis, 1907.

Parker, Carleton H. *The Casual Laborer and Other Essays.* New York: Harcourt, Brace and Howe, 1920.

Parker, Cornelia Straton. *An American Idyll: The Life of Carleton H. Parker.* Boston: Atlantic Monthly Press, 1919.

Parnell, W. W. "The Broom Corn Industry." *International Socialist Review* 16 (June 1916): 750–51.

Parr, Joy. *The Gender of Breadwinners: Women, Men, and Industrial Change in Two Industrial Towns, 1880–1950.* Toronto: University of Toronto Press, 1990.

Peake, George C. "The Ojibwas Used Firearms in Their Many Skirmishes." *The American Indian* 3 (November 1928): 13.

Peck, Gunther. "Reinventing Free Labor: Immigrant Padrones and Contract Laborers in North America, 1885–1925." *Journal of American History* 83 (December 1996): 848–71.

———. *Reinventing Free Labor: Padrones and Immigrant Workers in the North American West, 1880–1930.* New York: Cambridge University Press, 2000.

Peiss, Kathy. *Cheap Amusements: Working Women and Leisure in Turn-of-the-Century New York.* Philadelphia: Temple University Press, 1986.

Pifer, Caroline Sandoz, and Jules Sandoz, Jr. *Son of Old Jules: Memoirs of Jules Sandoz, Jr.* Lincoln: University of Nebraska Press, 1987.

Pinkerton, Allan. *Strikers, Communists, Tramps and Detectives.* New York: G. W. Dillingham Co., 1878.

Pittenger, Mark. "A World of Difference: Constructing the 'Underclass' in Progressive America." *American Quarterly* 49 (March 1997): 26–65.

Polivka, Anne E. "A Profile of Contingent Workers." *Monthly Labor Review* (October 1996): 10–21.

Preston, William. "Shall This Be All? U.S. Historians versus William D. Haywood, et al." *Labor History* 12 (Summer 1971): 435–53.

Quinn, D. Michael. *Same-Sex Dynamics among Nineteenth-Century Americans: A Mormon Example.* Urbana: University of Illinois Press, 1996.

Quirke, Bill. "Amongst the Home Guards." *Hobo News* 9 (July 1921): 5.

Radforth, Ian. *Bushworkers and Bosses: Logging in Northern Ontario, 1900–1980.* Toronto: University of Toronto Press, 1987.

Rammel, Hal. *Nowhere in America: The Big Rock Candy Mountain and Other Comic Utopias.* Urbana: University of Illinois Press, 1990.

Rand School of Social Science. *The American Labor Yearbook, 1919–1920.* New York: Rand School of Social Science, 1920.

———. *The American Labor Yearbook, 1923–1924.* New York: Rand School of Social Science, 1924.

Ream, Amanda. "New York Workfare Workers Vote Union: Unofficial Vote Held by Workers' Rights Board." *Labor Notes* 225 (December 1997): 1, 12.

Reckless, Walter C. *Vice in Chicago.* Chicago: University of Chicago Press, 1933.

Rediker, Marcus. *Between the Devil and the Deep Blue Sea: Merchant Seamen, Pirates and the Anglo-American Maritime World, 1700–1750.* Cambridge, England: Cambridge University Press, 1987.

Reid, Donald. "Reflections on Labor History and Language." In *Rethinking Labor History: Essays on Discourse and Class Analysis.* Ed. Lenard R. Berlanstein. Urbana: University of Illinois Press, 1993. 39–54.

Reitman, Ben. *Sister of the Road: The Autobiography of Box-Car Bertha, as Told to Dr. Ben L. Reitman.* 1937. Reprinted, New York: Harper Colophon Books, 1975.

Report of the General Secretary-Treasurer to the Second IWW Convention, 1906, Chicago, Illinois, n.p. [1906?].

Richardson, Henry P. "Scientific Organizing and the Farmer." *International Socialist Review* 15 (March 1915): 554–58.

Riebe, Ernest. *Mr. Block: Twenty-Four IWW Cartoons.* 1913. Reprinted, Chicago: Charles H. Kerr, 1984.

Ringenbach, Paul T. *Tramps and Reformers, 1873–1916: The Discovery of Unemployment in New York.* Westport, Conn.: Greenwood Press, 1973.

Robinson, Elwyn B. *History of North Dakota.* Lincoln: University of Nebraska Press, 1966.

Rodgers, Daniel T. *The Work Ethic in Industrial America, 1850–1920.* Chicago: University of Chicago Press, 1974.

Roediger, David. *Towards the Abolition of Whiteness: Essays on Race, Politics, and Working-Class History.* New York: Verso, 1994.

———. *The Wages of Whiteness: Race and the Making of the American Working Class.* New York: Verso, 1991.

Rølvaag, O. E. *The Boat of Longing.* Trans. Nora O. Solum. 1933. Reprinted, St. Paul: Minnesota Historical Society Press, 1985.

Rönning, Gerald. "Miners on the Warpath: The Wobbly Menace in Arizona, 1917." Paper presented at the American Historical Association Annual Meeting, January 2001.

Rose, Sonya O. "Class Formation and the Quintessential Worker." In *Reworking Class.* Ed. John R. Hall. Ithaca, N.Y.: Cornell University Press, 1997. 133–66.

Rosemont, Franklin, ed. *From Bughouse Square to the Beat Generation: Selected Ravings of Slim Brundage, Founder and Janitor of the College of Complexes.* Chicago: Charles H. Kerr, 1997.

———. *Juice Is Stranger Than Friction: Selected Writings of T-Bone Slim.* Chicago: Charles H. Kerr, 1992.

Ross, Carl. *Radicalism in Minnesota, 1900–1960: A Survey of Selected Sources.* St. Paul: Minnesota Historical Society Press, 1994.

Ross, Dorothy. *The Origins of American Social Science.* New York: Cambridge University Press, 1991.

Rowan, James. *The I.W.W. in the Lumber Industry.* Seattle: Lumber Workers Industrial Union No. 500 [1919?].

Ruff, Allen. *"We Called Each Other Comrade": Charles H. Kerr and Company, Radical Publishers.* Urbana: University of Illinois Press, 1997.

Salerno, Salvatore. *Red November, Black November: Culture and Community in the Industrial Workers of the World.* Albany: State University of New York Press, 1989.

Saloutos, Theodore, and John D. Hicks. *Agricultural Discontent in the Middle West, 1900–1939.* Madison: University of Wisconsin Press, 1951.

Salvatore, Nick. *Eugene V. Debs: Citizen and Socialist.* Urbana: University of Illinois Press, 1982.

Sandburg, Carl. *Always the Young Strangers.* New York: Harcourt, Brace and Co., 1952.

———. *The Complete Poems of Carl Sandberg, Revised and Expanded Edition.* New York: Harcourt Brace Jovanovich, 1970.

Sautter, Udo. "North American Government Labor Agencies before World War One: A Cure for Unemployment?" *Labor History* 24 (Summer 1983): 366–93.

Schmahl, Julius. *Address by Julius Schmahl (Secretary of State of Minnesota) at New Ulm.* Minneapolis: Syndicate Printing Co., 1919.

Schneider, John C. "Omaha Vagrants and the Character of Western Hobo Labor, 1887–1913." *Nebraska History* 63 (Summer 1982): 255–72.

———. "Tramping Workers, 1890–1920: A Subcultural View." In *Walking to Work: Tramps in America, 1790–1935.* Ed. Eric Monkkonen. Lincoln: University of Nebraska Press, 1984. 212–34.

Schob, David E. *Hired Hands and Plowboys: Farm Labor in the Midwest, 1815–60.* Urbana: University of Illinois Press, 1975.

Schoenfeld, W. A., and Nils Olson. "The Wheat Situation." *Yearbook of the U.S. Department of Agriculture, 1923.* Washington, D.C.: GPO, 1924.

Schrager, Samuel Alan. "'The Early Days': Narrative and Symbolism of Logging Life in the Inland Northwest." Ph.D. diss., University of Pennsylvania, 1983.

Schwantes, Carlos A. *Coxey's Army: An American Odyssey.* Lincoln: University of Nebraska Press, 1985.

Schwartz, Harold. *Seasonal Farm Labor in the U.S. with Special Reference to Hired Workers in Fruit and Vegetable and Sugar-Beet Production.* New York: Columbia University Press, 1945.

Scott, James C. *Weapons of the Weak: Everyday Forms of Peasant Resistance.* New Haven, Conn.: Yale University Press, 1985.

Scott, Joan Wallach. "The Evidence of Experience." *Critical Inquiry* 17 (Summer 1991): 773–97.

———. *Gender and the Politics of History.* New York: Columbia University Press, 1988.

Searle, R. Newell. *Saving Quetico-Superior: A Land Set Apart.* Minnesota Historical Society Press, 1977.

Seidman, Michael. *Workers against Work: Labor in Paris and Barcelona during the Popular Fronts.* Berkeley: University of California Press, 1991.

Sellars, Nigel Anthony. *Oil, Wheat and Wobblies: The Industrial Workers of the World in Oklahoma, 1905–1930.* Norman: University of Oklahoma Press, 1998.

Sewell, William H., Jr. "How Classes Are Made: Critical Reflections on E. P. Thompson's Theory of Working-Class Formation." In *E. P. Thompson: Critical Perspectives.* Ed. Harvey J. Kaye and Keith McClelland. Philadelphia: Temple University Press, 1990. 50–77.

Shannon, Fred. *The Farmer's Last Frontier: Agriculture, 1860–1897.* New York: Farrar and Rinehart, 1945.

Shor, Francis. "Masculine Power and Virile Syndicalism: A Gendered Analysis of the IWW in Australia." *Labour History* 63 (November 1992): 83–99.

———. "'Virile Syndicalism' in Comparative Perspective: A Gender Analysis of the

IWW in the United States and Australia." *International Labor and Working-Class History* 56 (Fall 1999): 65–77.
Short, Mrs. Wallace M. *Just One American* (n.d., n.p.).
Short, Wallace M. "How One Town Learned a Lesson in Free Speech." *Survey* 35 (30 October 1915): 106–8.
Shover, John L. *Cornbelt Rebellion: The Farmers' Holiday Association.* Urbana: University of Illinois Press, 1965.
Sideman, Michael Samuel. "The Agricultural Labor Market and the Organizing Activities of the IWW, 1910–1935." Master's thesis, University of Illinois, 1965.
Silag, Bill. "The Social Response to Industrialism in Sioux City." *Annals of Iowa* 50 (Winter 1990).
The Sioux City Commercial Club. *Annual Report for the Year 1915.* Sioux City: Deitch and Lamar Co., 1915.
Sklar, Martin J. *The Corporate Reconstruction of American Capitalism, 1890–1916.* New York: Cambridge University Press, 1988.
Slichter, Sumner. *The Turnover of Factory Labor.* New York: D. Appleton, 1919.
Solenberger, Alice Willard. *One Thousand Homeless Men. A Study of Original Records.* New York: Charities Publications Committee, 1911.
South Dakota Department of History. *Fourth Census of the State of South Dakota, 1925.* Sioux Falls, S.Dak.: Mark D. Scott, 1925.
Speek, Peter Alexander. "The Psychology of Floating Workers." *The Annals of the American Academy of Political and Social Science* 69 (January 1917): 72–78.
Stallybrass, Peter, and Allon White. *The Politics and Poetics of Transgression.* Ithaca, N.Y.: Cornell University Press, 1986.
Stanley, Amy Dru. "Beggars Can't Be Choosers: Compulsion and Contract in Postbellum America." *Journal of American History* 78 (March 1992): 1265–93.
Stansell, Christine. *City of Women: Sex and Class in New York, 1789–1860.* Urbana: University of Illinois Press, 1987.
Stearns, Peter N. *Be a Man! Males in Modern Society,* 2nd Ed. New York: Halmes and Meier, 1990.
———. "The Unskilled and Industrialization: A Transformation of Consciousness." *Archiv für Sozialgeschichte* 16 (1976): 249–82.
Stock, Catherine McNicol. *Main Street in Crisis: The Great Depression and the Old Middle Class on the Northern Plains.* Chapel Hill: University of North Carolina Press, 1992.
Stowell, David O. *Streets, Railroads, and the Great Strike of 1877.* Chicago: University of Chicago Press, 1999.
Sugrue, Thomas J. *The Origins of the Urban Crisis: Race and Inequality in Postwar Detroit.* Princeton, N.J.: Princeton University Press, 1996.
Swierenga, Robert P. "Agriculture and Rural Life: The New Rural History." In *Ordinary People and Everyday Life: Perspectives on the New Social History.* Ed. James B. Gardner and George Rollie Adams. Nashville: American Association for State and Local History, 1983. 93–94.
Syrjamaki, John. "Mesabi Communities: A Study of Their Development." Ph.D. diss., Yale University, 1940.

Taft, Philip. "The Harvest Hand Passes: Ushering Out Labor Color." *Labor History* 19 (Winter 1978): 76–81.

———. "The IWW in the Grain Belt." *Labor History* 1 (Winter 1960): 53–67.

———. "Mayor Short and the IWW Agricultural Workers." *Labor History* 7 (Spring 1966): 173–77.

Takaki, Ronald. *Pau Hana: Plantation Life and Labor in Hawaii, 1835–1920.* Honolulu: University of Hawaii Press, 1983.

Tanenhaus, Sam. "Gus Hall, Unreconstructed American Communist of 7 Decades, Dies at 90." *New York Times,* October 17, 2000.

Taylor, Paul S. "The American Hired Man: His Rise and Decline." U.S. Department of Agriculture, Bureau of Agricultural Economics, *Land Policy Review* 7 (Spring 1943).

———. "Origins of Migratory Labor in the Wheat Belts of the Middle West and California." *U.S. Senate Subcommittee on Migratory Labor, Migrant and Seasonal Farmworker Powerlessness, Part 8-C.* Washington, D.C.: GPO, 1971. 6258–98.

Taylor, William Bayard. "The Labor Market for the Northwest: A Study Based Chiefly upon the Records of Minneapolis Private Employment Agencies for the Period 1919–1922." MA thesis, University of Minnesota, 1923.

Thernstrom, Stephen. *Poverty and Progress: Social Mobility in a Nineteenth Century City.* Cambridge, Mass.: Harvard University Press, 1964.

Thompson, Carl W., and G. P. Warber. *Social and Economic Survey of a Rural Township in Southern Minnesota.* Minneapolis: University of Minnesota, 1913.

Thompson, Edward P. *The Making of the English Working Class.* New York: Vintage Books, 1963.

Thompson, Fred, and Patrick Murfin. *The I.W.W., Its First Seventy Years (1905–1975).* Chicago: Industrial Workers of the World, 1976.

Trotter, Joe William, Jr., ed. *The Great Migration in Historical Perspective: New Dimensions of Race, Class, and Gender.* Bloomington: Indiana University Press, 1991.

———. "Race, Class, and Industrial Change: Black Migration to Southern West Virginia, 1915–1932." *The Great Migration in Historical Perspective: New Dimensions of Race, Class, and Gender.* Ed. Joe William Trotter. Bloomington: Indiana University Press, 1991.

Tuttle, William. *Race Riot: Chicago in the Red Summer of 1919.* New York: Atheneum, 1970.

Tyler, Robert L. *Rebels of the Woods: The IWW in the Pacific Northwest.* Eugene: University of Oregon Press, 1967.

Uchitelle, Louis. "Gap between Full-Time and Part-Time Workers Has Widened." *New York Times,* August 8, 1997.

Ulonska, Carl. "Wheat, Wages—and You!" *International Socialist Review* 16 (October 1915): 205.

"Unorganized: The Militant Harvest Workers." *International Socialist Review* 17 (October 1916): 229–30.

U.S. Bureau of Labor Statistics. "Unemployment in the United States." *Bulletin No. 195.* Washington, D.C.: GPO, July 1916.

U.S. Bureau of the Census. *Fifteenth Census of the United States, 1930.* Vol. 4: *Occupations.* Washington, D.C.: GPO, 1933.

———. *Fifteenth Census of the United States, 1930: Agriculture,* Vol. 2, Pt. 1: *Northern States.* Washington, D.C.: GPO, 1932.

———. *Fourteenth Census of the United States, 1920.* Vol. 5: *Agriculture, General Report and Analytical Tables.* Washington, D.C.: GPO: 1922.

———. *Fourteenth Census of the United States, 1920.* Vol. 6, Pt. 1: *Agriculture, Northern States.* Washington, D.C.: GPO, 1922.

———. *Fourteenth Census of the U.S., 1920.* Vol. 4: *Population, 1920: Occupations.* Washington, D.C.: GPO, 1923.

———. *Special Reports: Occupations at the Twelfth Census, 1900.* Washington, D.C.: GPO, 1904.

———. *Thirteenth Census of the United States, 1910.* Vol. 6: *Agriculture, Reports by State (Alabama–Montana).* Washington, D.C.: GPO, 1913.

———. *Thirteenth Census of the United States, 1910.* Vol. 7: *Agriculture, Reports by State (Nebraska–Wyoming).* Washington, D.C.: GPO, 1913.

———. *Thirteenth Census of the United States, 1910: Abstract of the Census.* Washington, D.C.: GPO, 1914.

———. *Thirteenth Census of the United States, 1910: Statistics for North Dakota.* Washington, D.C.: GPO, 1913.

———. *Thirteenth Census of the United States, 1910: Statistics for South Dakota.* Washington, D.C.: GPO, 1913.

———. *Thirteenth U.S. Census.* Vol. 9: *Manufacturers, 1909.* Washington, D.C.: GPO, 1912.

U.S. Commissioner of Labor. *Eleventh Special Report, Regulation and Restriction of Output.* Washington, D.C.: Government Printing Office, 1904.

U.S. Commission on Industrial Relations. *Final Report and Testimony.* Washington, D.C.: GPO, 1915.

U.S. Department of Commerce and Labor, Bureau of Labor. "Statistics of Unemployment and the Work of Employment Offices." *Bulletin No. 109.* Washington, D.C.: GPO, 1913.

U.S. Department of Labor. *Report of the Secretary of Labor and Reports of Bureaus, 1920.* Washington, D.C.: GPO, 1921.

———. *Reports of the Department of Labor, 1918.* Washington, D.C.: GPO, 1919.

U.S. Department of Labor, Employment Service. *Annual Report of the Director General to the Secretary of Labor for the Fiscal Year Ending June 30, 1918.* Washington, D.C.: GPO, 1919.

———. *Annual Report of the Director General to the Secretary of Labor for the Fiscal Year Ending June 30, 1919.* Washington, D.C.: GPO, 1919.

———. *Annual Report of the Director General to the Secretary of Labor for the Fiscal Year Ending June 30, 1920.* Washington, D.C.: GPO, 1920.

U.S. Federal Trade Commission. *Report of the Federal Trade Commission on the Meat-Packing Industry.* Washington, D.C.: GPO, 1919.

U.S. Industrial Commission. *Reports.* Vol. 10: *Report of the Industrial Commission on Agriculture and Agricultural Labor.* Washington, D.C.: GPO, 1901.

U.S. Immigration Commission. *Reports of the Immigration Commission, Immigrants in Industries.* Vol. 18, Pt. 22: *The Floating Immigrant Labor Supply.* Washington, D.C.: GPO, 1911.

———. *Reports of the Immigration Commission, Immigrants in Industries.* Vol. 21, Pt. 24, Nos. 1 and 2: *Recent Immigrants in Agriculture.* Washington, D.C.: GPO, 1911.
U.S. Senate. *Hearings Before the Senate Committee on Indian Affairs on Matters Relating to the Wisconsin Indians.* 61st Cong., 2d sess., 1910.
———. *Report of the Country Life Commission.* 60th Cong., 2d sess., 1909.
Valdés, Dennis Nodin. *Al Norte: Agricultural Workers in the Great Lakes Region, 1917–1970.* Austin: University of Texas Press, 1991.
———. *Barrios Norteños: St. Paul and Midwestern Mexican Communities in the Twentieth Century.* Austin: University of Texas Press, 2000.
———. "Betabeleros: The Formation of an Agricultural Proletariat in the Midwest, 1897–1930." *Labor History* 30 (Fall 1989).
Vargas, Zaragosa. *Proletarians of the North: A History of Mexican Industrial Workers in Detroit and the Midwest, 1917–1933.* Berkeley: University of California Press, 1993.
Veblen, Thorstein. *The Theory of the Leisure Class: An Economic Study of Institutions.* 1899. Reprinted, New York: The Modern Library, 1934.
Wagman, David. "The Industrial Workers of the World in Nebraska, 1914–1920." *Nebraska History* 56 (Fall 1975): 295–337.
Walker, Charles Rumford. *American City: A Rank-and-File History.* New York: Farrar and Rinehart, 1937.
Wallace, Samuel. *Skid Row as a Way of Life.* Totowa, N.J.: The Bedminster Press, 1965.
Way, Peter. *Common Labour: Workers and the Digging of North American Canals, 1780–1860.* New York: Cambridge University Press, 1993.
———. "Evil Humors and Ardent Spirits: The Rough Culture of Canal Construction Laborers." *Journal of American History* 79 (March 1993): 1397–1428.
———. "Labour's Love Lost: Observations on the Historiography of Class and Ethnicity in the Nineteenth Century." *Journal of American Studies* 28 (April 1994): 1–22.
Webb, John N. *The Migratory-Casual Worker (WPA Research Monograph 7).* Washington, D.C.: GPO, 1937.
Wedge, Frederick R. *Inside the IWW: A Study of the Behavior of the IWW, with Reference to Primary Causes.* Berkeley: F. R. Wedge, 1924.
Weiner, Lynn. "Sisters of the Road: Women Transients and Tramps." In *Walking to Work: Tramps in America, 1790–1935.* Ed. Eric Monkkonen. Lincoln: University of Nebraska Press, 1984. 171–88.
West, Jim. "Big Win at UPS! Strike Puts Part-Timers on National Agenda." *Labor Notes* 222 (September 1997): 1, 14.
———. "UAW Strike against Johnson Controls Targets Vast, Non-Union Auto Parts Sector." *Labor Notes* 216 (March 1997): 3–4.
———. "Union to Drop 441 Unfair Labor Practice Charges in Return for Contract at Caterpillar." *Labor Notes* 228 (March 1998): 7.
Whipp, Richard. "Labour Markets and Communities: An Historical View." *The Sociological Review* 33 (November 1985): 768–91.
White, William Allan. "The Business of a Wheat Farm." *Scribner's Magazine* 22 (November 1897): 538, 532, 547.
Wiebe, Robert H. *The Search for Order, 1877–1920.* New York: Hill and Wang, 1967.

Williams, Raymond. *Keywords: A Vocabulary of Culture and Society.* New York: Oxford University Press, 1983.

———. *Problems in Materialism and Culture.* London: Verso, 1980.

Williams, Whiting. "Hail Columbia, Hopeful Land!" *Collier's* 69 (25 March 1922): 5, 26–27.

———. "In the Strike Breakers' Camp." *Collier's* 70 (21 October 1922): 9–10.

———. "A Job for Every Man Every Day." *Collier's* 69 (14 January 1922): 9–10, 21–23.

———. "The Job and Utopia." *American Labor Legislation Review* 11 (1921): 13–23.

———. *Mainsprings of Men.* New York: Charles Scribner's Sons, 1925.

———. "Unsteady Jobs—High Rents. Three Million Families Need Homes: Yet Many Building Trades Workers Are Idle." *Collier's,* 69 (27 May 1922): 18, 28–29.

———. "We Were Pals, but We Got in a Jam: Why Railroad Men Fight and Why They Work for Peace." *Collier's* 70 (18 November 1922): 11, 28–29.

———. "What I Know Now about Railroaders." *Collier's* 70 (4 November 1922): 13, 29.

———. "What the Worker Thinks." *Collier's* 65 (21 February 1920):. 9–10, 27–28; 65 (20 March 1920): 9–10, 47–50; 65 (22 May 1920): 10–11, 60–62; 65 (3 July 1920): 7, 36–38, 40; 66 (7 August 1920): 8–9, 36–37.

———. *What's on the Worker's Mind: By One Who Put on Overalls to Find Out.* New York: Charles Scribner's Sons, 1920.

———. "Who's to Blame for a Coal Strike? The Truth about an Amazing Stupidity That Threatens the Comfort and Safety of All of Us." *Collier's* 69 (1 April 1922): 7–8, 29–30.

———. "Why My Buddies Will Strike Again." *Collier's* 70 (14 October 1922): 13–14, 32.

———. "The Workers' Speakeasy." *Survey* 65 (15 January 1931): 493.

Wilson, Robin. "For Some Adjunct Faculty Members, the Tenure Track Holds Little Appeal." *Chronicle of Higher Education* (24 July 1998): A9–A10.

Wilson, William B. *Report of President's Mediation Commission to the President of the United States.* Washington, D.C.: GPO, 1918.

Winstead, Ralph. "Organizing the Harvest Workers." *Labor Age* 11 (June 1922): 18–20.

Wixson, Douglas. *The Worker-Writer in America: Jack Conroy and the Tradition of Midwestern Literary Radicalism, 1898–1990.* Urbana: University of Illinois Press, 1994.

Woirol, Gregory. *In the Floating Army: F. C. Mills on Itinerant Life in California, 1914.* Urbana: University of Illinois Press, 1992.

Woodruff, Abner. *The Advancing Proletariat: A Study of the Movement of the Working Class from Wage Slavery to Freedom.* Chicago: IWW, 1919.

———. *The Evolution of American Agriculture.* Chicago: Agricultural Workers Industrial Union, No. 400, IWW, 1919.

Woodward, Mary Dodge. *The Checkered Years: A Bonanza Farm Diary, 1884–1888.* 1937. Reprinted, St. Paul: Minnesota Historical Society Press, 1989.

Workman, E. *History of "400": A.W.O., The One Big Union Idea in Action.* New York: One Big Union Club, 1930.

Wren, Daniel. *White Collar Hobo: The Travels of Whiting Williams.* Ames: Iowa State University Press, 1987.

Wright, Gavin. "American Agriculture and the Labor Market: What Happened to Proletarianization?" *Agricultural History* 62(3) 1988: 182–209.

———. *Old South, New South: Revolutions in the Southern Economy since the Civil War.* New York: Basic Books, 1986.

Wyckoff, Walter A. *The Workers: An Experiment in Reality, the East.* New York: Charles Scribner's Sons, 1898.

———. *The Workers: An Experiment in Reality, the West.* New York: Charles Scribner's Sons, 1898.

Zorbaugh, Harvey W. *The Gold Coast and the Slum: A Sociological Study of Chicago's Near North Side.* 1929. Reprinted, Chicago: University of Chicago Press, 1969.

INDEX

FRANK TOBIAS HIGBIE is director of the Newberry Library's Dr. William M. Scholl Center for Family and Community History. His articles have appeared in *Social Science History* and *Labor History.*

The Working Class in American History

Worker City, Company Town: Iron and Cotton-Worker Protest in Troy and Cohoes, New York, 1855–84 *Daniel J. Walkowitz*

Life, Work, and Rebellion in the Coal Fields: The Southern West Virginia Miners, 1880–1922 *David Alan Corbin*

Women and American Socialism, 1870–1920 *Mari Jo Buhle*

Lives of Their Own: Blacks, Italians, and Poles in Pittsburgh, 1900–1960 *John Bodnar, Roger Simon, and Michael P. Weber*

Working-Class America: Essays on Labor, Community, and American Society *Edited by Michael H. Frisch and Daniel J. Walkowitz*

Eugene V. Debs: Citizen and Socialist *Nick Salvatore*

American Labor and Immigration History, 1877–1920s: Recent European Research *Edited by Dirk Hoerder*

Workingmen's Democracy: The Knights of Labor and American Politics *Leon Fink*

The Electrical Workers: A History of Labor at General Electric and Westinghouse, 1923–60 *Ronald W. Schatz*

The Mechanics of Baltimore: Workers and Politics in the Age of Revolution, 1763–1812 *Charles G. Steffen*

The Practice of Solidarity: American Hat Finishers in the Nineteenth Century *David Bensman*

The Labor History Reader *Edited by Daniel J. Leab*

Solidarity and Fragmentation: Working People and Class Consciousness in Detroit, 1875–1900 *Richard Oestreicher*

Counter Cultures: Saleswomen, Managers, and Customers in American Department Stores, 1890–1940 *Susan Porter Benson*

The New England Working Class and the New Labor History *Edited by Herbert G. Gutman and Donald H. Bell*

Labor Leaders in America *Edited by Melvyn Dubofsky and Warren Van Tine*

Barons of Labor: The San Francisco Building Trades and Union Power in the Progressive Era *Michael Kazin*

Gender at Work: The Dynamics of Job Segregation by Sex during World War II *Ruth Milkman*

Once a Cigar Maker: Men, Women, and Work Culture in American Cigar Factories, 1900–1919 *Patricia A. Cooper*

A Generation of Boomers: The Pattern of Railroad Labor Conflict in Nineteenth-Century America *Shelton Stromquist*

Work and Community in the Jungle: Chicago's Packinghouse Workers, 1894–1922 *James R. Barrett*

Workers, Managers, and Welfare Capitalism: The Shoeworkers and Tanners of Endicott Johnson, 1890–1950 *Gerald Zahavi*

Men, Women, and Work: Class, Gender, and Protest in the New England Shoe Industry, 1780–1910 *Mary Blewett*

Workers on the Waterfront: Seamen, Longshoremen, and Unionism in the 1930s
Bruce Nelson
German Workers in Chicago: A Documentary History of Working-Class Culture from 1850 to World War I *Edited by Hartmut Keil and John B. Jentz*
On the Line: Essays in the History of Auto Work *Edited by Nelson Lichtenstein and Stephen Meyer III*
Upheaval in the Quiet Zone: A History of Hospital Workers' Union, Local 1199
Leon Fink and Brian Greenberg
Labor's Flaming Youth: Telephone Operators and Worker Militancy, 1878–1923
Stephen H. Norwood
Another Civil War: Labor, Capital, and the State in the Anthracite Regions of Pennsylvania, 1840–68 *Grace Palladino*
Coal, Class, and Color: Blacks in Southern West Virginia, 1915–32
Joe William Trotter, Jr.
For Democracy, Workers, and God: Labor Song-Poems and Labor Protest, 1865–95
Clark D. Halker
Dishing It Out: Waitresses and Their Unions in the Twentieth Century
Dorothy Sue Cobble
The Spirit of 1848: German Immigrants, Labor Conflict, and the Coming of the Civil War *Bruce Levine*
Working Women of Collar City: Gender, Class, and Community in Troy, New York, 1864–86 *Carole Turbin*
Southern Labor and Black Civil Rights: Organizing Memphis Workers
Michael K. Honey
Radicals of the Worst Sort: Laboring Women in Lawrence, Massachusetts, 1860–1912
Ardis Cameron
Producers, Proletarians, and Politicians: Workers and Party Politics in Evansville and New Albany, Indiana, 1850–87 *Lawrence M. Lipin*
The New Left and Labor in the 1960s *Peter B. Levy*
The Making of Western Labor Radicalism: Denver's Organized Workers, 1878–1905
David Brundage
In Search of the Working Class: Essays in American Labor History and Political Culture *Leon Fink*
Lawyers against Labor: From Individual Rights to Corporate Liberalism
Daniel R. Ernst
"We Are All Leaders": The Alternative Unionism of the Early 1930s *Edited by Staughton Lynd*
The Female Economy: The Millinery and Dressmaking Trades, 1860–1930
Wendy Gamber
"Negro and White, Unite and Fight!": A Social History of Industrial Unionism in Meatpacking, 1930–90 *Roger Horowitz*
Power at Odds: The 1922 National Railroad Shopmen's Strike *Colin J. Davis*
The Common Ground of Womanhood: Class, Gender, and Working Girls' Clubs, 1884–1928 *Priscilla Murolo*

Marching Together: Women of the Brotherhood of Sleeping Car Porters *Melinda Chateauvert*

Down on the Killing Floor: Black and White Workers in Chicago's Packinghouses, 1904–54 *Rick Halpern*

Labor and Urban Politics: Class Conflict and the Origins of Modern Liberalism in Chicago, 1864–97 *Richard Schneirov*

All That Glitters: Class, Conflict, and Community in Cripple Creek *Elizabeth Jameson*

Waterfront Workers: New Perspectives on Race and Class *Edited by Calvin Winslow*

Labor Histories: Class, Politics, and the Working-Class Experience *Edited by Eric Arnesen, Julie Greene, and Bruce Laurie*

The Pullman Strike and the Crisis of the 1890s: Essays on Labor and Politics *Edited by Richard Schneirov, Shelton Stromquist, and Nick Salvatore*

AlabamaNorth: African-American Migrants, Community, and Working-Class Activism in Cleveland, 1914–45 *Kimberley L. Phillips*

Imagining Internationalism in American and British Labor, 1939–49 *Victor Silverman*

William Z. Foster and the Tragedy of American Radicalism *James R. Barrett*

Colliers across the Sea: A Comparative Study of Class Formation in Scotland and the American Midwest, 1830–1924 *John H. M. Laslett*

"Rights, Not Roses": Unions and the Rise of Working-Class Feminism, 1945–80 *Dennis A. Deslippe*

Testing the New Deal: The General Textile Strike of 1934 in the American South *Janet Irons*

Hard Work: The Making of Labor History *Melvyn Dubofsky*

Southern Workers and the Search for Community: Spartanburg County, South Carolina *G. C. Waldrep III*

We Shall Be All: A History of the Industrial Workers of the World (abridged edition) *Melvyn Dubofsky, ed. Joseph A. McCartin*

Race, Class, and Power in the Alabama Coalfields, 1908–21 *Brian Kelly*

Duquesne and the Rise of Steel Unionism *James D. Rose*

Anaconda: Labor, Community, and Culture in Montana's Smelter City *Laurie Mercier*

Bridgeport's Socialist New Deal, 1915–36 *Cecelia Bucki*

Indispensable Outcasts: Hobo Workers and Community in the American Midwest, 1880–1930 *Frank Tobias Higbie*

The University of Illinois Press
is a founding member of the
Association of American University Presses.

University of Illinois Press
1325 South Oak Street
Champaign, IL 61820-6903
www.press.uillinois.edu